Fr. Kilian Healy (1912-2003)

INSTITUTUM CARMELITANUM
VACARE DEO - VOL. 1

INSTITUTUM CARMELITANUM
VACARE DEO - VOL. 1

Methods of Prayer in the Directory of the Carmelite Reform of Touraine

by

KILIAN J. HEALY, O. CARM.

EDIZIONI CARMELITANE
ROMA 2005

First printing: 1956
Second printing: 2005

Revised by: William Harry, O. Carm.
Joachim Smet, O. Carm.

Edizioni Carmelitane
Via Sforza Pallavicini, 10
00193 Roma - Italia

ISBN: 88-7288-085-8
ISSN: 0394-7807

To
OUR LADY OF MOUNT CARMEL
Mother and Model of the Interior Life

PRIORE GENERALE DEI CARMELITANI
VIA GIOVANNI LANZA, 138
00184 ROMA - (ITALIA)

8 December 2004
Solemnity of the Immaculate Conception

I am very pleased to present this edition of the classic, "Methods of Prayer in the Directory of the Carmelite Reform of Touraine", written by the former Prior General, Fr. Kilian Healy, in 1956. This work began life as a doctoral dissertation at the Gregorian University in Rome. It is a tribute to the book's great influence that it has been republished almost fifty years later.

Throughout the long history of the Carmelite Order there have been many reforms, the most famous of which being that initiated by St. Teresa of Avila in the 16th century. Due to various political reasons, the Discalced Reform and the original Order went their separate ways. Next in importance is the Touraine Reform in the 17th century, and it is this reform that spread to the whole Order and had a profound effect on its spirituality. Fr. Healy makes it clear that the spiritual writers of the Touraine Reform esteemed St. Teresa and her teaching on prayer greatly.

The present work is a study of the manual used to teach novices about the way of prayer. It is historically fascinating in that Fr. Healy reveals how 17th century Carmelites understood their vocation as a life of "continual loving conversation with God". It is also still spiritually refreshing after so many years and I have no hesitation in commending it to you.

Joseph Chalmers O. Carm.

Joseph Chalmers, O. Carm.
Prior General

CONTENTS

Contents ix
Introduction xiii
Abbreviations xviii

SECTION ONE
THE REFORM OFTOURAINE

Chapter   I – Origin of the Reform 1
Chapter II – The Spirit of Touraine. 15
Chapter III – The Spiritual Directory for Novices . . . 22
    I – The Authors 22
        1. Father Bernard of St. Magdalen 24
        2. Father Mark of the Nativity of the Blessed Virgin . . . 27
    II – Editions and Translations 34
    III – The Style of the *Méthode* 38

SECTION TWO
THE WAYS OF PRAYER IN THE *MÉTHODE*

Chapter IV – Meditation. 39
    I – The Preface 39
    II – Prayer and Its Divisions 40
    III – Mental Prayer 41
        1. The Parts of Mental Prayer 42
        2. Reading 44
        3. Meditation 44
        4. Affections 46
        5. Resolutions 48
        6. Petition 49
    IV – Meditative Reading 50
    V – Affective Prayer 50

VI –	Prayer of Simple Regard	51
VII –	Prayer of Recollection	51
VIII –	Difficulties in Prayer	52
Commentary		53

Chapter V – Mixed Prayer 57
Commentary 58

Chapter VI – Aspirative Prayer, or the Exercise of the Presence of God 60
    I – Aspirative Prayer 60
    II – The Presence of God 64
    III – The Four Ways 67
    IV – Counsels 71
Commentary 73

    V – Summary of the Three Ways of Prayer 74
    VI – Prayer and Mortification 74

SECTION THREE
THE SOURCES OF THE *MÉTHODE*

Chapter VII – Sacred Scripture, the Fathers, the Rule and Tradition of Carmel 76
    I – Sacred Scripture 77
    II – The Fathers 78
    III – The Rule and Tradition of Carmel 79

Chapter VIII – The Ignatian School of Prayer 84
    I – St. Ignatius and the Spiritual Exercises 84
    II – Francis Arias, S. J. 91
    III – Alphonsus Rodriguez, S. J. 97
    IV – Luis de la Puente, S. J. 99
    V – Alvarez de Paz, S. J. 105
        Conclusion 106

Chapter IX – Louis of Granada 109
        The Presence of God 119

Chapter X – Louis de Blois (Blosius) 121

Chapter XI – St. Teresa and the Discalced Carmelite School	125
I – St. Teresa	125
St. Teresa's Concept of Prayer	127
II – Spanish Discalced Carmelites	131
III – John of Jesus and Mary, of Calahorra (1564-1615)	132
The Presence of God	139
Aspirative Prayer	139
Chapter XII – St. Francis de Sales	141
The Presence of God	144
Chapter XIII – Carmelites of the Touraine Reform	147
I – Ven. John of St. Samson	147
Aspirative Prayer	153
II – Ven. Dominic of St. Albert	159
The Exercise of the Presence of God	166
Conclusions	171
Bibliography	175
Index	181
Biography of Kilian Healy	185

INTRODUCTION

The human soul was made to love God with all its strength. And it is the avowed p u r p o s e of every religious Order to help its members to attain the perfection of this love, even though there will never come a moment in this valley of tears when the soul will not be able to love a little more perfectly and serve a little more faithfully.

All Orders use the same essential means to conduct their members to perfection, but they apply them differently, depending upon the particular work for which the Order was instituted. Every Order, for instance, recognizes prayer as a normal, ordinary means to grow in charity. But because each Order has a special aim, it gives more or less emphasis to the various exercises of prayer. For the Jesuit, prayer, both oral and mental, is necessary, but precisely for the inspiration and perfection of action to which it is ordered. Whereas for the Carmelite the various exercises of prayer are means *par excellence* to attain the contemplative spirit which is not ordered as a means to the active life. The Jesuit seeks the glory of God and his own perfection as well as that of his neighbor through the active apostolate. The Carmelite seeks the same end especially through zeal for prayer or the contemplative life. It is zeal for prayer fostered by silence, solitude, self-abnegation and a tender devotion to Mary as Mother and Patroness of the contemplative life that helps to give Carmel its distinctive nature.

To this contemplative ideal the Order has joined the active apostolate, but in such a way that the contemplative spirit predominates and ever remains the *pars principalior*, governing and limiting the active apostolate which may vary from age to age depending upon the needs of the Church. Today, the apostolate, is exercised by the friars in parishes, in schools, in preaching, in writing and in the conducting of foreign missions. Moreover, just as the contemplative life of the Order is marked by its Marian spirit, so also is its active life, so that wherever the Order labors, devotion to Our Lady of Mount Carmel is surely to be found.

No one will doubt that there is a pressing need in the Church today for a more intense active apostolate, and that the Order must respond to this need with enthusiasm. But to be engaged in active work and at the same time retain the primacy of the contemplative life is no easy task. Yet the problem must be faced honestly and directly, for there is a real problem. We believe it can only be solved successfully by taking a firm stand on the fundamental principle that within the Order activity depends upon the contemplative spirit as the branch upon the vine, and if ever divorced from it, the life of Carmel will wither and die. The Carmelite, therefore, must be taught to be first and foremost a man of solitude and prayer. He must become personally convinced that the success of his apostolic labors depends upon his fidelity to the contemplative life.

Originally Carmel had no such problem, for the Order was eremitical, and apostolic activity played little part. But in the middle of the thirteenth century, when the religious were forced by the Saracens to flee from Mount Carmel and to seek refuge on the shores of Europe, they built monasteries near the cities and took a greater interest in the care of souls. Pope Innocent IV in 1248 during the generalate of Saint Simon Stock approved this new mode of mendicant life with its broadened apostolate, although the Order remained devoted to the contemplative ideal. Even today, seven centuries later, the eremitical life is encouraged, and the Constitutions recommend monasteries for those who wish to withdraw permanently or at least for a period of time from the active life to give themselves to prayer and solitude. For example, the hermitage "Mons Carmeli" in Wölfnitz, Austria, dedicated to the Blessed Virgin Mary, Mother of Carmel and Patroness of the contemplative life, has for its sole purpose the pursuit of contemplation.

The struggle to retain the primacy of the contemplative life can be traced in every phase of the Order's history – a history that has known moments of anxiety and even of occasional bitterness. At times weakened from within by the loss of fervor, and again assailed from without by wars, plagues and economic chaos the Order has had to resort to reforms to restore zeal for prayer as the primary and fundamental characteristic of daily life.

In the fifteenth and sixteenth centuries the Order experienced the reforms of Mantua (1412-1413), of Albi (1419), and of Monte Oliveto (1516). These were followed by the most publicized and successful of all reforms, that of St. Teresa of Avila and of St. John of the Cross, which after their deaths separated from the Order under Father Nicholas of Jesus (Doria). For over two hundred years the reform of the Discalced, as it is known, was carried on in two distinct congregations, the Spanish and the Italian, until finally united by Pope Pius IX in 1875.

After the departure of the Discalced the effort continued within the Order and one of the most important and influential reforms took place in the seventeenth century in the French province of Touraine – a reform destined to leave its mark on the whole Order. But aside from its universal influence, Touraine retains a place in the history of spirituality, because it has given to the Church one of the most exalted mystics of France, the blind brother, Venerable John of St. Samson, whose example and teaching molded the spiritual life of the reform.

Planting its roots in the monastery of Rennes, the reform of Touraine grew into a mighty oak spreading its branches into the seven provinces of France and even beyond its border into the Low Countries, Germany and Poland. In the year 1645, less than fifty years after the inception of the reform, Touraine drew up a new set of Constitutions that was adopted by the General Chapter of the Order not only for monasteries and provinces directly under the influence of Touraine, but even for independent reforms that were going on simultaneously in Latin countries. This federation of all reformed houses in the Order, based on the monastic discipline and the interior life that had its origin in Touraine, became known as the *Strictior Observantia*, and when in 1789 the French Revolution had mercilessly suppressed the provinces of France, it was the *Strictior Observantia* in other countries that kept alive the spirit of Touraine. Finally, when new Constitutions for the whole Order were being drawn up in 1930 they were based on the Constitutions of the *Strictior Observantia*.

The debt that the Order of today owes to Touraine is quite evident, but it is even greater when we consider that not only its monastic discipline but also its interior life emanates from Touraine. For the concept of prayer and the ways of prayer taught to the novices of the reform are being taught today in every province of the Order, since they have been reproduced almost literally in the new official directory for novices, the *Directorium carmelitanum vitae spiritualis* (1940). This new directory, although original in many things, was inspired by and based on the *Directoires des novices* (1650-1651), the official directory of the reform of Touraine, which in the course of time was translated into different languages and used extensively, if not universally, in the *Strictior Observantia*.

It takes but a moment of reflection to see that the bridge that joins the Order of the twentieth century with Carmel of the past is the reform of Touraine. To it we owe in great part our heritage. If, then, a Carmelite wishes to acquire a deeper appreciation of the life and the ways of prayer that characterize the spirit of the Order; he must acquaint himself with the spirit and the directory of Touraine. To help him to do this is the purpose of this book. We have written it with the hope that it will bring into relief the traditional spirit of the Order, uncover some of its hidden treasures, and inspire others to make more profound studies. We have limited our investigation to the fourth volume of the *Directoires,* which is entitled: *Methode claire et facile pour bien faire raison mentale et pour s'exercer avec fruict la presence de Dieu.* We believe that this treatise, called the *Méthode* for the sake of brevity, reflects not only the contemplative spirit of the French Carmelites of the seventeenth century and the *Strictior Observantia* but also the traditional life of the Order.

In particular, we have tried to answer the following questions: Who composed the *Méthode?* What are the ways of prayer that it teaches? What is their nature and purpose? From what sources are they derived?

To attain this goal we divided the work into three sections. In the first section we considered the history of the reform of Touraine. and its spirit. We have not given a detailed account, but simply presented certain facts that are useful for a better knowledge of the *Méthode*. In the second section we explained and then commented on the three ways of prayer that make up the *Méthode*. If our exposition seems lengthy, the reason is that we wanted to give the reader an adequate picture of these ways of prayer, which otherwise would be impossible since copies and translations of the *Méthode* are extremely rare.

In the last section we have unearthed the most influential doctrinal sources. We believe this part of the study is important for two reasons. First, it helps us to understand the *Méthode* in its original and authentic sense. It is said that if we know the parents, we can better understand the child. So too, from a knowledge of the sources of the *Méthode* we grasp more perfectly the ways of mental prayer, their comparative value and the purpose which they wish to attain. Secondly, a knowledge of the sources restrains us from making any exaggerated claims to the singularity of a Carmelite method of prayer, and helps us to establish definitively its roots in the sound teaching of Catholic tradition.

Throughout the book we refrained from examining the relationship of Touraine to the Jansenistic movement; (there is evidence of its opposition), or to the Prequietist movement in the first part of the seventeenth century. Both these questions would take us too far afield.

Furthermore, there is no mention in our work of the possible infuence of Cardinal Bérulle. While it is well known that Bérulle exercised tremendous influence on seventeenth century French spirituality, there is no evidence to indicate that this influence penetrated the methods of prayer in the *Méthode,* although he was known and greatly esteemed by Father Philip Thibault, the father of the reform.

Finally, whatever the merits of our research may be, it has helped us to establish two general facts. First, the reform of Touraine was a determined corporate effort to mold men of prayer, who like Elias would always stand in the sight of God, lovingly conversing with Him, unless otherwise called to other labors. To explain the steps that lead to the fullness of this contemplative life is the sole purpose of the *Méthode.* The history of the reform bears ample witness to the success of this undertaking and to the truth that where zeal for prayer reigns, the fruits of Carmel are abundant. Secondly, the *Méthode* is not a manual of mere historic value that belongs on the shelf of outmoded books, but a work that has had a steady if varying influence in the Order over a span of three centuries – an influence which has come down to us through the *Strictior Observantia* and is now at its peak because for over a decade its doctrine and methods have been taught in the novitiates of the whole Order.

It is our conviction that the *Méthode* in its basic and essential teaching on the primacy of prayer and the contemplative life, which has been preserved in the new *Directorium carmelitanum,* has the same potential today as it did in Touraine. It can direct souls in the first steps of prayer that will lead them to the threshold of new mansions of the interior life in which with Elias they will stand continually in the loving presence of God.

It is only fitting that we conclude our introduction with a word of thanks to those who in any way helped us complete this study. We are grateful to the late Very Reverend John Brenninger, O. Carm. and the late Reverend Joseph de Guibert, S.J. for their help in the first stages of this work, and to Father Valerius Hoppenbrouwers, O. Carm. for his interest and advice. Special thanks, however, are due to Reverend Arnold Lanz, S. J. and Reverend Charles Truhlar, S. J. of the Gregorian University for their patient guidance and helpful suggestions.

ABBREVIATIONS

AOC   *Analecta Ordinis Carmelitarum.* Rome, 1909-

BC   *Bibliotheca carmelitana* edited by Cosmas de Villiers, Orléans, 1752, new edition by Gabriel Wessels, Rome, 1927, 2 Vols.

DSp   *Dictionnaire de spiritualité ascétique et mystique.* Marcel Viller, Paris, 1935-

DTC   *Dictionnaire de théologie catholique.* A. Vacant, E. Magenot, Paris, 1903-

Méthode   *Méthode claire et facile pour bien faire oraison mentale, et pour exercer avec fruict en la présence de Dieu.* Paris, 1651.

RAM   *Revue d'ascétique et de mystique.* Toulouse, 1920-

Section One

THE REFORM OF TOURAINE

Chapter I

ORIGIN OF THE REFORM

At the dawn of the seventeenth century the Carmelites of the Ancient Observance underwent a spiritual reform in France that has become known to future generations as the reform of Touraine. This was one of the most efficacious reforms in the history of Carmel, and its good effects have reached down even to the present day.

This spiritual revival of Carmel in France was greatly aided by external circumstances. For when Pope Clement VIII accorded absolution to King Henry IV in 1595, the government of France began to take a more favorable attitude to the promotion of the Catholic faith. Henry entered Paris and began fifteen years of excellent administration, one of the most prosperous in the history of France.[1] It was during these years of outstanding leadership especially in the political, economic and religious fields that the spiritual life of Carmel so long dormant in France began to stir, grow and finally blossom forth like a new flower in spring.

In the year 1600 Carmel of the Ancient Observance was represented in France by seven provinces: Narbonne, France, Aquitaine, Provence, Toulouse, Gascony and Touraine. It was in the province of Touraine,[2] not the least of the seven provinces, that the first signs of spiritual restlessness began to show themselves. The province of Touraine at that time included under its jurisdiction fifteen

---

[1] Jean Dagens, *Bérulle et les origines de la restauration catholique* (Paris, 1952), 169-178.

[2] At this time the Carmelites of the Ancient Observance numbered throughout the world 37 provinces which do not include some 54 houses that belonged to the Mantuan reform. Cf. *Constitutiones strictioris observantiae* (Antwerp, 1656), 374.

The Discalced Carmelite nuns did not arrive in France until the end of the year 1604. The Discalced friars opened their first monastery in Avignon on March 19, 1609. Cf. Silverio di Santa Teresa, O.C.D., *Historia del Carmen Descalzo* (14 vols., Burgos, 1935-1949), VIII, 154.

monasteries, but many of them lacked a vigorous spiritual life, a state of affairs which in great part had been brought about by the miserable economic conditions of France. The monasteries were located in the following places: La Rochelle, Angers, Tours, Plöermel, Nantes, Orléans, Loundun, St. Pol-de-Léon, Poitiers, Pont-L'Abbé, Hennebont, Vivonne, Dol, Le Boudon, Rennes and Aulnay.[3]

Three men in particular were chosen by God to have a special place in the organization and propagation of the reform of the province of Touraine. They were Fathers Peter Behourt, Louis Charpentier and Philip Thibault. The first two took part in organizing the reform, and the latter insured its growth. The monastery at Rennes was chosen as the cradle of the reform, and for this reason the reform of Touraine is sometimes called the Observance of Rennes.[4]

Peter Behourt and Louis Charpentier were not outstanding perssonalities, and neither was destined to leave a profound influence upon the spiritual growth of Touraine. Charpentier was the weaker of the two, and quicky sought refuge in retirement once the machinery of the reform was set in motion. Behourt was a more determined and relentless reformer and in the face of opposition refused to relinquish the path he had undertaken until he had safely entrusted the reform into the hands of the young but capable Father Philip Thibault, who has justly merited the title of "Father of the Reform of Touraine."

Philip Thibault was born at Brain-sur-Allone near Angers in 1572.[5] He entered the Carmelite monastery at Angers, and in later years was fortunate to study theology, at least for one year, at the Jesuit University of Pont à-Mousson, which is well known among other things for the number of reformers of French monasteries who were educated there toward the end of the sixteenth century.[6]

---

[3] During the course of the reform the following eleven monasteries were founded: Chalain, Quintin, Le Guildo, St. Malo, Josselin, Auray, Blessed Sacrament in Paris, Basses Loges, Fontainebleau, La Flèche, La Flocelière. Four convents of nuns also belonged to the Province: Notre Dame des Coüets near Nantes, Nazareth near Vannes, Holy Sepulchre at Rennes, Bethléem at Ploërmel. Cf. Suzanne-Marie Bouchereaux, *La Réforme des Carmes en France et Jean de Saint-Samson* (Paris, 1950), 31.

[4] Father Benedict Zimmerman mistakenly thought that the reform of Touraine and the Observance of Rennes were two differents reforms. B. Zimmerman, O.C.D., "Les Réformes dans l'Ordre de Notre Dame du Mont-Carmel," *Études Carmélitaines*, 19 (Oct., 1934), 195.

[5] For more detailed biography consult Bouchereaux, *La Réforme des Carmes*, 36.

[6] The Jesuit University of Pont-à-Mousson was founded in 1572. About 1580 many young men who were to take part in various religious reforms in France received their theological training there. Peter Fourier, who reformed the Augustinians, and founded the Congregation of Notre Dame for the education of young girls; Didier de la Cour, reformer of

How did Philip Thibault come to choose Pont-à-Mousson for his studies? It is not easy to say, but if we may believe Father Abram, historian of the University, who however errs in some facts regarding Thibault (he calls Thibault a Norman), then it was on the advice of Father André Duval, famous professor of theology at the Sorbonne, and one of the most influential figures in the spiritual revival of France in the first part of the seventeenth century. It seems that Thibault was troubled about his vocation. He felt called lo leave Carmel for the solitude of the Carthusians. He sought advice from Dom Richard Beaucousin at Paris, who urged him at that time to remain in the Order of Carmel and work for its reform.[7] Following this advice, Thibault turned to André Duval, who counseled him to go to the Jesuits, to find what course of action he should take. It is believed he remained at Pont-à-Mousson for one year, either in 1595 or 1596.[8]

According lo Father Abram, Thibault, like other reformers who had frequented Pont-à-Mousson, made the Spiritual Exercises of St. Ignatius, and obtained the inspiration to begin the great work of reform that he was destined to accomplish in the course of time.[9]

In the Jubilee year of 1600 Thibault was among those who made the Holy Year pilgrimage to Rome. He went to seek pardon for his premature ordination to the priesthood which had unnecessarily caused him many scruples. Thibault had been ordained before the age of twenty-four which was the canonical age established by the Council of Trent. He had been given this permission because the decrees of Trent had not yet been promulgated in France, although they had been promulgated in the Order. At the same time he wanted to inform the General of the Order of his intention to join the Carthusians or Discalced Carmelites, or else obtain in the province of Touraine a house following the strict observance of Carmel.[10]

---

the Benedictines of St. Vanne, and the initiator of the reform of St. Maur; Servais de Lairuels, reformer of the Premonstratensians; and later Philip Thibault, reformer of the Carmelites. Cf. Henri Bremond, *Histoire littéraire du sentimcnt religieux en France* (11 vols., Paris, 1916-1935). 11, 2.

[7] Beaucousin is given credit by some spiritual writers as being the hand that guided the whole spiritual revival of France at the beginning of the seventeenth century while he himself remained in the background. He directed the great St. Francis of Sales, the saintly Bérulle and many reformers of religious orders. J. Huijben, "Aux sources de la spiritualité française du XV11 siècle," *Vie Spirituelle*, supplément, 26 (1931) 21-46: Lézin de Sainte Scholastique, O. Carm., La *vie du V.-P. Philippe Thibault* (Paris, 1673), 254.

[8] Bouchereaux, *La Réforme dcs Carmes*, 45.
[9] *Ibid.*, 43.
[10] *Ibid.*, 45.

At Rome Thibault had an audience with Pope Clement VIII, who did much for the reformation of religious Orders in the Church. The Pope advised him to remain in the Order and to work for its reform. He made known to Thibault his intention to send the General of the Order into France as soon as possible with authority to establish a reform.

On the same day Philip had an audience with the General, Father Henry Sylvius, who was also reluctant to see Philip leave the Order, and promised he would on his next trip to France reform the Province.[11]

Returning to France, Philip informed Beaucousin of the will of his superiors. The latter had already made some preparations to send Philip to the charter house at Grenoble, but recognizing the will of God in the advice Philip received at Rome, he was happy to see the young Carmelite remain in his Order.[12]

On the occasion of the baptism of the future King Louis XIII in 1601, the Cardinal de Joyeuse presented some Carmelites of the province of Touraine to King Henry IV. They had come to ask for assistance in the reform of the province. The king promised to help, and wrote to Pope Clement VIII asking His Holiness to send the General of the Carmelites to France to set up the reform.

Meanwhile in 1602 Father Peter Behourt was elected provincial of the province of Touraine at the provincial chapter held at Angers. Known to be a reformer, Behourt was not well received in his office by many of the religious, but nevertheless. was confirmed in office by Rome.[13]

Finally in 1603 the Prior General, Henry Sylvius, arrived in France. He immediately sought out Philip Thibault, and made him his companion during his stay. He convoked a chapter at Nantes on June 20, 1604, and published the first regulations of the reform, which were inspired for the most part by the decrees of Pope Clement VIII for the reform of religious orders.[14]

The monastery of Rennes was chosen to be the cradle of the reform. Sylvius appointed Peter Behourt as the first prior. Philip

---

[11] Fr. Antoine-Marie de la Présentation, O.C.D., *Le Carmel en France, étude historique* (7 vols., Toulouse, 1936-1939), I, 98. Fr. Antoine-Marie states that Philip spent two years at this time in the Discalced monastery of S. Maria della Scala to learn the method of prayer taught to the novices. We have not been able to find any verification of this statement.

[12] Bouchereaux, *La Réforme des Carmes,* 47.

[13] Bouchereaux, *La Réforme des Carmes,* 31. She gives a short biography of Behourt.

[14] The decrees refer to the divine office in choir, the vow of poverty, the habit, the cloister, the novices, the administration. Cf. J. de la Servière, "Clement VIII," in DTC, III, 286.

Thibault, who assisted the General during the chapter, remained in the background. There were only five religious who immediately accepted the reform at Rennes. They were: Peter Behourt, prior; Father Plumelet, sub-prior; Father Guerchois, sacristan; and two novices, one of whom was Mathurin Aubron.

In the chapter of 1607 Louis Charpentier was elected prior of Rennes. He wanted the reform, but unlike Behourt he was timid and easily discouraged and drawn to compromise. He was definitely not the type to inspire and lead the new movement.

Behourt then turned to Philip Thibault in whom he saw the ideal leader. Thibault was at Paris studying for the licentiate in theology. Behourt and Charpentier prevailed upon him to come and preach the Lenten course at Rennes in 1608. His presence in the community was a boon to all, and Thibault was persuaded to stay as subprior and master of novices. He fell to the work of guiding the novices with great zeal. Whereas Behourt had depressed the young men by his continual insistence on mortification and exterior practises so that many were discouraged, Thibault inspired their souls with joy and confidence as he directed them in the ways of prayer, teaching them to live in the presence of God and to love silence and solitude.

Finally on April 21, 1608, the religious of Rennes renewed their profession, and signed a document to the effect that they willingly submitted themselves to follow the new regulations of the reform. Among those who signed were: Louis Charpentier, prior, Peter Behourt, Philip Thibault, William Guerchois, Francis Odiau, Noël de Mardeaux, P. Demart, Anthony Dupuy and Mathurin Aubron. Later the following added their names to signify their intention to observe the strict observance: Matthew Pinault, Charles of St. Agatha and Michael of Ave Maria.[15]

As was to be expected all did not go smoothly in the beginning, and Louis Charpentier was not able to cope successfully with the opposition. He gladly relinquished his post at Rennes to become prior of Angers.[16] Thibault, who in the meantime had returned to study at Paris, was elected prior, and came back to Rennes on November 15, 1608, where he received a joyful welcome.[17]

---

[15] Bouchereau, *La Réforme des Carmes*, 67.

[16] Toward the end of his life he returned to Rennes and took the name of Father Louis of St. Anne. He died there in 1640. *Ibid.*, 404.

[17] While at Paris Thibault was studying for the licentiate in theology. He obtained this degree on January 26, 1610, at the University of Paris. *Ibid.,*

Encouraged by this reception and imbued with the spirit of a reformer Thibault began to make some changes. The divine office hitherto grossly neglected was now chanted, and the ceremonial once so carelessly transgressed was now observed with care and reverence. Church feasts were again celebrated in the solemn manner with public processions that attracted favorably the attention of the lay populace of Rennes: The common life with insistence on the exact observance of the vow of poverty was introduced. This was most difficult since for years, due to plagues and wars, religious had to look out for themselves so that each cherished private possessions. Above all, Thibault insisted on set periods of mental prayer twice each day. Silence and solitude were also part of the new regime, since the interior life cannot flourish easily without these conditions. For this reason the number of visitors to the monastery was curtailed and the friars were permitted to visit only the sick and the afflicted. With these and similar regulations firmly established the restoration of the spiritual life of the province of Touraine was well on its way.[18]

The first members to be professed after their novitiate were Gabriel of the Annunciation, a clerical student, and Angelus of St. Paul, a brother, who made their profession in January 1609. They put aside their family names for religious names. In the future anyone who embraced the reform and made his novitiate according to its regulations would follow their example. By this practice Thibault hoped to inculcate more deeply in his subjects a taste for the interior life and withdrawal from the world. [19]

The reform next spread to the monastery of Angers, where Louis Charpentier was prior. Introduction of the reform by Charpentier and Thibault brought about a revolt that demanded the intervention of the civil authorities. It seems that the reformers acted a little imprudently in starting the reform at Angers when the provincial, Christopher Le Roy, who was hostile to the reform, was away in Rome attending the general chapter in 1609. On his return he refused to recognize the changes imposed at Angers, but finally submitted when the civil authorities threatened to bring the case to the ecclesiastical tribunal.

Further scandal was avoided when the Provincial ordered nine religious of Rennes to be transferred to Angers. Saddened but wiser, Thibault avoided similar demonstrations in the future.

---

[18] Bouchereaux, *La Réforme des Carmes*, 70.
[19] *Ibid.*, 71.

Soon after this, uniform rules for both monasteries of Rennes and Angers were drawn up at Angers on May 13, 1610. These were the first statutes of the reform, and were later added to the new constitutions.[20]

In the provincial chapter of April 2, 1611 at Hennebont, Thibault succeeded in getting these statutes approved.[21] At this chapter Thibault was confirmed as prior of Rennes, and Francis Odiau as prior of Angers. The new provincial, Master Peter Chalumeau, did his best to oppose and impede the new movement but to no avail, for the general of the Order approved the statutes of the reform in 1615.

It should be noted that Thibault was reluctant to receive religious from unreformed houses. He feared they would only retard the revival. However, we know he made some exceptions, for he received from Dol two religious who were to become outstanding figures in the reform: Father Matthew Pinault, friend of Peter Behourt, was the first.[22] The other was the blind lay brother John of St. Samson. The blind brother was a holy man, a master of masters in the spiritual life, and destined to be the soul of the reform of Touraine. At Rennes he would teach all, including Thibault, the father of the reform, the true spirit of Carmel.

In 1614, led by Thibault, some religious of the new observance met at the monastery of Loudun, to draw up common rules for Rennes, Angers and Loudun. This was the first Congregation of the reform.

At the meeting Thibault succeeded in bringing about a common fund between the three monasteries, a new program of studies for the students, the naming of Advent and Lenten preachers, and the establishment of the regular life at Loudun modelled on Rennes.[23]

In 1615 the reform was blessed with the beginning of a new monastery; the gift of Christopher Fouquet, "premier Président de la séance d'Août au Parlement de Rennes," who had been drawn to love the Order by the piety of the religious of Rennes. The new monastery was called St. Joseph of Chalain and was consecrated in 1618 by the Archbishop of Angers.

---

[20] These regulations are found in the work of Hugh of St. Francis, *La Véritable idée d'un supérieur religieux, formée sur la vie et les conduites du vénérable père Philippe Thibault avec les maximes spirituelles pour acquérir la perfection chretienne et religieuse* (2 vols., Angers, 1663-1665), I, 102.

[21] Cf. Hugh of St. Francis, *La Véritable idée*, I, 105; Bouchereaux, *La Réforme des Carmes*, 329.

[22] Bouchereaux, *La Réforme des Carmes*, 329.

[23] *Ibid.*, 78.

The success of the reform was assured by the number and quality of the novices who entered the observance. The college of the Jesuits at Rennes became the source of many solid vocations and brilliant men. Dominic of St. Albert, one of the glories of the reform and a true mystic, entered the observance in these early years and was professed in 1614.

As the reform grew Thibault found it necessary to draw up a set of new Constitutions. The original manuscript is preserved in the Archives of Rennes.[24] It bears the title: *Constitutiones, seu Exercitia spiritualia per Reverendos Patres·Priorem et caeteros gremiales Carmeli Rhedonensis, quae per plures annos in eodem Carmelo non sine magno spirituali fructu sunt observata, ac in posterum, favente Deo et annuentibus Reverendis Ordinis Superioribus observanda, in praedicto conventu, nec non in aliis eiusdem Observantiae.*

These Constitutions have a prologue and twenty-six chapters. They tell us that the reform is placed under the protection of St. Charles Borromeo. Thibault had great devotion to this saintly reformer. The Constitutions are drawn up in accordance with the Rule of St. Albert of Jerusalem, according to the mitigation of Pope Eugene IV and the decrees of Pius II and Sixtus IV. They are signed by the fathers of the conventual chapter at Rennes on April 25, 1615.[25]

It is interesting to note some observations on the background of these Constitutions, which were approved at Rome by the General, Sebastian Fantoni (1612-1623) on November 22, 1615.[26] In a book of controversies addressed to the Jesuits, a religious of the reform, Father Gregory of St. Martin, openly confessed:

> We know that our humble reform, which with the blessing of God has spread through France, the Netherlands, Germany, Poland and the New World, has taken its happy beginning in Brittany under the leadership of Father Thibault, assisted by your counsel, after having accommodated our Constitutions to those of the Society of Jesus, in so far as the humble solitary spirit of Elias-would permit. [27]

Thibault did not forget the essential life of the Order, which is prayer, when drawing up the Constitutions with the aid of Jesuit

---

[24] Bouchereaux, *La Réforme des Carmes*, 79. Archives départementales d'Ille-et-Vilaine. Fonds des Grands Carmes, 9 H 25.

[25] *Ibid.*, 79.

[26] Bouchereaux, *La Réforme des Carmes*, 82.

[27] Gregory of St. Martin, *Apologie pour l'antiquité des religieux Carmes* (Douay, 1685), preface.

counsel. He was thoroughly Carmelite. From his novitiate days he had been inspired by the life and earlíer reform of Blessed John Soreth.[28] The Discalced reform also inspired him. He spent six weeks in their novitiate at Paris following the strict life. He had great esteem and affection for the Discalced, and at various times sought their advice.[29] However, Thibault was bent upon a reform within the Order. He therefore retained the mitigation of the Rule granted by Eugene IV in 1432. Many of the practices that he had initiated at Rennes he now incorporated into the new Constitutions. In regard to the exterior life he brought back the strict observance of poverty which had been greatly abused in France. Privileges granted to those religious with academic degrees which had long been the bane of community life were abolished. On the other hand, the wearing of sandals, a sign of poverty and austerity, was not introduced because, as Thibault believed, sandals were not prescribed by the Rule or any of the older Constitutions. Besides, excessive austerity after a while seeks dispensations.[30]

The new legislation gave special attention to the interior life. The Carmelite liturgy emanating from the Holy Land and jealously guarded down through the centuries was retained in all its splendor. The daily practice of mental prayer, fasts, silence, solitude, matins at midnight, all these practices were incorporated into the Constitutions of 1615. The reform gained the admiration and the support of the hierarchy. The Archbishop of Rennes even offered some material aid to encourage the new observance. The bishops of Dol, St. Brieuc, St. Malo, and Vannes gave encouragement and protected the reform in their respective dioceses. Robert Berthelot, Carmelite and titular bishop of Damascus and suffragan of Lyon, expressed his interest, and on various occasions gave valuable counsel to Father Thibault.[31] Secular authorities too rendered assistance, but as a general rule Thibault preferred to operate independently of all civil interference.

---

[28] Bouchereaux, *La Réforme des Carmes, 38-39*, Lézin, *Vie*, 14.

[29] Jean Marie de l'Enfant Jésus, O.C.D., "Deux siècles de vie carmélitaine," *Ètudes carmélitaines*, 20 (1935), 38; and Timothy of the Presentation, O. Carm., "Vita p. Philippi Theobaldi," *Analecta Ordinis Carmelltarum*, 7 (1930-1931), 52.

[30] Bouchereaux, *La Réforme des Carmes*, 70; Lezin, *Vie*, 110-111.

[31] Robert Berthelot was a friend of St. Francis de Sales. He was with the saint at the time of his death, and was later given the saint's episcopal robes: Cf. *BC;* 11, col. 686-691. He is not to be confused with Peter Berthelot, O.C.D., known as Dionysius of the Nativity. Cf. *BC*, I, col.401.

Finally, the Generals of the Order gave every encouragement to the reform. Amusing are the words written by the General to the provincial who refused to reform Ploërmel. *"Frivolae sunt omnes istae excusationes, et nisi curiae constituto plene satisfeceris, experieris, quam longas manus habeant generales."* [32]

With the reform solidly established and supported by the hierarchy and the Generals of the Order, Thibault turned his attention to the education of the young novices. The first novices were Bretons, Normans and Angevins. They received their spiritual formation from Thibault himself. Later he relinquished the position of novice master to Matthew Pinault, who continued to educate them as well as the young clerics according to the spirit of Thibault.

As regards their theological studies Thibault sent his students to the Jesuits at La Flèche. The Jesuits had returned to France and reopened their school in January 1604. They sent their own students to the college at La Flèche, and some of the better known professors, such as Fathers Brossart, Stephen Charlet and Louis Mairat, were already known to Thibault.

The students could have been sent to the Carmelite Studium at Place Maubert in Paris, but Thibault did not wish to send them to a house that did not admit the reform.

In 1617 Thibault gained the consent of the provincial to have a vicar provincial for the reformed houses. The provincial nominated Matthew Pinault. The general confirmed this choice, and ordered an annual congregation to choose the vicar in the future.

In 1618 Thibault himself became provincial of Touraine, and succeeded Peter Maillard. This was a further step toward the Reform of the entire province. Finally, the General obtained from Pope Paul V a brief naming Thibault as the commissary General apostolic for the reform of the province of Touraine. This was in 1620.

It was only natural that the work of Thibault should draw attention outside the Order. He won the respect of both lay and clerical groups. His name was even mentioned for a bishopric. In fact, we are told that he refused the bishopric of Nantes and recommended for this see Philip Cospéan, bishop of Aire, who was finally chosen bishop of Nantes on January 17, 1621.[33]

In 1620 Thibault, as provincial of Touraine, went to the General Chapter in Rome, fortified with many letters of recommendation

---

[32] Hugh, *La Veritable idée*, I, 147.
[33] Boucheaux, *La Réforme des Carmes*, 87.

from the French court including letters from the queen mother, Marie de Medicis. At Rome he was welcomed by the Prior General, Sebastian Fantoni.

It is suggested that while at Rome Thibault was in a position to make the reform a separate Congregation, as the Discalced did, since he, like they, enjoyed the favor of the court. It would have meant independence and unity in progressing with his ideas of reform. Thibault however refused, believing that the observance of Rennes would spread to the whole Order.[34]

Meanwhile (1623) the General urged Thibault to extend the reform into other provinces. Thibault often hesitated, and sometimes did not act upon the suggestions of the General. He seemed often reluctant to go to other provinces. After continual urging he did go to Flanders, where he was welcomed by the religious of Valenciennes. This was the beginning of the reform that eventually spread to all the houses of Belgium.[35]

In 1632 Father Archangelus of St. Luke became provincial. He was ordered by the General, Theodore Strazio (1631-1642), to begin tlle reform of the provinces of Toulouse and France. The General desired also the reform of the general house of studies on Place Maubert in Paris, but to no avail.[36] Finally, in 1634 the provincial received instructions to reform the province of Provence.

By 1633 all the houses of the province of Touraine had been received into the fold and the vicar provincial became useless. His work done, Thibault retired the same year from all administrative duties, and went to live and work with the nuns. The reform was left in the hands of men whom he had formed over the years. Five years later he died a holy death on January 24, 1638.[37]

The pioneer work of Touraine spread and the provinces of Narbonne, Aquitaine, France and Gascony were soon reformed. The provinces of Provence and Toulouse joined later so that by the middle of the century the provinces of France had all fallen under the spell of Touraine.

---

[34] *Ibid.*, 89.

[35] Lézin, *Vie*, 254. Cf. also *AOC*, 7 (1930-1931), 53.

[36] This house was never successfully reformed. Cf. Bouchereaux, *La Réforme des Carmes*, 424-431.

[37] It is the opinion of Bouchereaux (in which we do not concur) that the reform of Touraine would have been more successful if Thibault had set up a separate congregation. His failure to do so, she says, shows a weakness in his character which ultimately hurt the future of the reform. Cf. *La Réforme des Carmes*, 89.

The new Constitutions for the reform were first printed in Paris by Jean Guillemot in 1636 with the title: *Regula et Constitutiones Fratrum B. Dei Genetricis et Virginis Mariae de Monte Carmeli pro conventibus reformationis gallicae in provincia Turonensi.*

At the general chapter in Rome in 1645 Leo of St. John, provincial of Touraine, and one of the most prominent men in the history of the reform,[38] formed part of the committee that revised these Constitutions for use by all the reformed convents of the Order.[39] The *Regula et Constitutiones Fratrum B. Dei Genetricis et Virginis Mariae de Monte Carmeli Strictioris Observantiae pro conventibus reformatis* appeared that same year (without name of place or publisher). Certain alterations were later deemed necessary and resulted in a fresh edition in 1650 (Paris, Joseph Cottereau).

Despite many problems the work of the reform continued and we find it finally spreading outside France. We have seen that Thibault brought the reform to Flanders in 1624, where it took deep root and in time produced some remarkable religious. Among them we mention the historian, Daniel of the Blessed Virgin Mary, and the spiritual writer, Venerable Michael of St. Augustine, whose Marian writings are of outstanding merit.[40] The two provinces of Germany accepted the reform. It was received into Poland first in the monastery of Corpus Christi in Poznan in 1647,[41] and later in 1672 in Danzig and Bydgoszcz.[42] Some of the religious of France even brought the reform with them to the missions in the Antilles. These missionaries continued in relations with the reform up to 1788.[43]

After the death of Thibault and John of St. Samson other prominent men took a very active part in keeping alive the reform, and have won for themselves a place in the history of spirituality. Besides Dominic of St. Albert, to whom we shall have occasion to refer later, the following Carmelites are worthy of mention: Leo of St. John, Maurus of the Child Jesus and René of St. Albert.

---

[38] *Ibid.*, 337-352.

[39] *Ibid.*, 96. We note that the Constitutions of 1636 have no date and no place, but the year 1636 can be sufficiently established. Cf. *AOC*, 15 (1950), 349, no. 1.

[40] *BC*, I, col. 375, col. 446.

[41] Ex articulis pro introducenda, confirmanda ac promovenda Strictioris Observantiae in conventibus et Provinciis Ord. Carmelitarum nondum totaliter reformatis. (1672) Ms. Archives O. Carm., Rome.

[42] Decreta pro introducenda reformatione ad conv. Bydgostensem et Gedanensem. Ms. (1672) Archives O. Carm., Rome.

[43] Bouchereaux, *La Réforme des Carmes*, 418.

Father Leo of St. John was an eloquent preacher and prolific writer.

He was the court preacher of King Louis XIII and of King Louis XIV, as well as a close friend of the great Cardinal Richelieu. He heard the last confession of the Cardinal, and was with him at his deathbed. We shall have ocasion to speak of him later.

Maurus of the Child Jesus was another spiritual writer of the reform. His works were highly esteemed by the Quietists, Madame Guyon and Father Bertot, although the writings of Maurus seem free from Quietistic teaching.[44]

René of St. Albert, one time prior of the monastery of the Blessed Sacrament in Paris, where he died in 1691, was the friend and confessor of Bossuet. According to Father Levesque, who has published some notes of Bossuet on the prayer of simplicity, Bossuet had written in his own hand beside the title of his work, the name of René of St. Albert, the Carmelite prior of the monastery of the Blessed Sacrament. It seems that Bossuet took from his confessor this prayer of simplicity that is described in these notes.[45]

To continue with a more detailed history of the reform after 1650 would be going beyond our task. Suffice it to say that the following years brought much success and some failures to the work of Thibault. The monastery of Rennes that could scarcely support twelve religious in 1600, was able to house comfortably one hundred religious only forty years later. In the middle of the seventeenth century the province of Touraine had increased its membership to seven hundred.[46] The reform continued on into the eighteenth century, but political strife in the nation began to take its toll upon Carmel as well as upon other religious Orders. Thus, in 1766 the reform of Touraine had 25 houses and 199 religious. The Carmelites of France at that time had 129 houses and numbered 1,194 religious.[47]

While it is true that the French Revolution of 1789 saw the Carmelite provinces of France completely destroyed, we would be in error if we were to believe the reform of Touraine ceased entirely to exist. For the reform of Touraine had spread not only throughout

---

[44] Pourrat, *La Spiritualité chrétienne* (4 vols., Paris, 1926-1930), IV, 180.

[45] *Ibid.*, 160.

[46] Matthias of St. John, O. Carm., *Genius Carmelitanae reformationis in antiquo ordinis coetu institutae* (Bordeaux, 1666), 4-5.

[47] Bouchereaux, *La Réforme des Carmes,* 31.

France, but into many other countries. In later years together with other reforms in the Order it developed into the *Strictior Observantia*. No one has yet written the history of this reform or of its dependence on the reform of Touraine. This is a task which we hope to see done within a few years. Yet, one thing is certain. Many of the spiritual writings of Touraine were translated into other languages, and thus the spirit of Touraine passed into many provinces of the Order. As we shall see, the official directory of novices, which contains the spirit of Touraine, was used extensively in the novitiates of the *Strictior Observantia*. But before we examine this official directory let us first analyse the spirit of the reform.

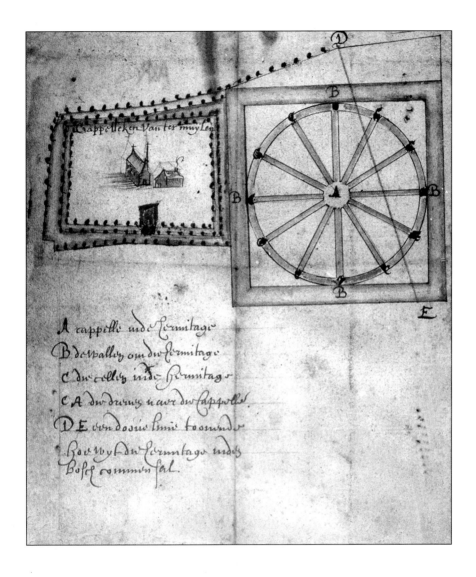

THE HERMITAGE OF LIEDEKERKE
of the Flemish Belgian Province in Termuylen, Belgium

A.   the Chapel in the hermitage.
B.   the walls around the hermitage.
C.   the cells in the hermitage.
CA. the lanes to the chapel.
DE. a dead line showing how the hermitage will lead into the forest.

Chapter II

THE SPIRIT OF TOURAINE

In the light of the historical development of the reform of Touraine we pose the following question: Was this reform a mere return to common life and the practise of the three vows – a return to a life of regularity free from scandal and bad example, or was it more than this? Was it also a return to the true primitive spirit of the Order of Carmel?

We ask this question for two reasons. First, a clear understanding of the spirit of Touraine will shed light on the ways of prayer that were taught to the novices and which will be the special object of study in this book. Secondly, it has been alleged, and we believe erroneously, that the reform of Touraine was not a reform in the true sense, that is, a return to the primitive spirit of the Order, but that it was essentially only a determined effort to return to the common life and regular observance. This latter opinion seems to be that of Father Antoine Marie de la Présentation, O.C.D., who proposed the following question in 1932 which he said had not been answered satisfactorily. "In what did the essence of the reform of Touraine consist?" His solution was that it consisted in a return to the common life. *"La stricte observance consistait en somme dans l'établissement de la vie commune telle qu'elle venait d'être imposée par les décrets de Clement VIII renouvelés et augmentés sous Urbain VIII, par la Congrégation du Concile."*[1]

We wish to take issue with this opinion. There can be no doubt that the provinces of France needed reform. The Protestant reformation, plagues and wars had left their mark on the whole Order including the houses of France.[2] Not only were the houses in a deplorable

---

[1] "La réforme de Touraine," *Études carmélitaines*, 17 (Oct., 1932), 201.
[2] L. Cognet, "Les origines de la spiritualité française au XVIIe siècle." *Culture catholique* (Sept. 1949), 19-123.

economic condition, but the spiritual life was also at a low ebb. Often the divine office was not celebrated. There was no real solitude. Each religious took care of his own material needs. Private ownership of property, which is the ruin of mendicant Orders, was generally tolerated. The friars were regulars without a rule. They were supposed to be men of prayer, but some of them had never been taught the meaning and the necessity of mental prayer. Touraine did not escape this common decadence, and Rennes, the birthplace of the reform, was in a miserable state when Peter Behourt made his profession there in 1578.

But it seems to us after an examination of some of the more important documents of the reform[3] that this was not merely a return to the common life, but that it was much more, it was above all a return to the primitive spirit of Carmel – a return to a life that was primarily (but not exclusively) contemplative wherein the spirit of solitude, silence and prayer would reign supreme.

We have many authentic documents to substantiate our position. But before we examine them, it is all-important to remember that the reform of Touraine was taking root at the very time that the spiritual terrain of France was being deluged by what Bremond has rightly called the "mystical invasion" from Spain, Italy, the Netherlands and the German Rhineland. The spiritual influence of these countries was tremendous, and can be measured at least partially by the manifold translations of spiritual books that flooded France.

It was during these years and those just prior to the reform of Touraine that the Spanish writers (Grenada, Arias, John of Avila, St. Teresa, etc.), the Italian writers (Bellintani, Capiglia, Pinelli, Scupoli, etc.), and the Germanic mystics (Tauler, Suso, Ruysbroeck, Harphius, Denis the Carthusian, Lansperge, Louis de Blois, etc.) were translated into French, and began to slowly indoctrinate not only the French clergy and religious, but the devout laity. So great was this foreign influence that in his earlier letters of spiritual direction (prior to the publication of his *Philothea*) St. Francis of Sales recommended many of these foreign books for spiritual reading, but never once recommended a French author.[4]

In the molding of the interior life of seventeenth century France the mystics from the North wielded tremendous influence. We find not only the Benedictines, but the Jesuits and Capuchins adopting the *In-*

---

[3] Father Antoine-Marie cites only the report of the annual congregation (1619) of Rennes and two excerpts from the General Chapter of 1620.

[4] Jean Dagens, *Bérulle*, 104.

stitution Spirituelle of Blosius as a manual for their novices. Madame Acarie also succumbed to the charm of Blosius, and carefully recopied many of his mystical writings. Should we not, then, be surprised if the Carmelites of the Ancient Observance did not look to these same spiritual writers for direction in carrying on their reform? Would the Carmelites attempt a reform based on a mere return to the common and regular life, and thus cut themselves off from the mystical atmosphere that was penetrating almost every religious Order in France?

History proves that the Carmelites of Touraine also fell under the spell of the mystical invasion. We find this point adequately demonstrated by Miss Bouchereaux in her doctoral dissertation *La Réforme des Carmes en France et Jean de Saint-Samson*. Here we see the tremendous influence of Ruysbroeck, Harpius, Blosius, etc. especially in the writings of John of St. Samson, who had more influence than any other man in forming the spiritual life of the reform of Touraine.

But the dissertation of Miss Bouchereaux proves much more. It clearly demonstrates that Thibault and John of St. Samson sought to give to Touraine the true primitive spirit of Carmel. Her own conclusion is that "the reform of Touraine, authentically Carmelite, had no other ambition than to see the true spirit of Carmel revive among its sons."[5]

Although we could consider this issue settled by Miss Bouchereaux, we think it important to cite some documents of the reform that clearly picture the true nature of the Touraine reform.

The Constitutions of an Order are always an authentic proof of its purpose and spirit. The new Constitutions of the reform (1636) reveal its contemplative spirit, especially in its advice to the newly professed clerics.

It is necessary that a convenient time and place be given to the newly professed so that they may be more deeply imbued with the spirit of our holy Institute, and implant virtues in their minds, and transfer all their affections totally in God, so that in time they may advance in internal conversation with God and in the sweet presence of God, which beyond a doubt constitutes and makes the true Carmelite. [6]

---

[5] Bouchereaux, *La Réforme des Carmes*, 355.

[6] *Regula et Constitutiònes Fratrum Beatae Dei Genatricis et Virginis Maria-de Monte Carmelo.* (Paris, [1636]), Part I, chap. vi, p. 73. The ideal expressed here is traditional in the Order and was clearly expressed before Touraine in the *Institutio primorum monachorum* of at least the fourteenth century. The ascetical part of this work was edited by G. Wessels, O. Carm. *AOC*, 3 (1916), 346-367.

The true nature of Touraine is perhaps nowhere better stated than in the *Directoires des novices,* the official manual for the formation of novices in the reform. Here we read:

> The first and principal obligation of our Institute is to attend and stand with God in solitude, silence and continual prayer, following the wish of our first father and founder St. Elias, the prophet.
>
> For this reason our dwelling has been placed in the desert, where the express command of our Rule orders us to remain continually withdrawn in our cells, meditating day and night on the law of God. And although after many centuries we have been transported from the deserts of Palestine to the cities and populated towns of Europe, nevertheless, this obligation of continually being attentive to God in prayer has always remained the same. Our Rule on this point has never been changed. Hence, the principal work of the Order is prayer, solitude and silence, all other work should be considered accessory, and should never destroy or be prejudicial in any manner to the principal work.
>
> The purpose of anyone entering our Order therefore should not be to study to become a learned man, or to live in community life precisely to perform good works in order to merit heaven, but to become a spiritual man, a man of prayer. One should try to live with God and himself in total ignorance of worldly things, striving to avoid all useless and frivolous thoughts, directing and holding his spirit continually united to God, walking always in his presence, completely taken up by prayer which is the true and delightful food of the soul.[7]

Philip Thibault did not write much, but we can thank Hugh of St. Francis, an historian of Touraine, for preserving the following words of Thibault that express clearly his understanding of the reform.

> Although the popes have dispensed with certain points of strictness in the primitive Rule, for example, in regard to solitude, in order to serve our neighbor better, in performing ecclesiasical duties, still, they have not in any way moderated this point of meditating day and night on the law of God, which is the principal spirit of our holy religion.[8]

This same truth is expressed in all the writings of John of St. Samson, and is clearly summarized in his exhortation to superiors on humility. "The question often arises," he says, "as to what is the spirit of

---

[7] *Direttorio spirituale de' Carmelitani* (2nd. ed., 4 v., Torino, 1757), I, 300-301. We use the Italian translation, because the original French text is not available to us. Cf. also *Ibid.*, III, 23. Italics ours.

[8] Hugh, *La Véritable idée*, I, 265.

our profession. It does not consist in external appearances, but in humility and interior occupation with God."[9]

The interior life of Carmel was handed down by John of St. Samson to his disciples. Although he was only a lay brother, his knowledge and sanctity was so superior that the spiritual formation of the novices was partly entrusted to his care. His most beloved disciple was Father Dominic of St. Albert, who for many years was the master of novices and young professed, and a true mystic in his own right. Father Dominic has this to say about the spirit of the reform:

> Whoever wishes to embrace our reform should know before everything else, that the perfection of it does not consist only in a certain honest and well regulated manner of life, and in the sole exterior observance of vows, punctuality at divine office and in its ceremonies, and in an exact discipline alone of all things, but principally consists in the assiduous study of holy prayer and meditation, and in a continual and perfect denial of oneself. In these two foundations of true religion consists principally monastic perfection. [10]

Leo of St. John, foremost orator in the reform, in his brief history of Touraine bears witness to the same truth.

> If one directs his attention to the spiritual and mystical theology which the spirit teaches, then our religious must (and so they are taught) dedicate themselves wholly and entirely to silence, solitude, spiritual reading, penance, mental prayer and other related works.[11]

Finally we have the testimony of one of the greatest Carmelites of the seventeenth century, Daniel of the Virgin Mary, a noted historian of the Order and a member of the reformed province of Belgium. Daniel, who died in 1678, lived through some of the most crucial years of the reform, and therefore writes from experience when he says:

> To live the reformed Carmelite life it is necessary to return to the principal end of our Institute. What do we find in our leader and founder Elias? Solitude, silence, prayer, and conversation with God in whose presence he always stood. And it is the primary precept of our Rule: "To meditate day

---

[9] *Oeuvres spirituelles et mystiques du divin contemplatif F. Jean de S. Samson religieux Carme de la réform et observance de Rennes en la province de Touraine,* ed. by Donatian of St. Nicholas. (Rennes, 1658-1659), II, 884.

[10] *Opuscula pro novitiis et professis studentibus,* ed. Joannes a Cruce Brenninger, O. Carm., *AOC,* 11 (1940-1942), 24.

[11] *Delineatio observantiae Carmelitarum Rhedonensis in provincia Turonensi* (Paris, 1645), 60.

and night on the Law of God." It is necessary, therefore, to recognize and to assimilate the interior life as the proper nourishment and spiritual food of the Order.[12]

From this array of documentary evidence there can be no doubt that Touraine had set for its goal a return to the primitive spirit of the Order. But did Touraine really succeed? We believe it did, because just as we judge a tree by its fruits, so we can judge Touraine by the type of religious it produced. The reformed religious of Touraine, as we shall see, actually followed a mode of life that was conducive to contemplation, and they were indoctrinated from their novitiate year to dispose themselves to receive the gift of infused contemplation. This contemplative mode of life in itself, regardless of whether the religious attained contemplation, is sufficient to demonstrate that the religious of Touraine lived according to the primitive spirit of Carmel.[13]

Yet the truth of the matter is that some religious of Touraine actually had the gift of infused contemplation. It is not always easy to judge whether or not one has received this heavenly gift, which cannot be acquired, and which often remains hidden. Nevertheless, we do know that some of the religious of the reform were repututed to have this gift, and they were known during their life to be true mystics. Their fame as mystics spread even beyond the Order. The two outstanding mystics of Touraine were Brother John of St. Samson and his disciple, Father Dominic of St. Albert. The former is considered by Bremond to be one of the most profound mystics of France. From the writings of these two Carmelites and from their biographers it is easy to see how deeply the contemplative spirit entered into their lives, and how keenly they desired that it permeate every member of the reform. Their lives and their writings were not without influence. There were many disciples who followed the spirit of these men, who at one time or another were placed in charge of the spiritual formation of young novices and clerics. The disciples also became contemplatives, lesser lights perhaps, who may or may not have received infused contemplation, but men, nevertheless, who learned to live an intense interior life. We recognize their contemplative spirit in their writings which often simply repeat the ideas of John and Dominic.

---

[12] Daniel of the Virgin Mary, *Vinea Carmeli, seu historia Eliana B.V. Mariae de Monte Carmelo contracta in variis opusculis* (Antwerp, 1662), 361-362.

[13] Matthias of St. John, O. Carm., *Genius,* in Chapter fifteen on mental prayer explains the prayer of the reform (92-102).

Among these writers the following are worthy of mention: Maurus of the Child Jesus,[14] Bernard of St. Magdalen,[15] Mark of the Nativity of the Blessed Virgin,[16] Peter of the Resurrection,[17] Michael of St. Augustine [18] and Mary of St. Teresa (Petyt),[19] a Carmelite Tertiary under the direction of Michael of St. Augustine. It is of special interest to note that Father Michael and Mary of St. Teresa developed the contemplative life in union with the Marian life of Carmel.[20] Mary of St. Teresa, especially, describes her mystical experiences which are inseparable from her Marian devotion.[21] Today she is recognized as a true mystic.

We believe that there is only one conclusion to be drawn from all this testimony that we have gathered from the Constitutions, the directory for novices, the various historical accounts of Touraine, and from the lives and writings of its most eminent religious. The conclusion is that the reform of Touraine is characterized by its intense interior life in which God is the loving object of contemplation. It is, therefore, more than a return to the common life. It is a return to the interior life which is nothing else than the primitive spirit of the Order that once animated the hermits of Carmel. These hermits and their disciples of Touraine desired above all else solitude, silence and mortification in order to live, like their spiritual father, Elias, in the continual presence of God. In this heavenly atmosphere they longed to be lifted up one day, if God so willed, to enjoy and taste the delights of mystical contemplation.

---

[14] *BC*, II, col. 426.
[15] *Ibid.*, I, col. 275.
[16] *Ibid.*, II, col. 312.
[17] *Ibid.*, II, col. 597.
[18] *BC*, II, col. 446.
[19] *Ibid.*, II, col. 359.
[20] Michael's work anticipates by several years the doctrine of St. Grignion de Montfort. It is entitled: *De vita Mariae-forma et mariana in Maria propter Mariam*. It can be found as an appendix to his work: *Introductio ad vitam internam et fruitiva praxis vitae mysticae*, ed. by G. Wessels, O. Carm. (Rome, 1925). Available in two English translations. *Life in and for Mary*, tr. by Rev. Venard Poslusney, O. Carm. (Chicago, 1954). *Life with Mary*, tr. by Rev. Thomas McGinnis, O. Carm. (New York, [1953]).

[21] *Union mystique á Marie*, tr. from Flemish by Louis van den Bossche. (Juvisy [n.d.]). Available in an English translation. *Union with Our Lady; Marian Writings of Ven. Marie Petyt of St. Teresa*, tr. by Rev. Thomas McGinnis, O. Carm. (New York, [1954]).

CHAPTER III

THE SPIRITUAL DIRECTORY FOR NOVICES

I – THE AUTHORS

The greatest spiritual master of the observance of Rennes was Brother John of St. Samson. Although he was a lay brother, he was allowed to teach the novices in the ways of prayer. His conferences were most helpful and led many like his beloved disciple, Dominic of St. Albert, to the heights of contemplative prayer. For Brother John the true spirit of the Order, which he desired to see in the reform, consisted in the contemplation of divine things. For him Elias, standing in the presence of God, was the true model of the Carmelite. He has left us a true and masterly description of Carmel in his treatise: *Vrai esprit du Carmel*.[1]

There can be no doubt that the spiritual conferences and writings of Ven. John helped to lay the foundation of the edifice of the reform that would weather many a storm in the course of time. Still, in themselves, these conferences and writings were not sufficient. They were often beyond the grasp of a simple novice, and the writings especially were not drawn up in an orderly and pedagogical fashion. Moreover, John and his more faithful disciples would one day die, and there was danger that their spirit and doctrine might die with them and thus deprive the reform of its richest spiritual heritage. Hence, we are not surprised to find a desire for a spiritual directory for the novices and young religious, wherein they would be able to study all the principles and practical exercises of religious life as well as the interior and contemplative spirit of the reform. And so directories for novices were begun. Philip Thibault, John of St. Samson and his beloved disciple Dominic of St. Albert, who for some time was a novice master, all took part in preparing directories for novices. Leo of St. John in his history

---

[1] Oeuvres, I, 1-133.

of, the reform, without mentioning names, tells us that others, still among the living (1663), also took part in composing directories.[2]

The first official directories for novices in the province of Touraine were printed in Paris. They appeared in four volumes under the general title of *Directoires des novices,* and the name of the author or authors was not given.[3] In the preface of the fourth volume we read that the directories do not bear the name of any author because they were meant to express the teachings of the whole reform and not those of any particular religious.

Yet, in the course of time the *Directoires des novices* have come to be considered the work of Father Mark of the Nativity of the Blessed Virgin, a member of the province of Touraine.[4] Was Father Mark the author of the *Directoires?* Or was it the work of others? In this chapter we hope to solve this problem. In doing so we shall use three special sources: 1) Several unpublished letters of Father Mark;[5] 2) the biography of Father Mark written by his friend and companion for thirty years, Father Michael Joseph of St. Mark,[6] 3) the biographical sketches in the *Bibliotheca Carmelitana.*[7]

In 1636 the provincial chapter met at Orleans, and among other things decreed that Father Bernard of St. Magdalen, novice master, should complete the directory for novices that he had already begun.[8] Father Bernard never finished this directory. He handed his writings over to Father Mark of the Nativity of the Virgin. Father Maurus of the Child Jesus was designated to assist Mark.[9] Father Mark finally published four volumes of the *Directoires des novices* in 1650 and 1651.

Thus, three Carmelites are explicitly mentioned as collaborators of the official *Directoires des novices.* What part did each play in com-

---

[2] *Delineatio,* 60.

[3] *BC,* II, col. 316-317.

[4] *Ibid.,* II, col. 312; Bouchereaux, *La Réforme des Carmes,* 109.

[5] *Scriptores Ordinis Carmelitarum,* manuscript in Archives of Carmelite Order, Rome, under the indication AO 42. Contains six unedited letters written by Father Mark to the General of the Order and to his friend, Father Louis Perez, O. Carm. They were written between 1674 and 1686. Other letters of Mark in II AO 37, II AO 94, II AO 221, II AO 222. Cf. Bibliography.

[6] Mark of the Nativity of the Blessed Virgia, *Traité de la Componction* (Tours, 1696) edited by Father Michael Joseph of St. Mark; the preface is a biography of Father Mark written by the editor.

[7] *BC,* I, col. 275 ff; II, col. 312 ff.

[8] *Ibid.,* I, col. 275. "Perficiat R. Pater Bernardus a S. Magdalene quod iam suscepit directorium pro novitiis."

[9] *Ibid.,* II, col: 317.

posing these directories? Perhaps an investigation into their lives will give us the answer.

1. *Father Bernard of St. Magdaden*

The first one to put his hand to the composition of the official *Directoires des novices* was Father Bernard of St. Magdalen. We know this from the testimony of Father Mark, who says of Bernard "that he outlined all the treatises of the directory."[10]

Fr. Bernard was known as James Rou before his entrance into religious life. He was born in the village of Le Coudray Macoard near Saumur in the diocese of Angers in the year 1589.[11] His parents were poor, but Bernard was able to receive an elementary education from a pious priest, his uncle, who was attached to the celebrated Abbey of Florence near Saumur, where he taught Benedictine novices.

At the age of twenty, James Rou went to Rennes, the capital of Lower Brittany, to study at the Jesuit college that had recently been founded there. The reformation of the French Carmelites was just beginning to take root; and Father Philip Thibault, the leader of the reform, was well known for his zealous preaching. A group of young men from the college, who often visited the Carmelite Church at Rennes, requested entrance to the Order, and James Rou was among them. He entered in 1609 and was professed on the feast of St. Mary Magdalen, July 22, 1610. He became known in religion as Bernard of St. Magdalen.[12]

History records the name of Father Bernard of St. Magdalen among the strongest pillars of the reform of Touraine. For sixty-two years he helped to form and stabilize the spirit of Carmel in his province. He held various offices in the reform, being elected twice prior of Rennes, and once vicar provincial of the reform. In 1629 he was elected provincial and fulfilled his office with great skill and modesty,

---

[10] Archives O. Carm., II AO 42, letter 70, Nov. 4, 1676, written to Louis Perez.

[11] *Ibid,* The *BC*, I, col. 275, says that Bernard was born in 1588. We are inclined to follow the dates given by Mark. The *BC* is often inaccurate in giving dates.

[12] We note that Bernard, unlike Thibault, Behourt, etc., dropped his fanily name. The reason for this difference seems to have been a mutual understanding whereby those who had been members of the Order in France before the reform and then wished to join it without making another novitiate, as was the case of the leaders like Thibault and Behourt, retained their family name. All those who made their novitiate according to the reform of Touraine dropped their family names for a saint's name. Hugh, *La Véritable idée, I,* 69. The *BC,* I, col. 275, says Bernard took the habit in 1610 and pronounced his vows in 1611, in the hands of Thibault, being the seventh to make vows in the new reforrn. We prefer the dates above given by Mark, letter 70. Hugh, *La Véritable idée,* I, 102, agrees with Mark.

winning not only the admiration of his own brothers, but even that of outsiders. He was also instrumental in making the foundations at La Flèche and the Blessed Sacrament at Paris.

But his most significant work was with the novices and young professed clerics. He was in charge of them for nearly forty years, though not consecutively. He possessed the gift of discernment of spirits and could probe the secrets of the heart with unusual ability. But his most outstanding virtue was meekness,[13] and to the novices and young clerics he was always a kind father.[14] Hugh of St. Francis testifies to the deep interior life of Bernard, who taught his novices how to lift their hearts to God, not only by teaching them from books but by giving them his own experiences in the life of prayer.[15]

For fifteen consecutive years (1632-1647) he was novice master of the clerics and this gave him the opportunity to prepare the *Directoires des novices*. About the year 1634 he began to design and outline this manual. As we have seen, he was encouraged in this work by the provincial chapter of 1636. But Bernard never completed these directories. They were used in the reform for the novices and bore the title: *Collectanea nonnulla novitiorum usui conducibilia*.[16]

In 1646 Father Leo of St. John, provincial of Touraine, and his definitorium held their annual meeting in Rennes and ordered that the writings of Father Bernard should be published. Their directive was not immediately carried out because the next year the fathers of the province gathered at Orleans and commanded Mark of the Nativity of the Blessed Virgin to complete the directories. Bernard then placed all his work into the hands of his beloved disciple, Mark, as the latter himself tells us.

He [Bernard] was especially a master of mystical prayer, and wrote an inspired method on remaining and conversing interiorly with God.[17] Moreover, he outlined all the treatises of the directory which he entrusted to his singularly beloved disciple, Father Mark of the Nativity of the Virgin. He was under the spiritual direction of the very divinely inspired blind brother, John of St. Samson, and drew from him the interior spirit which he said was the soul of the reformation and of all religious life. He also wrote a trea-

---

[13] Mark, Archives O. Carm., II AO 42, letter 70.

[14] Hugh, *La Véritable idée*, II, 2.

[15] *Ibid.*, II, 80.

[16] Mark, Archives O. Carm., II AO 42, letter 70. "Extremum usque ad unguem perficere non potuit."

[17] It seems that this was never published. The *BC* makes no mention of it among the works of Bernard.

tise for novice masters entitled: *Directorium Magistri Novitiorum*, which he also entrusted to Father Mark, who intends to publish it.[18]

Although Father Mark does not mention it, Hugh of St. Francis tells us that Bernard had the greatest esteem for Thibault and expressed it in his work *Relatio de gestis et virtutibus R. P. Philippi Thibault*.[19]

Besides preparing the four spiritual directories for the novices (*Directoires des novices*), Bernard also began *Le Directoire des petits offices de la religion* which Mark of the Nativity edited in four volumes. Mark writes:

> All these little offices, as well as the treatises of the spiritual directory for novices, were begun and in some manner outlined by our R. Father Bernard of St. Magdalen, of holy memory. They were begun about 1634, and this holy father, who was one of the strongest pillars of the reform, continued to perfect them throughout his life by his great experiences, having been employed for nearly forty years in the direction of novices or young professed clerics in the seminary.[20]

In an unpublished manuscript fragment that contains the names of writers in the province of Touraine we find an added confirmation of Father Bernard's part in the composition of the directories.

> Bernard of St. Magdalen, of the diocese of Angers, a man of the greatest meekness, who composed the directories of the reformation, which Father Mark afterwards organized into better form and then published.[21]

This is practically all the information that we have been able to gather about Father Bernard, who throughout his long life in religion always took an active part in the affairs of the reform. He was present at all the provincial chapters of the reform until his very holy death at Tours on August. 6, 1669, at the age of 82. One of his last wishes was

---

[18] Archives O. Carm., II AO 42, letter 70. "Orationis mysticae apprime magister fuit, divinamque methodum interius cum Deo conversandi ac manendi edidit. Insuper omnes Directorii tractatus adumbravit quos reliquit discipulo suo singulariter dilecto Patri Marco a Nat. V. perficiendos. Sub disciplina spirituali fuit illuminatissimi caeci fratris Joannis a S. Sampsone hausitque ab eo spiritum interiorem, quem reformationis, immo et religionis totius animam esse dicebat. Edidit etiam volumen egregium scilicet Directorium Magistri Novitiorum quod eidem P. Marco dimisit aliquando typis mandatum." It seems this latter directory was never published. It is not mentioned in the *BC*.

[19] Hugh, *La Véritabler idée*, I, 69.

[20] *Le Directoire des petits offices* (Angers, 1677), I, 14-15.

[21] Scriptores Ordinis Carmelitarum, MS in the Archives of the Carmelite Order, Rome, AO II 42. This particular item, No. 58, has no date.

that Father Mark would finish the *Directoires des petits offices,* which he (Bernard) believed most important for the growth and stabilization of the reform.[22] His untiring interest in the novices and clerics merited for him the title of the spiritual father of the reform.[23]

2. *Father Mark of the Nativity of the Blessed Virgin*

Father Mark is generally cited as the author of the *Directoires des novices.* But, as we have just seen, he was not the original author, but completed and edited the work that was begun by the veteran novice master Father Bernard of St. Magdalen.

Father Mark was born in the village of Cuno near Saumur in the diocese of Angers on January 9, 1617.[24] He was known in the world as Mark Genest and came from a family of substantial means. His father's name was Philip and his mother's Barbara Bouré.[25] He received his early education at the hands of the Benedictines, and at the age of eight was sent with his older brother to the Jesuit College at La Flèche, which at that time, according to Mark, was the most famous in all France. While at the college he was attracted to the Carmelite Order by the singular piety of some young Carmelite priests, who had been sent from the province of Touraine to study theology. At the age of fifteen he went to Rennes to receive the Carmelite habit on September 8, 1631, from Father Bernard, the provincial. He took the name of Mark of the Nativity of the Blessed Virgin, because of his special devotion to Our Lady, a devotion he retained throughout his long life. His novitiate was prolonged more than a year because of his youth. He finally made his profession on February 8, 1633.[26] He remained in the novitiate house under the watchful guidance of Father Bernard for three years. Mark himself declares his indebtedness to Bernard for guiding him along the path of the interior life.[27]

At no time does Mark refer in these letters to his relations with Brother John of St. Samson, with whom he lived at Rennes. He credits the formation of his religious life to Bernard, who, as we have mentioned, had drawn deeply from the spiritual well of Brother John. However, elsewhere we are informed that Mark also was under the direct in-

---

[22] *Le Directoire des petits offices,* I, 20.

[23] Mark, *Componction,* preface (no pagination).

[24] Mark, Archives O. Carm, II AO 42, letter 70.

[25] Mark, *Componction,* preface.

[26] Mark, Archives O. Carm., II AO 42, letter 70. We prefer Mark's dates to those in the *BC*, II, col. 312, and to those of Michael Joseph in the preface of the *Componction.*

[27] *Ibid.,* "Sub disciplina dicti P. Betnardi tres annos continuos, permansit, qui tanta patientia usus est erga puerum, ut nisi bonum patrem nactus fuisset protervus et licentiosus." Mark writes here about himself in the third person.

fluence of Brother John. Mark's friend and biographer, Father Michael Joseph of St. Mark, relates that both Bernard and Brother John took special efforts to form the interior life of Father Mark. Mark became the secretary of the blind mystic and copied some of the divine and mystical books that the blind brother has left us. At the same time Brother John inspired the youth with solid principles of the interior life.[28]

After being well grounded in the principles of the reform, Mark was sent to the house of studies at the Place Maubert in Paris to study philosophy. This famous studium in the Order never was successfully reformed. Cardinal de Richelieu, who had great esteem for the Order, wanted this studium to join the reform. In accordance with his wishes fifty religious from Touraine were sent there, and among them was Mark. The attempt at reform was unsuccessful and, after some violence, the reformers were ejected.[29] Mark then went to Angers for his philosophy and in 1638 went to Rennes for his theology. At Rennes he was a most proficient student. In 1640 he defended in the presence of the Breton Parliament a number of theses, which were dedicated to the Marechal de la Milleraye. Because of his extraordinary intellectual ability and other talents Mark would have been a good teacher or a successful preacher. But because of his attraction to the interior life and his ability to direct souls his superiors placed him in charge of the novices.

The depth of his knowledge of the spiritual life finally appeared in 1647 at the provincial chapter held at Poitiers, where Mark brilliantly defended a thesis on the nature of mystical theology. From that time on (he was only thirty years old) he was regarded as a master of the spiritual life in his province. It was at this same chapter that he was given the important task of preparing for publication the spiritual directories for novices begun by Father Bernard, and which had been used by the novices for some years.[30] No doubt Father Bernard, who was present at the chapter, had much to say in the choice of his disciple. Father Maurus of the Child Jesus was designated to assist Mark. But the following year Father Maurus was sent to the province of Gascony, where he became the spiritual father of the reformation of the province. Hence, his assistance to Father Mark could not have been great, if indeed, any at all.[31] Meanwhile, Mark went to the monastery of Aulnay, where in two years he completed four volumes of the directory.

---

[28] Mark, *Componction*, preface.
[29] *Ibid*.
[30] Mark, Archives O. Carm., II AO 42, letter 70.
[31] Mark, *Le Directoire des petits offices*, I, 17-18. We shall not give a biography of Maurus because of the small part, if any, which he had in the composition of the

While at Aulnay he preached, heard confessians and gave catechetical instructions to the people in surrounding districts, who had been exposed to Calvinism. He was recognized by the people as an apostolic man.[32]

Leaving this place of solitude, he journeyed to Paris, where he had the *Directoires des novices* published by Joseph Cottereau in 1650 and 1651. They were an immediate success. As we shall see, they were reprinted and often translated. Other religious Orders eagerly accepted these manuals for the instruction of their own novices. The year following their completion Father Mark was elected superior of the monastery of Tours, and during his priorship restored it to its pristine glory.[33]

The archbishop of Tours, His Excellency Victor le Bouteiller, esteemed him highly and made him one of his confessors, consulting him frequently on spiritual matters. He asked Mark to promise to be with him at his deathbed. Mark kept this promise. When the archbishop was dying in 1690, Mark hastened to his bedside and gave great comfort to him.[34]

But Mark's time was not given wholly to the interior life and to studies. He became involved in the political rule of the province. Both he and Hugh of St. Francis were singled out in the General Chapter at Rome in 1660 as rebellious, and leaders of a seditious movement for which they were promptly condemned.[35] They were cleared of all guilt in the following General Chapter in 1666.[36] The controversy arose when the established custom in the province of Touraine of electing alternately a native of Brittany and a native of France to the provincialate was disregarded. Mark and Hugh fought for the continuation of this custom, as well as a separate novitiate for the French and Bretons. After much controversy these customs were retained and approved by Father Jerome Ari, the General of the Order.[37]

Directoires. However, it is well to state that he was one of the better-known Carmelites of the reform of Touraine, as we have already mentioned in chapter one.

[32] Mark, *Componction*, preface.

[33] *Ibid*.

[34] Mark, *Componction*, preface.

[35] *Acta Capitulorum Generalium ordinis Fratrum B. V. Mariae de Monte Carmelo*, edited by G. Wessels, O. Carm. (2 vols., Rome, 1912-1934), II, 109.

[36] *Ibid.*, II, 121.

[37] Mark gives his own account of this controversy in a letter to Perez, Archives O. Carm., II, AO 42, letter 68, written from La Flèche, April 15, 1676. Bouchereaux, *La Réforme des Carmes,* 445 (footnote), gives only evidence that is very adverse to Father Mark. She does not refer to Father Mark's absolution in the General Chapter of 1666, and therefore does not give a complete or accurate picture of the controversy. This controversy is found in the Archives Departmentales Ille-et-Vilaine, Rennes, 1 H 4, Codex 16 bis, 18, 96.

Although Mark may have had many enemies in his province during this time, he nevertheless enjoyed the favor of the General of the Order, Jerome Ari, who made him general visitator for the provinces of Narbonne and Gascony in 1662. Mark travelled from house to house on foot. He practised great austerity and said Mass each day, sometimes after fasting for many hours. He became seriously ill while in the province of Gascony and showed great resignation to the will of God. While doing this work he drew up decrees for reformed provinces that were still being used thirty years later as models not only for Narbonne but for the provinces of Poland, Italy and Brazil.[38]

After his reappointment as master of novices in 1672 Mark decided to complete the directories that explained the manner of performing the external duties in religious life, such as caring for the altar, serving Mass, serving in the dining room, etc. These new directories were to be a continuation of the spiritual directories published in 1650 and 1651. The original plan, with the approval of the Generals of the Order, had been to publish manuals which would contain the principles, practical exercises and rules that would guide not only the interior life of the reform, but also safeguard the regular exterior observance. Burning with a strong desire to finish this work begun by Father Bernard of St. Magdalen, Mark immediately began to seek a dispensation from the duties of novice master, and from all responsible duties. His untiring interest in this work is obvious from the letters he wrote to the General in Rome and to Louis Perez, regent of studies in the monastery of Santa Maria in Traspontina, Rome.[39]

In the years 1677 and 1679 the new directories were published in four volumes at Angers and entitled: *Le Directoire des petits offices de la religion devisé en quatre parties à l'usage des couvents réformés de l'Ordre de Notre Dame du Mont Carmel.* The preface to the first volume was written by Mark, although (like the other directories edited by him) it does not bear his name. It tells of the work begun by Bernard and his interest and guidance in the completion of all the treatises even after they were consigned to Mark in 1647.

---

[38] Mark, *Conponction*, preface.

[39] The friendship of Mark and Louis Perez is easily explained. Perez was collecting data on Carmelite writers and their works in France. Hence, he often wrote to Mark for information on contemporary writers. Although he wrote much and well, Perez never published any works. Many of his manuscripts are preserved today in the archives of the Carmelite Order in Rome. For a list of these works see the *BC*, II, col. 296.

These new directories were well received and even found their way into other provinces. They were quickly accepted in the province of Gascony. "The Definitorium accepts the directory of Father Mark of the Nativity of the Blessed Virgin and recommends its practise to the whole province."[40]

Mark was also a zealous promoter of the Third Order Secular of Mount Carmel. It is said, although with a bit of exaggeration, that he revived the Third Order in France. Father Michael Joseph of St. Mark, his biographer, said of this work: "In the whole kingdom of France Mark was the remarkable promoter of the Third Order of Mount Carmel, which had almost completely died out."[41] This remark was occasioned by the publication of Mark's *Le Manuel du Tiers Ordre du Mont-Carmel* (Angers, 1681).

Some years after Mark had edited the last of his directories he became involved in a rather strange and bitter controversy with Anthony Arnauld, the fierce promoter of Jansenism in France. The whole controversy centered around a derogatory statement against Jansenius that Mark had made in writing, and which he had given to two Jesuits. The statement later appeared in a book, and Arnauld bitterly attacked it as a being not only unfair but untrue.[42]

It seems that Mark, when he was a young man in his early thirties (1652), was told a very strange story by a nobleman of Tours named de Razilly. Razilly had been present in Gascony at a meeting which included Bérulle before he became cardinal, Bishop Cospéan, who later became bishop of Nantes, Jansenius, who had returned from Spain, and the future Jansenist Abbe of St. Cyran. The conversation of the group concerned the possibility of lessening the power of the Mendicants with the laity and restoring the prestige of the hierarchy. Each member of the group expressed his opinion. Bérulle's solution was to organize a group of secular priests, who by the goodness of their lives would restore the confidence of the people in the secular clergy. Actually Bérulle later founded the Congregation of the Oratory. Cospéan's solution was to curtail the privileges of the Mendicants. He later wrote a book or had one written, says Mark, on the jurisdiction of bishops. Jansenius suggested an attack against the Jesuits, accusing them of Semipelagianism, which would be easy after the recent quarrel in Spain on the nature of effica-

---

[40] *Acta Provinciae Vasconiae*, 1 maii 1678. In the Archives of the Postulator General of the Carmelite Order, Rome.

[41] Mark, *Componction*, preface. This statement seems exaggerated, since others had written Third Order manuals. Cf. *BC*, II, col. 320.

[42] *BC*, 11, col. 322-325.

cious grace. Jansenius later wrote his *Augustinus*. The future Abbé of St. Cyran suggested curtailing the use of the sacraments for the laity, for the prestige of the Mendicants was due in part to the easy access to the sacraments which they offered the faithful. He later issued his precepts on confession and communion.

This story, Mark says, was confirmed again by de Razilly shortly before his death. It had also been related to others, especially to Nicholas of the Visitation, who was a well-respected superior among the Carmelites. It was also known for many years by the members of the Carmelite province of Touraine.

Mark gave this story to Father Cornelius Hazart, a Belgian Jesuit in 1678. It was this incident that caused the outburst of Antony Arnauld. He accused Mark of perpetrating a false and vicious story.

Arnauld's arguments against Mark, as related by the editor of the *Bibliotheca carmelitana*, are far from convincing. We mention this incident to indicate Mark's attitude as well as that of some members of the province of Touraine toward the infiltration of Jansenism in the Church of France.[43]

Mark was held with high esteem outside the Order as well as within. On the recommendation of King Louis XIV Father Jerome Ari, Prior General of the Order, made Mark a member of his secret council. He was also held in honor by the bishop of Poitiers. Laymen in high stations of life often consulted him as did theologians, mystics and religious of other Orders.

Mark, especially toward the latter part of his life, showed also that he had some administrative ability. In 1687 he was made provincial of Touraine at Angers, an office which he filled well, bringing to completion the hermitage of Fontainebleau and even sending missionaries to England and Brazil. Surely this new office would have impeded progress in his writings.[44] Three years later he was made prior of the monastery of the Blessed Sacrament at Paris: It was while prior of this monastery that be was attacked by Arnauld. In 1693 he is numbered among the definitors of the province of Touraine and shortly before his death he accepted for the fourth time the duty of master of novices.

---

[43] *Ibid*.

[44] Archives O. Carm., II AO 222, letter written by Mark from La Flèche, April 28, 1677, to Father Seraphinus of Jesus and Mary in Rome. In this letter Mark explains his plans for future books after finishing the *Directoires des petits offices*. He planned to publish four more treatises for novices, six for professed clerics and four for priests. Actually, none of these were published by Mark. Only one of these was published after his death, the *Traité de la compoction*, which he composed for the novices.

An unfortunate accident brought his long life to a tragic end. One evening, while returning to the monastery from a visit he had made to a nearby convent of Ursuline nuns, he fell from his horse into a ditch of poisonous water. He swallowed some of the water and this proved fatal. A few days later, February 23, 1696, his strength exhausted, he passed to his eternal reward at Tours fortified by the sacraments. He was seventy-nine years of age.[45]

After Mark's death, his friend and companion, Father Michael Joseph of St. Mark, edited the last work of Mark, the *Traité de la componction*. The preface is meant to be a biography of Father Mark, but it is in the nature of a eulogy. Nevertheless, it does contain many facts which we have used in this chapter.

Father Michael believes that of all his writings the *Traité de la componction* was the most pleasing to Mark. Perhaps the reason is that it was more his own than the others. According to Michael Joseph, the true spirit of Mark is revealed here more than in the other works. Did Bernard of St. Magdalen also have a hand in preparing this treatise? It is quite possible, because it was meant to be the fifth volume of the *Directoires* of 1650, as Mark tells us in volume four.[46]

The *Bibliotheca carmelitana* that has used the biography of Michael Joseph for its sketch of Father Mark of the Nativity believes the style of the *Traité de la componction* does not attain the simplicity and unction of the *Directoires des novices*, and therefore shows the interference of the editor Father Michael Joseph. However, the latter in his preface states that he has edited the *Traité de la componction* just as Mark had written it.

In this fifth volume of the *Directoires des novices* (although it never seems to have been officially accepted as such), we find many affective colloquies with God which are reminiscent of the earlier volumes of the *Directoircs*. Mark wrote this volume, so Father Michael Joseph informs us, because he believed a young novice could not approach God and climb the mountain of perfection unless he were first cleansed of his sins and had a pure heart to offer God.

From the foregoing information we reach the following eonclusions:

The *Directoires des novices* (the first four volumes) were composed for the novices of Touraine and contained the spiritual doctrine on which the first members and leaders of the reform had been nourished. This doctrine was gathered systematically by Father Bernard of St.

---

[45] Mark, *Componction*, preface.
[46] *Méthode*, chap. v, p. 88.

Magdalen, who gave it to Father Mark of the Nativity of the Blessed Virgin to complete and edit. Bernard was a recognized disciple of the blind mystic, Brother John of St. Samson, who was the soul of the reform of Touraine. Father Mark also was greatly influenced by Brother John, since he was for a few years his secretary and copied down much of the spiritual doctrine that Brother John has left us. Father Mark admits, however, that he was the immediate and beloved disciple of Father Bernard, to whom he was greatly indebted for his direction in the interior life. It is difficult to say just how much of the *Directoires* is due to the authorship of each man. We must be content with the following testimony of Father Mark:

> Likewise he [Mark speaks of himself in the third person] lent a hand to the formation of the directories, first outlined by Father Bernard of S. Magdalen, whom he always cherished as a father. But in truth these directories should not be attributed to any religious in particular, but should be considered the product of the whole reform, so that they may be of greater authority.[47]

II - Editions and Translations

The success of the *Directoires* can be gaged in some measure by the number of its editions and translations. First printed at Paris in 1650 and 1651 by Joseph Cottereau in four volumes, it was again printed at Paris by Simon Piget, 1664-1668. Father Philippinus, the General who presided at the provincial chapter at Tours in 1651, issued the following order:

> The four volumes of the directory, namely, 1) "Preparation for Religious Life," 2) "Christian Instruction or Catechism for Novices," 3) "Regular Life or Religious Way of Life," 4) "On Mental Prayer and Aspirative Prayer," which have been printed, are approved. They are recommended to novice masters for their own use, and they should take care that the novices use them also.[48]

Copies of the original French editions of the *Directoires* are extremely rare. The only copy of the first edition known to me, which forms the basis of the present study, is preserved in the Carmelite

---

[47] Letter of Mark to Perez, April 15, 1676, letter 68 in Archives O. Carm. II AO 42. "Similiter et Directoriis manu admovet, prius adumbratis per R. P. Bernardum a S. M. quem ut patrem semper coluit, necque vero ulli religioso particulari ascribi debent Directoria, nam a tota reformatione credi debent prodisse, ut majoris sint auctoritatis."

[48] *Le Directoire des petits offices*, I, 18-19. Cf. also *BC*, II, col. 317.

monastery of Merkelbeek in the Netherlands;[49] of the second edition, which is known through allusions in the *Bibliotheca carmelitana*,[50] no copies have come to my notice. A number of translations, partial or entire, have appeared.

The title pages of the original edition read as follows:

Volume I: *Préparation à la vie religieuse, où sont exposés les principaux motifs de renoncer au monde pour embrasser l'état de la religion. Faisant le premier traitté de la conduitte spirituelle des novices pour les convens reformez de l'Ordre de Nostre Dame du Mont-Carmel.* A Paris, chez Ioseph Cottereau, 1650.

Volume II: [*Instruction chrestienne, contenant l'explicatian des misteres et veritez de la foi sur la croiance & pratique desquelles on doit ietter les fondemens de la vie religieuse. Faisant le second traitté de la conduitte spirituelle des novices pour les convens reformez de l'Ordre de Nostre Dame du Mont Carmel.* A Paris, chez Ioseph Cottereau, 1651].

Volume III: *La vie reguliere, où enseignemens necessaires pour pratiquer sainctement toutes les actions de la religion. Faisant le troisiéme traitté de la conduitte spirituelle des novices pour les convens reformez de l'Ordre de Nostre Dame du Mont-Carmel.* A Paris, chez Ioseph Cottereau, 1651.

Volume IV: *Méthode claire et facile pour bien faire oraison mentale et pour s'exercer avec fruict en la presence de Dieu. Faisant le quatriesme traitté de la conduitte spirituelle des novices pour les convens reformez de l'Ordre de Nostre-Dame du Mont-Carmel.* A Paris, chez Ioseph Cottereau, 1650.

The fourth volume will be the subject of this study. It is entirely devoted to mental prayer. For the sake of brevity we shall refer to it hereafter as the *Méthode*. The *Conduite spirituelle* itself we shall continue to call the *Directoires des novices,* a name by which it is also commonly designated.

Italian Translations and Editions

Direttorio spirituale de' Carmelitani, diviso in quattro parti, nelle quali si tratta con brevità e chiarezza di quanto appartiene alla vita religiosa circa la preparazione, fondamenti, pratiche di tutte le azioni regolari ed esercizio d'orazione. Dato in luce in lingua italiana a comodo de' noviziati d'Ita-

---

[49] The title page of volume two is wanting; it has been supplied below from the *imprimatur* and by analogy from the title pages of the other volumes. I wish here to acknowledge the kindness of the fathers of Merkelbeek in making the work available to me.

[50] *BC*, II, 316.

lia... In Venetia, appresso Gio. Battista Tramontin, 1684. 4 v. The translator is Fr. Jerome of St. Clement Aimo, O. Carm.[51]

Direttorio spirituale de' Carmelitani, diviso in quattro parti, nelle quali si tratta con brevità e chiarezza di quanto appartiene alla vita religiosa circa la preparazione, fondamenti, pratiche di tutte le azioni regolari ed esercizio d'orazione. Dato in luce in lingua italiana a comodo de' noviziati d'Italia. Seconda edizione... In Venezia ed in Torino, per Francesco Antonio Mairesse, 1757. 4 v.

Lo spirito delle azioni religiose, in cui contengonsi pie considerazioni per ben animarle, le direzioni interiori prima di cominciarle, e varie divote aspirazioni, dalle quali esser debono accompagnate; opera utilissima ad ogni sorta di persone claustrali dal francese nell'italiano traslata... In Torino, per Gio. Francesco Mairesse, 1732. This is a compendium of vol. III of the *Directoires,* comprising 63 chapters, one less than the Latin compendium (see below). The editor is Fr. Theobald of the Annunciation Ceva, O. Carm [52]

Latin Translations

Methodus clara et facilis vacandi orationi mentali atque exercendi se cum fructu in praesentia Dei, cui pro majori animum in praesentia Dei continendi facilitate in fine additur Spiritus actionum religionis; opuscula antehac gallice conscripta, nunc ... latinitate donata & in lucem emissa studio & opera cujusdam Ordinis Fratrum B. V. Mariae de Monte Carmelo in provincia Allemanniae Inferioris alumni. Coloniae Agrippinae, sumptibus haeredum Joannis Widenfelt & Godefridi de Berges, 1687. The translator is Fr. George of the Queen of Angels. [53]

---

[51] This appears from the preface of vol. I of the second edition.

[52] *BC*, II, col. 782. In the preface we read that this is a translation from the original French. But we have not been able to find a French edition of *Lo Spirito delle azioni.* It may be that it was never published, although we cannot doubt its existence, at least in manuscript, since even the Latin edition was translated from the French. Furthermore, we know that an eighteenth century manuscript bearing the same title by an unknown author can be found in the public library of Monthéliard in France. *L'esprit des actions de la religion extrait du Directoire des religieux reformés de l'ordre de Nostre-Dame du Mont Carmel,* composé par un religieux de la Province de Touraine, 1678, 242ff. Beginning fol. 195 is the treatise *Méthode pour bien faire l'oraison mentale, traduction du canon de la sainte messe, méthode pour reciter l'office divin et "orationes".*

We also have a French adaptation of the *L'esprit des actions* prepared for Carmelite nuns in France by Father Alexis of St. Anne. *L'esprit des actions de la religion pour servir de directoire aux religieuses Carmélites de Bretagne.* Rennes, Nicolas Paul Vator, 1760.

[53] The *Methodus* does not mention the name of the translator, but we found this information in a manuscript written in 1684 and preserved in the Archives of the Carmelite Order, Rome, II AO 37, no. 479. Here we read that Father George of the Angels

Methodus meditandt atque exercendi se in praesentia Dei, ex Directorio novitiatus FF. B. Mariae Virginis de Monte Carmelo. A recent ms. copy of the *Methodus clara* (Cologne, 1687) in the Archives of the pastulator general O. Carm., Rome, codex I, 10. This work omits a number of chapters, but faithfully produces the whole theory of prayer in the *Methode*.

Flemish and German Translations

The preface of the second edition of the Italian *Direttorio spirituale* mentions Flemish and German translations.[54] So does Fr. Michael Joseph of St. Mark in the preface of his *Traité de la componction*. We have not been able to locate any copies.

Compendium of the Directoires

Nova schola virtutum, exhibens regulas, praxim & usum vacandi Deo per meditationes, actus virtutum, victoriam passionum, nec non praesentiae divinae & alia consueta religionis praesertim novitiatus exercitia, in gratia juniorum religiosorum in hanc formam redacta per quendam sacerdotem S. Ordinis Fratrum B. V. Mariae de Monte Carmelo provinciae Germaniae Superioris. Bambergae, typis viduae Georg. Andr. Gertner [1764]. The author seems to be Fr. Hyacinth of the Mother of God.[55] The work contains a digest of the methodical meditation in the *Méthode* and faithfully explains all the different parts. Aspirative prayer it explains under the exercise of the presence of God, which is taken partly from the *Méthode* and partly from Dominic of St. Albert and other sources.

Adaptations

Vademecum. Voor de novicen der orde van Onze Lieve Vrouw van den berg Carmel Genomen uit het directorium. Breda, 1892.

(George Gaillard), a reformed Carmelite of the German province, was born in Vianden, Luxembourg, Nov. 25, 1628. Besides teaching philosophy and theology within the Order, he taught at the University of Cologne. A preacher of renown, he edited many of his sermons on Our Lady and the scapular. His translation of the *Méthode,* so the ms. states, was to be published the following year in 1685. Actually it was not published until 1687. This manuscript gives more information than the *BC*, I, col. 545.

[54] "...le provincie di Germania, e di Fiandra avevanla già trasportata nel loro idioma." (No pagination in the preface.)

[55] The *BC (I, col.* 161) mentions another edition: Vienna, Johann Jakob Kurner, 1707. A third edition known to me is that of Würzburg, 1740.

Directorium carmelitanum vitae spiritualis, praesertim novitiis instruendis. Typis polyglottis Vaticanis, 1940. The author is Fr. John Brenninger, O. Carm. Part IV has borrowed almost verbatim the method of meditation and the exercise of the presence of God from volume IV of the *Directoires*. Fr. Brenninger used the *Methodus clara,* as the original French was not available at the time.

Translations of the Directorium

The Carmelite Directory of the Spiritual Life: translated from the Latin. Chicago, The Carmelite Press, 1951. The translator is Fr. Leo J. Walter, O. Carm.

Dottrina spirituale del Carmelo. Tipografia poliglotta vaticana, 1952. The translator is Fr. Tarcisio M. Giuliani, O. Carm.

Directorio carmelita de vida espiritual, copilado y dado a luz especialmente para la instruccion de los novicios. Zaragoza, tip. La Editorial, 1951.

III – The Style of the *Méthode*

The style of the *Méthode* is very simple. In fact, Father Mark of the Nativity apologized in the preface for the simplicity of language, reminding the reader that it is meant for young novices. The whole volume is arranged and divided in an orderly fashion. It is the work of a teacher, a pedagogue. Yet the simplicity and unction of the style make the book easy to read.

The *Méthode* is divided into three parts, corresponding to the three ways of prayer that make up the material of the book; that is, the meditation, mixed prayer and aspirative prayer. This last way is joined with the exercise of the presence of God. The book opens with a preface and contains thirty-six chapters: chapter one on prayer in general, chapters two to twenty-four on meditation, chapters twenty-five to twenty-seven on mixed prayer, chapters twenty-eight to thirty-six on aspirative prayer and the presence of God.

The *Méthode's* style renders it suitable for translation. Both the Italian translation of Jerome Aimo and the Latin translation of George of the Queen of Angels are accurately done from the original French. But copies of these works, like the original French, are very rare.

Section Two

THE WAYS OF PRAYER IN THE *MÉTHODE*

Chapter IV

MEDITATION

The *Méthode is* divided into three parts: 1) methodical meditation, 2) mixed prayer, and 3) aspirative prayer, which is also called the exercise of the presence of God: These parts are preceded by a preface and a chapter on prayer in general.

I – The Preface

The Méthode opens with a preface in which the purpose of the manual is clearly and precisely explained. Every religious is obliged to acquire perfection which consists in an affective union with God.[1] One of the most powerful means to acquire perfection is the practise of prayer by which we can break the bonds of sin, overcome vice, and thus remove the obstacles that hinder affective union with God.[2] The

---

[1] Perfection and affective union with God are identified in the *Méthode,* although it is the latter expression that we continually find. Affective union means that the will as well as the intellect of man is united with God. It is the product of sanctifying grace and habitual charity. It grows stronger and more perfect the more the will is moved to make acts of love, hope, adoration, etc. These affections of the will in turn move the soul to effective action in the spiritual life. The *Méthode* does not make the clear distinction between affective and effective charity, nor does it make a distinction between sanctifying grace and the virtue of charity. It is not concerned with such fine distinctions since it is a practical manual. However. it follows Catholic tradition in identifying Christian perfection with affective union with God. For a more detailed explanation of the relation between union with God and Christian perfection consult J. de Guibert, *Theologia spiritualis ascetica et mystica* (4th ed., Rome, 1952), nos. 87-91, pp. 80-83.

[2] Besides prayer, the *Méthode* presupposes other ordinary means that must be employed to obtain perfection, e.g., mortification, spiritual direction, spiritual reading, the use of the sacraments, etc. None of these common means can be neglected. However, for the Carmelite, prayer, and especially mental prayer, is to be the distinctive means employed to attain perfection. All the other means, such as mortification, etc., should aid the Carmelite in perfecting his life of prayer that will lead to affective union with God.

Carmelites, more than others, if they wish to be faithful to the traditions of their Order and the spirit of their fathers, must practise prayer unceasingly. The ancient fathers of Carmel left the world for solitude to live a more intense interior life, meditating day and night on the law of God. The Carmelite Rule, chapter seven, says: "Let each one remain in his cell, or near it, meditating day and night on the law of God, and watching in prayer, unless occupied in other just works." A life of continual prayer is the legacy left to the sons of Carmel. To retain this true spirit of the Order, the Carmelite must strive continually to perfect himself in prayer. Those who persevere in prayer shall feel the powerful influence of God in the soul. They shall taste the sweetness of heaven in this life. They shall enjoy divine intimacy. Being detached from creatures, they shall be wholly transformed into God in so far as this is possible.

The *Méthode* has been written for novices and young Carmelites to help them acquire this interior life which will lead them to affective union with God.

This manual and no other should be used by the young Carmelites. There are two reasons for this command: 1) all instructions both theoretical and practical, including ready-made meditations, are contained here; 2) this method has been practised, says the author, in the reform from the beginning (1608) until the present time (1650).

II - Prayer and its Divisions

Prayer *(precatio seu oratio)* may be considered in three senses: 1) Petition, which is prayer in the strict sense; 2) Elevation of the heart to God *(Élevation de notre coeur à Dieu)*; 3) Conversation or colloquy with God, which is prayer in its widest sense and embraces all forms of prayer. Throughout the *Méthode* prayer in its widest sense, conversation with God, will ordinarily be understood.[3]

Prayer is an elevation of the heart to God. This includes the uplifting of both intellect and will; but Carmelites should give emphasis to

---

[3] These definitions are traditional in the Church, although we should notice that the *Méthode* uses the word "heart" *(cor)* where others use the word "mind" *(mens)*. The Latin translation of the *Méthode* page 9, uses the word "mens". The first two definitions of prayer are found in the works of St. John Damascene, and the third is similar to the *locutio ad Deum* of St. Augustine. Cf. St. John Damascene, *PG*, 94, 1089; St. Augustine, PL, 37, 10.86; St. Jerome, *PL*, 22, 411; John Climacus, *PG*, 88, 1129. Cf. also Paul Philippe, O. P., "Mental Prayer in the Catholic Tradition," in *Mental Prayer and Modern Life, a Symposium*, translated by Francis C. Lehner (New York, 1950), 8. This book is translated from *L'Oraison (Cahiers de la Vie Spirituelle;* Paris, [1947]).

raising the will (or the heart) to God in prayer. This is the meaning of chapter seven of the Carmelite Rule. "Day and night they shall meditate on the law of God, and watch in prayer." That is, the Carmelite shall raise his heart to God continually in prayer. Young religious will not generally be able to practise this continual affective prayer, but this is the goal they must strive to attain.

Does the *Méthode* wish to minimize the part of the intellect in prayer? No. On the contrary, it includes the part of the intellect, and says he is truly praying who meditates or reasons on some spiritual truth with the purpose of making progress.[4] However, it subordinates the part of the intellect to that of the will. Even when reasoning on same divine truth, the Carmelite must realize that this is only a means to inflame his will to engage with God in loving conversation.

There are five different ways of prayer (conversing with God): 1) oral prayer, 2) mental prayer, 3) mixed prayer, 4) ejaculatory prayer, 5) unitive or contemplative prayer.

The *Méthode* presupposes a knowledge of oral prayer and hence omits it. Unitive prayer is usually beyond the grasp of the novices and, is likewise omitted. Hence, "in this tract we consider the three other kinds of prayer, mental, mixed and aspirative, because these are absolutely necessary for acquiring introversion and interior conversation with God."

III – Mental Prayer

Mental prayer is here restricted to what is commonly called meditation. "It is an interior conversation and a series of good thoughts and holy affections on a certain subject from which the soul desires to make some spiritual advancement."[5] This definition of mental prayer includes not only methodical meditation but affective prayer or meditation which has very little *discursus*.[6] This is a common definition found in the early part of the seventeenth century in many spiritual books.[7]

---

[4] Chap. i, p. 17. We shall always cite the chapters of the *Méthode* for the convenience of those who have the Latin or Italian translation.

[5] Oraison mentale, comme porte le mot, n'est autre chose qu'un entretien intérieur, et une suite de bonnes pensées et de sainctes affections sur quelque suiet, duquel l'ame veut tirer son edification." Chap. II, p. 20. Introversion and interior conversation with God mentioned above, will be fully discussed below, p. 122.

[6] Chap. ix, pp. 118 ff.

[7] Francis de Sales, *Traité de l'amour de Dieu*, in *Oeuvres de Saint François de Sales* (26 vols. Annecy, 1893) IV, 307.

Mental prayer is necessary for the religious.[8] It joins man with God. It obtains the remission of his sins; it is a bulwark in time of temptation. It is the singular treasure of the religious. All other means in religious life, for example, mortification, vows, etc., are only a means to help us pray better. The end of our Carmelite vocation is to acquire the state in which we pray well. Christ in the Gospel does not say that we must fast always, or work always, but that we must pray always. Prayer is the direct way to union with God in charity, that is, to perfection.

There are many means to perfection, but prayer is absolutely necessary. Some attribute the wickedness in the world to a lack of faith. Actually, faith is half dead only because souls fail to keep it alive by meditation and consideration of the divine truths.

Mental prayer is not easy. St. Teresa, says the *Méthode,* tells us in her autobiography of her own trying experiences. Before her total conversion she would have preferred to undergo any kind of penance rather than recollect herself for prayer.[9]

Why do souls find mental prayer so difficult? Some find it difficult because they lack fervor and devotion; others because they suffer from unbearable distractions; others still are tempted by the devil.

1. *The Parts of Mental Prayer*

The following method should help us to overcome our difficulties and should lead us to an intimate life with God. Mental prayer has three parts: preparation, meditation and affections. These correspond to the three faculties of the soul, i, e., memory, intellect and will. The memory arranges the subject matter and presents it to the intellect, which in turn meditates, ruminates, considers the matter, until the will is filled with holy affections, desires and practical resolutions to live a better life.

The *Méthode* then proceeds to explain each part which in turn is subdivided. We present the following outline which summarizes chapters three to thirteen.

---

[8] Mental prayer is not synonymous with discursive prayer. Chapter nine of the *Méthode* indicates many kinds of mental prayer by pointing out that discursive prayer is not always necessary.

[9] E. A. Peers, *The Complete* Works of *St. Teresa of Jesus* (3 vols., New York, 1949), I, *Life,* chap. viii, p. 51. This is a translation of the critical edition of *Teresa de Jesús, Obras,* ed. Silverio de Santa Teresa (9 vols., Burgos, 1915-1924). We shall refer to Peer's translation throughout this work.

OUTLINE OF MEDITATION

I **Preparation**
(memory; at least for immed. prep.)

- **Remote Preparation**
  1) aversion for sins and imperfections that impede access to God.
  2) seeking solitude; flight from useless works.
  3) detachment from all temporal things.
  4) avoiding vain recreation, vain thoughts; loss of time.

- **Proximate Preparation**
  intellect *a)* reading (eight rules are given)
  will *b)* desire to meditate.

- **Immediate Preparation** / **Entrance into meditation**
  1) act of presence of God (represent God as Father, Judge, King, etc. depending upon the subject of meditation).
  2) brief examen of conscience.
  3) acts of humility and other virtues; e. g., offer meditation for honor and glory of God. (This direction before prayer can be changed as often as we wish.)

II **Meditation**

- **Intellect** (considers sensible or spiritual subject)
  - Sensible subject. e. g. Incarnation. — History, time and place, persons, words, sentiments, end, effects, *personal application*.
  - Spiritual subject. — Nature, names, causes properties, effects, end, and *personal application*.

III **Affections**

- **Will**
  - Particular Affections — Love, hate, desire, hope, joy, sorrow.
  - General Affections (at end of meditation). — Thanksgiving, resolutions, oblation, petition.

Conclusion
(acts immediately following meditation) — Was meditation good or bad? the causes; resolve to be recollected during day by use of ejaculatory prayer; recall affections and resolution during day; write in book fruits received in prayer.

Place of Meditation: Usually in choir.
Time of Meditation: Twice daily.
    5:30 a. m. to 6:30 a. m.   5:30 a. m. to 6 a. m. In house of study: 5:30 a. m. to 6 a. m.
    3:00 p. m. to 3:30 p. m. after Vespers (during Lent 4:00 p. m. to 4:30 p. m. after Compline).

Introductory prayer: Veni Sancte Spiritus, etc. Oration: Deus qui corda fidelium, etc.
Closing prayer: Laudate Dominum omnes gentes, etc. Oration: Suscipe, clementissime, etc.

Each part of this method is explained in great detail. Well thought out meditations or model meditations are worked out for the navices. In conclusion, certain "doubts concerning meditation" are discussed. These "doubts" are actually most beneficial counsels.

There are certain elements in this method which we believe deserve further consideration. They are the reading, the actual meditation, the affections, resolutions and finally the other ways of prayer which are discussed among the "doubts."

2. *Reading*

The reading is not an actual part of the exercise of meditation.[10] It is part of the proximate preparation. For example, the reading for the morning meditation was usually (not necessarily) done in the cell after matins, which were chanted or said at midnight.[11] However, this was not an iron-clad rule, and Dominic of St. Albert speaks of the reading sometimes being performed in the designated place of prayer after entering into the presence of God.[12]

Eight rules for good reading are given. The reading should be moderate, sufficient for the presentation of the subject, attentive. If the religious has had experience, it is not necessary to follow the order of meditation in the book. Some time should be given to a few thoughts on the fruits to be expected from the meditation. However, it is not necessary to meditate on the subject prepared. The Holy Ghost is the supreme guide and master in prayer, and should be followed even though a subject is suggested that had not been prepared.

3. *Meditation*

The act itself of meditation pertains to the intellect and is an attentive and deliberate consideration of some truth.[13] It is a discursive act of the mind whose purpose is to excite the will to do good and avoid

---

[10] Chap. III, pp. 41 ff.

[11] *Directoires des novices, III, 152.*

[12] Dominic of St. Albert, *Exercitatio spiritualis* in *AOC,* I1 (1940-1942), 31. Mental prayer was performed twice each day in the reform of Touraine: one hour in the morning from five thirty until six thirty, and one half hour in the evening after vespers at three o' clock (during Lent after Compline at four o'clock). The meditation (usually in choir) began with the *Veni Sancte Spiritus,* etc., followed by the oration *Deus qui corda fidelium,* etc. The subject of the meditation was privately prepared "juxa formam misticam in nostris Directoriis praestitutam." At the end of the meditation the psalm *Laudate Dominum* etc., was said and it was followed by the oration *Suscipe clementissime,* etc. *Constitutiones [1636],* Part I, chap. xiv, 3, p. 110.

[13] Chap. v, p. *62.*

evil. After the intellect has understood some persuasive truth, it does nothing else but present it to the will. It ceases its reasoning action while the will produces the affections proper to it. The intellect therefore does not meditate merely to know truth, but to inflame the will to love, just as a dog does not kill the animal that it has tracked down, but guards it until captured by its master. Hence, the less consideration and the more frequent the affections, the more fruitful is the prayer. However, young novices will find it difflcult at first to inflame the will. They will have to give more time to the intellectual act, that is, to the *discursus*. "Nothing is able to be loved unless the intellect first knows it and proposes it to the will. "That is why they should follow some method, otherwise they waste their time in distractions.

The subject matter, which may be sensible or spiritual, should be simple. There should be no intention of producing beautiful and subtle thoughts. The following outlines will show how spiritual and sensible subjects may be handled.

Meditation on a sensible subject, e. g., the crucifixion.

1) The history of the fact. (how)
2) Circumstances of time and place. (how, where)
3) Persons and their characteristics. (who)
4) Words spoken or able to be spoken. (what)
5) The probable feelings of those who took part. (what)
6) The end or purpose of this fact. (why)
7) The effects derived from it. (what)
8) How do we conform with this practise? (why)
9) What fruit should be drawn from it? (what) [14]

Meditation on a spiritual subject (temperance).

1) The nature of the virtue or benefice.
2) The name, if there is anything remarkable about it.
3) Its causes, i.e., who produces it. God, etc.
4) Its properties and effects.
5) Its purpose.
6) Examples of it in the life of Christ. Christ's teaching.
7) How have we observed it?
8) Our attitude toward it for the future.
9) How draw profit from it?

---

[14] The *Méthode* does not use the words (what, who, why). We have added them for the sake of clarity and for comparison with other methods. However, the third volume of the *Directoires* uses these pronouns, *quis, quid, ubi, quibus auxiliis, cur, quomodo, quando*, as helpful for novices in the beginning of their novitate. Cf. *Directoires des novices*, III. 177.

It is not necessary to consider all these points in a meditation. One or two points may suffice to inflame the will.

What truths should be the subject matter of meditation? The subject will often differ according to the spiritual age of the one who meditates. Beginners ordinarily will meditate on sin, the four last things. The advanced will find the life and virtues of Christ most suitable. And in the unitive way no subject in particular is prescribed, but the perfection of God and divine providence will prove helpful.[15]

4. *Affections*

The third act of this exercise is the act of the will, that is, the production of affections and resolutions.[16] This is the most important act of mental prayer because both the memory and the intellect serve to move the will. The greater the acts of the will, the better the prayer. For the will is the queen of all the faculties.

Knowledge and love are not to be given equal standing in prayer. And if you have love of God, it shall be an inexhaustible source of excellent enlightenment and holy thoughts, as Father Dominic mentions in his exercises.[17]

The Holy Spirit can inflame and move the will without much reasoning of the intellect, but ordinarily He presupposes human effort. It is after deep reasoning and consideration (with the aid of grace) that the soul perceives some truth, loves it, desires it and proposes to embrace it.[18]

The affections or motions of the will should not be forced. No affections are better than artificial affections.[19] The will may produce affections of love, hate, desire, etc. These are called particular affections, and are usually distinguished from the general affections, e. g., thanksgiving, resolutions, oblation and petition, which are called general be-

---

[15] Chap. vii, pp. 90-91.

[16] Chap. ix, p. 118. Cf. P. Pourrat, "Affections," *DSp*, I, 235-240. Affections are actions of the will, such as faith, hope, charity, adoration, gratitude, sorrow for sin, joy, etc., which proceed from the consideration of the subject. Today modern experimental psychology speaks of three elements in the soul, the cognitive, the appetitive or volitive and the affective element. This tripartite division, of course, is not found in the *Méthode*, which includes the act of love as well as acts of joy, sorrow, etc., as affections. On this tripartite division in the mystical life consult C. Truhlar, S. J., *De experientia mystica* (Rome, 1951), 15-20.

[17] Chap. v, p. 65; chap. xxiv, p. 586. The exercises referred to are in his *Théologie mystique*, edited in *Études carmélitaines*, 22 (1937) 258, 269. Dominic refers to this point on p. 263. His reference is to the prayer of contemplation.

[18] Chap. ix, pp. 122-123.

[19] Chap. xxiv, p. 386.

cause they are found in almost all meditations and usually come at the end of the meditation. We shall speak of these general affections later. All affections are not produced in every meditation. One affection may suffice, if it is strong and durable. Ordinarly, the affections will correspond to the subject of the meditation.[20] However, the Holy Spirit being our principal master may at times prompt us to elicit affections foreign to the subject of the meditation. We should always follow these divine inspirations. Often God may give to perfect souls affections of contrition and contempt of the world that, properly speaking, belong to the beginner's state.[21] However, young religious should be cautious. Experience teaches that beginners are sometimes inflamed with such great love that they think they have arrived at perfection. These affections, however, are transitory, and the young religious or beginner will soon find himself again trodding the hard long way of dryness to perfection.[22]

In prayer it is possible and useful to prolong the meditation (*discursus*) in order better to move the will by conversing with God, the Blessed Virgin or the saints. So also it is possible and most useful to prolong the affections by carrying on affective conversations or colloquies with Our Lord, the Blessed Virgin or the saints. Once a religious has acquired the habit of affective conversation with God, he is living in the atmosphere of the true spirit of Carmel.

A novice, of course, is not ordinarily expected to practise continual conversation with God. This is what he is striving for. But he must learn how to produce affections which lead to this conversation. Therefore, he should follow the method that is explained here and be faithful to it at least for several months.

Those who persevere in this method will dispose themselves eventually to the higher state of prayer that is practised by those who are perfect. Indeed, no human effort or artifice will bring them to the prayer of perfect souls. But human effort (ordinary grace is understood) is able to dispose them to the heights of perfection wherein the affections consist in a nude and simple adhesion to God or in a total abandonment to His will.

---

[20] Chap. ix, pp. 127-128.

[21] Here again the *Méthode* cites St. Teresa as its authority. "D'autant que saincte Térèse a très bien dit, que iamais on ne doit se depouillés des sentiments d'une très humble et sincere componction, qui est le pain quotidien, avec lequel on doit manger toutes les viandes des autres sainctes affections." Chap. xxiv, p. 392.

[22] Chap. ix, p. 131.

No rule is given here for perfect souls. They will receive their direction from God, being moved interiorly by the Holy Spirit in their exercises. Their affections are very intimate: either the total loss and resignation of themselves into the hands of God, or a simple and bare adhesion to His Majesty, or a transformation, uniformity and the like, which cannot be attained by human effort, although they are able to *dispose* themselves for it, since one comes to the eminetnt degree of prayer by practising the very low degree of prayer, of which we speak here.[23]

Hence, the humble exercises of prayer that are presented in the *Méthode* are the way by which religious arrive at this eminent grade of prayer. Meditation is the way to contemplation.[24] There is no doubt that the *Méthode* refers here to infused contemplation which cannot be strictly merited because it is a pure gift of God. It is quite clear, too, that the *Méthode* conceives infused contemplation as the normal end toward which the Carmelite disposes himself.

After this digression the *Méthode* explains the time of making the affections. Following the general law that it is the Holy Ghost Who is our principal guide in prayer, the *Méthode* grants the greatest freedom. Some religious (especially beginners) elicit affections immediately after each point or consideration. Others wait and elicit affections after having considered all points. Still others join affections with the considerations and make each consideration affective. This is common among those who are advanced in prayer.[25] In chapters seventeen and eighteen the authors give examples of these three ways.

At the end of the period of mental prayer it is customary to make acts of thanksgiving, resolutions, oblation and petition.[26] These acts do not have to follow the above order. But beginners should follow this order for a short period of time to familiarize themselves with the method. After some time, a religious may omit some of these acts, such as thanksgiving, petition, etc., although they are always helpful.

5. *Resolutions*

The *Méthode* gives special importance to resolutions. Just as the whole fruit of the meditation *(discursus)* consists in eliciting affections,

---

[23] Chap. ix, pp. 130-131.

[24] *Ibid.* The *Méthode* does not mean that the step from discursive prayer to infused contemplation is immediate. For it teaches that discursive meditation is followed by affective prayer and the prayer of simple regard (acquired contemplation). These ways of ordinary prayer gradually dispose the soul for infused contemplation. Cf. chap. xxiv, pp. 375-377.

[25] Chap. ix, pp. 132-133.

[26] Chap. xi, p. 134.

so the whole fruit of affections consists in making good and efficacious resolutions.[27]

Resolutions to be helpful must be 1) specific, 2) few in number and made with discretion, 3) accommodated to the one who makes them, 4) prompt and free.

Resolutions are necessary not only for beginners but even for those well advanced in prayer. For he who finishes prayer without having made a good resolution is similar to the man invited to a banquet, who looks at the food-laden table, admires it, but eats nothing.[28] For those advanced in prayer the *Méthode,* speaking of resolutions, says: "Those advanced in prayer (*proficientes*) must learn to tolerate many things for God, holding themselves in total and entire resignation."[29] This total resignation to God's will is the effect of constant resolutions.

6. *Petition*

The act of petition usually closes the hour of prayer. The religious should humbly make known his needs to God.[30] He should stand before the Lord as a little dog before its master waiting to receive a few scraps from his hand. If repulsed, he should return the next day assuming the same humble attitude.[31] Actually, this petition can be made in two ways: humbly presenting the petition in the simple manner of a sick man or beggar, or entreating and pleading his cause as a criminal does before a judge or a subject in the presence of his king.[32]

After explaining the mechanics of mental prayer and giving many actual examples or models of meditation, the *Méthode* closes this first part of the tract with certain points of advice called "doubts" which form an apt conclusion to the treatise.

These doubts explain the relation of the imagination, the meditation and the affections to each other, at the same time they place the proper value on this method. Let us consider these points.

---

[27] Chap. xi, p. 144.
[28] Chap. xi, p. 145.
[29] "Les Profitans doivent tendre à la pratique solide de la vertu: et les Parfaits à endurer choses grandes pour Dieu, à se rendre souverainement attentifs à eux mesmes, à se tenir tousiours dans un total abandon, et entiere soumission de leur esprit, et de tout ce qu'els sont aux conduites divines." Chap. xi, p. 147.
[30] Chap. xiii, p. 163.
[31] Louis of Granada is cited as the authority for this example. The *Méthode* calls him "un excellent autheur." Chap xiii, p. 168.
[32] Chap. xiii, p. 174.

For beginners in prayer the use of the imagination is recommended. However, if one has a vivid imagination which tends to represent minute things, it should be checked lest disillusionment follow.[33] Furthermore, imaginary representations are to be as brief as possible. They are to be used only in so far as necessary to control the imagination from wandering. As soon as possible, one should pass to intellectual considerations.[34]

The intellectual considerations (the meditation) terminate in affections. The general rule is to cease meditating (*discursus*) as soon as the will is moved to make affections.[35] Hence, if the will is moved almost immediately with hardly any reflection, one should abandon the different points of the *discursus* and follow the attraction of divine grace.[36] For the method of prayer is only a help, and we must not stoop to formalism. If the method is only a hindrance to our freedom in prayer, we should abandon it. But a novice should first make a sincere effort to follow the method.

IV – Meditative Reading

Finally, what can be done for those who cannot meditate? They may use a book of meditations or a spiritual book of some value, and mingle the reading with reflection.[37] When they are moved by some passage of the book, they should close it and consider the matter that they may be able to elicit some fruit. Some may even resort to the practise of aspirations which we shall consider later.

So far the *Méthode* has considered mental prayer in its most simple forms and especially discursive prayer. Does the *Méthode* speak of higher grades of mental prayer? It not only mentions them but briefly describes them, for it is always aware that discursive prayer should with practise become more simple, so that affections take an ever more prominent part in prayer.

V – Affective Prayer

Affective prayer is explicitly taught in our manual.

When one has acquired great knowledge of divine things from many meditations, the soul becomes so enlightened that if it insists on too much

---

[33] Chap. vi, p. 77.
[34] Chap. xxiv, pp. 375-376.
[35] Chap. xxiv, pp. 376-377
[36] This is called affective prayer today. P. Pourrat, "Affective (Spiritualité)," *DeSp*, I, 240-246.
[37] Chap. xxiv, pp. 380-381.

reflection it becomes clouded and cold. In this state it should not want to meditate, but should rather enjoy the fruit of its previous labor, and give the whole time to affections. This practise is proper only to those advanced in prayer.[38]

VI – Prayer of Simple Regard

There is another type of higher prayer which the *Méthode* calls the prayer of simple regard. It sometimes happens that in a moment the soul understands some mystery, for example, the scourging of Christ at the pillar, and without further *discursus* comprehends the patience and meekness of Christ. What should the soul do in this state? Let the soul stand, as it were, attentive to the suffering Christ and strengthened by a living faith; "continue this simple intuition (*simple regard*) of the mystery without any *discursus*, and cherish the affection with which it is moved."[39]

VII – Prayer of Recollection

The *Méthode* presents only active ways of prayer or what we may call non-mystical ways of prayer to the novices. But it realizes the necessity of making known even higher ways of active prayer, since it wishes to explain all the stages of prayer that gradually lead to the threshold of infused contemplation. Hence, it presents what appears to be a prayer of recollection, but the brevity of the description makes it difficult to analyze this form of prayer. It seems to be the prayer of active recollection that precedes infused contemplation. It seems to coincide with the description of active recollection described by St. Teresa.[40] The *Méthode* says:

But if at some time you should notice that you are drawn by God to great interior quiet, leaving the *discursus*, follow this attraction of grace, quietly standing clearly and simply in the presence of God that you may converse with Him and enjoy Him, who is intimately present to you. In this state there is no need to produce any expressed act or to reflect on your actions. It is impossible for your soul to be lazy or inactive in this state, but simply allow it to be drawn by the movement or action within you.[41]

---

[38] Chap. xxiv, pp. 375-376.

[39] Chap. xxiv, p. 377. The *Méthode* calls this prayer *simple regard*. Other authors call it prayer of *simplicity* or *active* or *acquired contemplation*. Cf. Dom Lehodey, *The Ways of Mental Prayer*, trans. by a monk of Melleray (Dublin, 1917), 190-216; also A. Poulain, *The Graces of Interior Prayer*, trans. by L. Smith, 6th ed. (London, 1928), chap. ii, 37-38.

[40] *Complete Works*, I, *Life*, chap. xiv, p. 83.

[41] Chap. xxiv, pp. 377-378.

VIII – Difficulties in Prayer

Some of the most instructive and practical chapters in the *Méthode* deal with the difficulties in mental prayer.[42] These difficulties are many and come from different sources. There are trials from God, problems that rise from our own nature and temperament, and lastly there are the temptations and pitfalls of the devil.[43]

The general rule in all these trials is to remember that God is our principal director and, no matter what the problem, we must cooperate willingly and energetically with Him, if we wish to succeed in prayer.

God does not lead all souls the same way. His ordinary way of dealing with souls in mental prayer is to make them cooperate most diligently in order to obtain the fruits of prayer. He gives some consolation, but not often, nor does it last long. Sometimes God leads novices by the way of sensible consolation, giving them great spiritual joy. He does this to inspire them to a greater love of prayer and to strong and bold resolutions. This sensible consolation is good and helpful. But it can also come from the devil. If it lasts for a long time and turns us away from God so that we desire it above other things, then this consolation is dangerous and not from God. We pray to please God, and not to experience great joy. As the novice progresses, God usually withdraws this sensible consolation, because it is not necessary for effective prayer. If God should take it from us, let us realize that it was only a gift, and that He can dispose of it as He wishes.

God leads souls by a third way – the way or aridity and desolation. This is often the way of the saints. It is difficult and trying, but it is secure and advantageous. It is usually the way that leads to higher and more intimate union with God.

Distractions too will make prayer a burden. We must be resigned to them, although firm in our desire to rid ourselves of all of them. We must take a strong, determined stand against them. Involuntary, distractions are not sins. God often permits them to test our love. At all costs, we must persevere in prayer – persevere in times of great distractions and even during long periods of dryness.

If we are weighed down by sadness or tiredness and find it impossible to concentrate or to arouse our will, let us remember this can be a most fruitful state of prayer, because it can be a test of our real love of God. In this state we should kneel during the hour of prayer, and in the presence of God acknowledge our weakness and our helplessness.

---

[42] Chap. xxi, pp. 318 ff.
[43] On the discernment of Spirits consult De Guibert, *Theologia spiritualis*, no. 150, p. 138.

To simply kneel before God in this state of helplessness can be in itself a most efficacious act of love. "Lord, I kneel here because of love for you."[44] Who cannot see that this is a most profound prayer? For our heart remains close to God, even though the body and the mind would take us from Him. The "wasting" of this hour, is really a prolonged act of adoration; it is the consecration of self and of time to the Omnipotent God on Whom we depend for every grace and for every moment of our existence.

Commentary

The foregoing exposition of the method of meditation leads us to the following conclusions:

The method of meditation in the reform of Touraine contains three parts: preparation, meditation and affections. The method is predominantly *affective*. Its purpose is to lead the soul to affective conversation with God, which then disposes the soul for the prayer of contemplation. Meditation is the way to contemplation.

This method is most useful for the novice, and he should use it and no other as he begins the art of mental prayer. At first glance it is a very complicated, very rigid and precise method. This apparent formalism and rigidness disappears when we consider that the method should be adapted to the nature and grace of the individual. The mechanical form, that is, the coordinated steps of the meditation, is of secondary importance: Meditation should be free and easy. The various steps or parts of the method should be abandoned once they fail guide serve their purpose.[45] The Holy Spirit is the principal director and

---

[44] Chap. i, p. 13.

[45] This advice is in perfect harmony with present day teaching. It is interesting to compare the teaching of the *Méthode* with the words of the eminent theologian Garrigou-Lagrange, who writes: "What is simpler than prayer? Its spontaneity is, however, taken away at times by the use of excessively complicated methods, which draw too much attention to themselves and not enough to God, whom the soul should seek. A method is good as a way of finding the truth, on condition that it can be forgotten and that it lead truly to the end toward which one tends. To prefer the method to the truth, or, a certain intellectual mechanism to reality that should be known, would be a manifest aberration, similar to that of the meticulous man or of the pedant. Moreover, an over-complicated method provokes a reaction, and even an excessive reaction in some who, worn out by this complexity, often end up in a vague reverie that has scarcely any true piety about it except the name ... A method, or to speak more simply with Bossuet, a manner of making prayer, is useful, especially at the beginning, to preserve us from mental rambling. But that it may not by its complexity become an obstacle rather than a help, it must be simple, and, far from breaking the spontaneity and continuity of prayer, it should be content

guide of the soul in mental prayer, and we should always follow His inspiration and leave the method, if He chooses to lead us another way. But the novice should at least for some months make every sincere effort to learn and follow this method that has been proposed to him.

The method requires the use of the three faculties, namely, the memory, the intellect and the will. The memory is an aid to the intellect, and the intellect is the handmaid of the will. The will is the supreme faculty in prayer. The soul must always tend to a loving, intimate conversation with God. It should strive to come to God by way of affections rather than by reasoning powers. However, the uninitiated novice will find it necessary to use his reasoning powers extensively in order to awaken affections in his soul.

If his meditation is good, it will terminate in specific resolutions. No resolutions mean that the prayer is fruitless! It is good resolutions that place the soul on the road to a more perfect, affective union with God.[46]

It is important to observe that the *Méthode* requires the use of the three faculties of the soul in meditation. This is not the same as teaching the particular method of the three faculties that is found in the Spiritual Exercises of St. Ignatius, where he teaches many different methods. Among these, as we shall see, he makes a clearcut distinction between the method of the three faculties, the method of contemplation; the method of the application of the senses, etc. This division is not found in the *Méthode*. It uses the phrase "meditation of the three faculties" in a wide sense to indicate that mental prayer always requires these three faculties in prayer. It includes the meditations of sin, death, hell, the mysteries of Christ, virtues, vices, etc., under the general heading of meditation of the three faculties. It also considers the exercise of the presence of God as an exercise of the three faculties, as we shall see in chapter six.[47] At the same time the use of the three fac-

---

with describing the ascending movement of the soul toward God." *The Three Ages of the Interior Life,* trans. from the French by Sister Timothea Doyle, O. P. (2 vols., St. Louis, 1947-1948), I, 445-446.

[46] It is interesting to note that this practical effect of meditation in no way blinded the authors of our manual to the fact that meditation is just one section along the road of perfection and is just a preparation for a higher way of prayer. At no time does the *Méthode* consider meditation as an end in itself or as the only normal method of prayer for devout souls. It therefore follows faithfully the medieval concept of prayer, which ordains all meditation and prayer to contemplation. Cf. Philippe, *Mental Prayer,* 42, where he writes of the concept of prayer in the Middle Ages.

[47] We mention this distinction because Cardinal Lercaro in his excellent book *Metodi di orazione mentali* (Genoa, 1948), 318, fails to make this distinction when speaking of the Carmelite method of prayer in the Ancient Observance.

ulties in the wide sense would not exclude the use of the three faculties in the strict sense. Now the meditation on sin and other subjects in the *Méthode* may also be developed according to St. Ignatius' method of the three faculties in which the intellect is given a much greater part than the imagination.

In the exposition of meditation in the *Méthode* we find two problems that demand a solution. The first refers to the absolute necessity of meditation, mixed prayer and aspirative prayer for the novice; the second, to the necessity of resolutions in every meditation.

In reference to the first problem: Is mental prayer, especially meditation, absolutely necessary for the novice? The *Méthode* says that it is. "Therefore, in this tract we consider the three other kinds of prayer, mental, mixed and aspirative, because these three are absolutely necessary for acquiring introversion and interior conversation with God."[48]

We disagree with the word "absolutely" and believe that it is too severe. Now it may happen (to take the more obvious case) that a novice has no inclination to practise mixed prayer; and yet, if he practises mental prayer of some kind, there is no reason why he cannot come to perfect introversion. Why should mixed prayer be *absolutely* necessary, when there are some other ordinary ways to pray, for example, methodical meditation, or meditative reading?

Another question immediately comes to mind. Are any of the lower degrees of mental prayer exercised at set periods of time absolutely necessary to acquire continual interior conversation with God? It seems that some exercise of mental prayer, such as meditation, is at least morally necessary, since interior conversation with God, an advanced state of mental prayer, is the normal result of the lower degrees of mental prayer.[49] At the same time, we know that it is possible for God, although not in His ordinary providence, to grant a soul perfect interior conversation by a special grace, even though the soul may have never practised meditation, mixed prayer or aspirative prayer in its initial stages. However, we must bear in mind that the *Méthode* was written for novices and would naturally propose the normal, ordinary way to perfect interior conversation with God. Hence, we believe that some exercise of mental prayer, such as frequent meditation, is necessary for continual or perfect interior conversation with God, but we would omit the word absolutely.

---

[48] Chap. i, p. 13.
[49] De Guibert, *Theologia spiritualis,* no. 253, p. 228.

Our second problem concerns specific resolutions. Are specific resolutions necessary for every meditation, even for those advanced in prayer? The *Méthode* says they are. We must bear in mind that the *Méthode* is primarily for novices, and all spiritual writers would admit that novices should strive to produce specific resolutions for every meditation. But are they always necessary? Father de Guibert sees no reason why specific resolutions should be made for every meditation, although they are always helpful, and we agree with this opinion.[50] Now when the soul has made some advancement in prayer, it may occupy itself during the hour of meditation with a deeper appreciation of a divine mystery or with acts of adoration, thanksgiving, love, etc. This way of prayer, even though not ending with any specific resolutions, is an effective prayer and most pleasing to God.

---

[50] De Guibert, *Theologia spiritualis*, no. 294, p. 259.

Chapter V

MIXED PRAYER

We have seen in the discussion of the first part of the *Méthode* that the reform of Touraine grants great liberty in prayer. The second part of the *Méthode* is further proof of this liberty. It contains a very short treatise on mixed prayer.[1] In three chapters it explains the meaning and the usefulness of this prayer and the rules that govern it. Using the Our Father and the Hail Mary, it demonstrates how to make mixed prayer.

Mixed prayer is made up of internal thoughts (reasoning or considerations) and oral words. It is a mixture of oral and mental prayer. It is comparatively easy, requires little labor, and is most suitable for beginners who find it difficult to follow methodical meditation. Even the advanced and those who are perfect and live in the unitive way will find it to their advantage, especially when they are sick or unable to prepare their meditation.

Mixed prayer is not to be used indiscriminately. Therefore, beginners should heed the following advice. 1) The subject matter should be a psalm, a verse or vocal prayer which is *affective*. But any prayer in which we experience devotion will be suitable. 2) Single words or verses should be calmly and maturely weighed in order to elicit the will to affections. These latter acts should not be produced violently. Hence, when a word or a verse leaves the will unaffected, we should proceed to the next word or verse. 3) As in all mental prayer, so here, we are not striving to produce beautiful ideas or strange and unusual thoughts. We are striving to converse lovingly with God, and so we must use thoughts for that purpose. In purely affective prayer we speak with God in the second person. 4) We may strive to prolong both

---

[1] Chap. xxv-xxvii, pp. 396-425.

considerations and affections, just as explained above in ordinary meditation. 5) In producing affections we should ordinarily follow the order proposed by the subject matter. Resolutions should never be neglected. They are the fruit of prayer.[2]

Commentary

In this particular way of prayer we would like to make the following observations. Much of the counsel given here was mentioned also in the chapters on methodical meditation. This indicates there is only an accidental difference between these two ways of prayer, for both tend to lead the soul to more affective prayer. They are two different ways of reflection or meditation. The same *plan* of mental prayer would be used in both cases, namely, preparation, meditation and affections. The only difference would be in the second part, that is, meditation, which would not follow the points for a sensible or spiritual subject but would follow the rules of mixed prayer.

Resolutions are as necessary for mixed prayer as for methodical meditation. They should never be neglected and should correspond to the spiritual age of the religious.

Finally, one ought to foster [those affections] which lead the soul to the practise of virtue and mortification, without forgetting to make some resolutions which are the fruit of prayer. One should always ask God for the grace to put these resolutions into practise. In this matter each one should consider his state and need.[3]

The presentation of mixed prayer to the novices of Touraine is no innovation in the spiritual life. This same method is clearly explained by St. Ignatius in the fourth week of the *Spiritual Exercises* and by St. Teresa in her *Way of Perfection*.[4] It is of great psychological value, since it takes into consideration the different personalities and the varying needs of those engaged in prayer. It helps to do away with formalism that would adapt the religious to a determined method of prayer rather than the way of prayer to the needs of the religious.

In spite of the value of this way of prayer we are at a loss to explain why the authors of the *Méthode* have devoted the second section to mixed prayer, giving it almost equal importance with methodical meditation and aspirative prayer. It seems to us that mixed prayer

---

[2] Chap. xxv, p. 400.
[3] Chap. xxv, p. 400.
[4] *Complete Works*, II, chaps. xxviii to xxx, pp. 110-126.

could easily have been considered in section one along with the other ways of simple prayer, namely, meditative reading, affective prayer, prayer of simple regard and prayer of recollection. In this way the *Méthode* would have been divided into two sections, namely, ordinary meditation and aspirative prayer. This twofold division would then add more balance to the treatise of prayer in the *Méthode*.

Chapter VI
ASPIRATIVE PRAYER
OR
THE EXERCISE OF THE PRESENCE OF GOD

We now approach the third part of the *Méthode* which contains a treatise on aspirative prayer.[1] This kind of prayer is like mental prayer in so far as it is conceived in the mind, and like mixed prayer in so far as it is often mental and oral. It is different from both, however, because it is composed of a few words (oral or mental only) and, like an arrow that is directed toward its target, it ascends swiftly and directly to heaven. For this reason it is commonly called ejaculatory prayer.[2]

Aspirative prayer presupposes the exercise of the presence of God. It is therefore necessarily joined with this exercise. We shall first consider aspirative prayer and then the exercise of the presence of God.

In our consideration of aspirative prayer we shall answer the following questions : 1) What is an aspiration? 2) How is it produced in the heart? 3) Why practise this prayer? 4) What fruits does it produce?

I – Aspirative Prayer

The prayer of aspirations and ejaculatory prayer are terms that are used synonymously in the *Méthode*.[3] An aspiration is defined as: "A fervent elevation of the mind to God composed of a few words, that in a moment are hurled toward heaven to make known to God the good affection and holy desires of our heart."[4]

---

[1] Chaps. xxviii-xxxvi. Cf. De Guibert, *Thelogia spiritualis*, no. 303, p. 268.

[2] Chap. xxviii, p. 426.

[3] An aspiration, however, is not strictly the same as ejaculatory prayer. The former belongs to those advanced in prayer; ejaculations can be made in any state, even by people not given to much prayer. Cf. John Brenninger, O. Carm., "Ioannes a S. Samsone de animoet ingenio Ordinis Carmelitarum," *AOC*, 8 (1932-1936), 29, 32.

[4] Chap. xxviii, p. 426.

An aspiration springs from a heart of love, just as a flame from a burning furnace. It is a short prayer and composed of only a few words that may be mental or oral. When this movement of the heart (the will) is prolonged, it is called a colloquy rather than an aspiration. There are many degrees in this prayer. The grade of its perfection depends upon the advancement of the soul. If faithfully practised, the religious will reach the state when these fiery darts sent to heaven are returned one hundredfold. A battle takes place between God and man. It is a war of love. God is the victor, and the soul struck by shafts of divine love cannot but think of God and desires to please him continually.[5]

Continual attention to God comes only after the successful practise of meditation.

Those who love little and those who are negligent will think this practise is impossible. And indeed it is, until they give themselves seriously to mental prayer, and fill their minds with the good thoughts and affections that build up an arsenal from which they can draw fervent elevations, affective aspirations and inflamed desires.[6]

Occasionally it happens that God moves some novices at the beginning of their conversion to fervent affective prayer. Aspirations become easy for them and in a short time they make great progress in virtue.[7]

How are these aspirations formed in the soul? There are two ways: 1) Aspirations are formed in the soul without any determined effort on the part of the soul. (We do not say without *any* activity). Thoughts come into the mind and quickly inflame the will to make short acts of love. This is the work of the Holy Spirit, Who works in us and Whose guidance we follow. 2) The second way of forming aspirations depends much more upon human effort. The mind makes a determined effort to be recollected, and deliberately elevates itself to God. This act does not demand profound considerations, but only demands that we make ordinary daily events the occasion to praise and bless God, or that we recall some divine truth that in the past has deeply affected us, and soon the will is moved to aspirations. For example, if you perceive a fellow religious patiently bearing some hu-

---

[5] John of St. Samson, *Guerre d'amour,* cited by Bouchereaux, *La Réforme des Carmes,* 293.
[6] Chap. xxiii, p. 428.
[7] *Ibid.*

miliation, you can say: "How pleasing my brother is in your sight, O Lord, help me to practise this virtue."[8]

We must continually use daily occasions to say these short prayers, because this exercise will help us not only to remain in the way of perfection but it will also help us to progress. We must not permit an hour of the day to pass without raising our souls to God.

Those who make great progress in this exercise find that it becomes second nature, so that whether in the monastery or outside, night or day, alone or with others, engaged in work or living in solitude, they find their hearts continually turning to God. Almost naturally their hearts become a burning furnace from which sparks of love continually shoot forth. These fervent souls need no rules or aids to form aspirations. They do better left to themselves. Their life is a continual and actual affective conversation with God.

In this loving conversation with God, we find especially the spirit of the Carmelite Order. Novices should be taught the prayer of aspiration that they may attain the true spirit of Carmel which is expressed in chapter seven of the Rule: "Let them meditate day and night on the Law of God." The word "meditate" in the Rule should not be restricted to an act of the intellect, but indicates especially "affections of the heart and the ardor of the will."[9]

This state of affective prayer disposes the soul to contemplative prayer. It resembles the life of the blessed in heaven. For just as their life consists in a continual vision of God in most intense love and praise, so also the life of the Carmelite religious consists in seeing God by faith always and in all things, together with a continual uplifting of the heart to Him. The more actual and intense our love, the more it resembles the love of the blessed.[10]

This exercise of aspirations is most suitable for contemplative life, and is really a short cut to affective and continual union with God.[11]

Besides this, it will produce the following effects: 1) a disposition of the heart that prepares the soul to accept mortifications and practise virtue; 2) a state of almost sinlessness, since temptations to sin are overcome; 3) a purification of the mind, so that it attends first to God in all things and acts wisely and slowly in all things; 4) a soul that be-

---

[8] *Ibid.*, p. 431
[9] *Ibid.*, p. 434.
[10] *Ibid.*, p. 435.
[11] *Ibid.*, p. 438.

comes ever more inflamed with ardent affections, since God is a consuming fire.[12]

Novices must learn to follow certain rules, if they expect the prayer of aspirations to bring them to a loving conversation with God. The first rule for novices is to select a number of aspirations in the morning, so that when they think of God during the day they shall have something to say to Him. The second rule warns that they should observe great freedom in this practise and obey the impulses of the Holy Spirit. Ordinarily, a religious will produce aspirations accommodated to his state. The novice or beginner will be content with aspirations of sorrow for sin; the more advanced with desires for God; and the perfect with most fervent and unitive aspirations. However, there is no fast rule here. A religious may and should make aspirations that pertain to a higher state, if he feels invited by God to do this.[13]

The third rule refers to the manner of producing aspirations. As soon as the mind thinks of God, it should try to recollect itself with some good thought and affection, keeping itself and the will turned to God.

Finally, the novice must persevere in this practise. Even when indisposed he should practise aspirations, taking caution not to do any violence to the will. Nor should he allow distractions to discourage him, but should return time and again to recollect himself in God.

Certain defects should be avoided: 1) The number and diversity of the aspirations that are made are of little consequence. Attention should be given to the fact that they are made well. Mechanical aspirations that are made without any desire are useless. Therefore it is unwise to repeat them so often that they create disgust. They should be produced with attention, affection and sincerity. 2) It is not necessary to strive to penetrate truths, but rather to excite the will.

This is above all an exercise of love. For this exercise is not learned by subtle penetration, but by a loving elevation of the heart to God, so that a most simple affection is of more worth than all the thoughts that are written in books.[14]

Any attempt to formulate beautiful thoughts and phrases is consequently harmful to this exercise. 3) It is not necessary to look far

---

[12] *Ibid.*, pp. 439-441. St. Bonaventure, *Liber de theologia mystica*, chap. iii, is quoted as the authority for this final statement (on page 441). This is really the work of Hugh of Balma and was for a long time attibuted to St. Bonaventure. Cf. S. Autore, "Hugues de Balma," *DTC*, VII, 215-220.

[13] Chap. xxix. p. 443.

[14] *Ibid.*, p. 452.

off for God, as if He were absent, since He is near and actually in us. "He is not far from anyone of us. For in Him We live, and move and are."[15]

There are different ways of thinking of God's presence. Some like to think of God watching over them from heaven, and so they direct their aspirations heavenward (ejaculatory prayer). Others like to think of God present to all things by His immensity and therefore speak to Him as present with them (aspiration or familiar conversation). Still others, and this is the best way, think of God as within themselves and thus address Him residing in their souls (loving conversion). Although this last way is the most simple and is very helpful to recollection, not all novices can practise it immediately.

II – The Presence of God

It is obvious now that there is a connection between the presence of God and aspirative prayer. Indeed, the connection is so necessary that, unless God is in some way present to our minds, we will not be able to raise our hearts to Him in aspirations. Just as the will presupposes the operation of the intellect, aspirations presuppose the act of the presence of God.[16] Hence, the best way to be recollected and disposed to speak with God is to be always in His presence.

Walking in the presence of God cannot be too highly recommended to the Carmelite. Our father, St. Elias, worked wonders in the world through this practise; and he has left this holy exercise as his greatest gift, together with his twofold spirit, to his disciple Eliseus. "The Lord lives, in whose sight I stand."[17]

To be in the presence of God (in the restricted sense) means to continually have Him before our eyes, believing firmly that He sees us wherever we are. This kind of presence is necessary for meditation as well as for aspirative prayer. For the soul does not speak to God unless it believes Him to be present. And since the soul should speak frequently, it is necessary that the soul always lives in God's presence.[18]

There are different ways of defining the presence of God. As we mentioned above, in the strict sense it is only an act of the memory or of the intellect by which we recall or believe that God is present to us.

---

[15] Acts 17:28.
[16] Chap. xxx, p. 459.
[17] III Kings, 17:1.
[18] Chap. xxx, pp. 459 f.

This act in itself is often sterile and has little effect upon our spiritual life. The inflaming of the will by aspirations is needed, which in turn moves the soul to a more generous service of God.[19]

Because of this relation and mutual dependence both these exercises are united as parts of the one exercise of the presence of God.[20] In this sense "to be in the presence of God means to have God continually represented before us, to take care that this awareness of God rules all our actions and most secret thoughts, and to offer our hearts frequently to Him."[21] In other words, we build within us a secret oratory where we believe God resides, and there we dwell always recollected in Him, adoring Him frequently with interior aspirations.[22]

The presence of God is of great spiritual advantage, and a good part of chapter thirty is devoted to its fruit. "This exercise alone without any other is sufficient to withdraw us from every kind of vice and imperfection, and lead us to acquire every virtue."[23]

The fathers of the Church distinguish three acts of the presence of God, that is, imaginary, intellectual and affective.[24]

An imaginary presence of God may be formed in two ways. We may represent either the Sacred Humanity of Christ, and exercise all our actions in His presence, or we may represent God under a corporeal image, filling heaven and earth with His immensity just as the light of the sun fills the air. We may also consider Him dwelling in all creatures, giving motion to them just as the soul moves the body.

Finally, we may consider God surrounding, penetrating and filling the whole universe just as fishes immersed in the sea.

---

[19] These statements need to be clarified. When the *Méthode* says that the mere recollection of God's presence which is confined to the memory and intellect is sterile, it does not mean that it is useless, but rather that it lacks the perfection of an act of the presence of God that involves the will as well as the intellect. For an act of the intellect (union by faith with God) is an immediate and necessary preparation for the union of the will with God.

[20] This is found among other spiritual writers. E. Vansteenberghe, "Aspirations," *DSp*, I, 1017-1026, cites Alphonsus de Liguori; De Guioert, *Theologia spiritualis*, no. 303, p. 268, cites Francis de Sales. Brandsma, "Carmes," *DSp*, II, 162, says that the *Institutio primorum monachorum* attaches a particular importance to this exercise, which it considers a Carmelite practise inspired by the words of Elias: "Vivit Dominus in cuius conspectu sto:"

[21] Chap, xxx, p. 461.

[22] *Ibid.*, p. 162.

[23] *Ibid.*, p. 462

[24] *Ibid.*, p. 475. Cf. Cyprian of the Nativity (1605-1680), selection from "De l'exercise de la présence de Dieu," in *Études carmélitaines*, 20 (1935), 162. Cyprian considers imaginary and intellectual presence of God; quotes John of Jesus and Mary, and Alvarez de Paz.

Intellectual presence of God excludes, sensible images and representations, so that by an act of faith We believe God is present to us and in us, and that all things are disposed according to His will.

Affective presence of God ordinarily is the fruit of long practise of imaginary and intellectual presence. The will burns with love and elicits aspirations. God is not only present to the soul, but the will adheres to God.

The affective presence of God consists in an actual, clear and consoling sentiment whereby the soul dwells in a certain actual inclination toward God, which may be called the *state of adhesion,* because in this state the soul not only has God present but is really conjoined to Him.[25]

In this state the love of God burns so ardently in the soul that it breathes forth ardent aspirations. As a result we know how lovable God is, not because we have read it or understand it, but because we have experienced it. This experimental taste is the eternal voice which calls the soul to intimate union with God.[26]

Which kind of presence is more practical? Wisely we are told that we should practise the kind which is easiest and most fruitful. In other words, full liberty of spirit is again insisted upon in this holy exercise.[27]

Ordinarily the young novices do not know how to begin the exercises of the presence of God and aspirations, since they presuppose the successful practise of meditation. Wherefore, the *Méthode* has considered it prudent to outline a few rules [28] which we may sum up briefly: 1) Imaginary presence of God is more proper to their state. 2) Few aspirations should be practised in the beginning, at least for the first three months (more or less). But here again we cannot make any fast rule, since the action of the Holy Spirit and the nature of the individual must be considered. Violence should never be used to make aspiration. 3) It is sufficient to make a good intention before each task, renew it during the work, have a strong desire to please God in everything, making a short examination of conscience at the end of each task.

4) Since they may lack material to elicit ejaculations, the author has drawn up a lengthy list of aspirations principally from Holy Scripture. Why, we may ask, has the *Méthode* culled the aspirations from Scripture and not from other books ? Four reasons are given:[29] 1) The

---

[25] Chap. xxx, p. 475.
[26] *Ibid.*
[27] *Ibid.,* pp. 477-478.
[28] Chap. xxxi, pp. 486-489.
[29] Chap. xxxii, p. 496.

words of St. Paul the Apostle tell us how suitable is the word of God for ejaculatory prayers. "For the word of God is living and efficient and keener than any two-edged sword, etc." 2) The Carmelite Rule demands this use of Holy Scripture.[30] 3) The Savior Himself, when tempted by the devil in the desert, taught that all temptations of the devil should be met with the Holy Scripture. 4) Finally, the Word of God excites us to acquire virtues. David said to the Lord: "Thy word is exceedingly refined and thy servant hath loved it."[31]

III – The Four Ways

Having exposed in a general way the theoretical knowledge of the exercises of aspirations and of the presence of God, the *Méthode* presents four different practical ways to live in the presence of God and practise aspirations. 1) Exercise of aspirations (more properly, ejaculations) for the more important actions of the day. The aspirations are taken from Holy Scripture.[32] 2) Elevation of the mind to God through the visible things around us.[33] 3) Representation of the Humanity of Christ for all grades of the spiritual life. This is the doctrine of the fathers after Ps. Dionysius.[34] 4) The way of divine providence, i.e., seeing the hand of God in all things,[35] This last way consists in an act of faith, hope and charity, and is considered one of the most excellent exercises. Let us say a few words about each.

1. *Ejaculations.* Three series of aspirations are proposed: 1) aspirations for the more important actions of the day, e.g., after rising in the morning, going to mental prayer, returning to one's cell, for manual labor; 2) a selected list for warding off certain evil thoughts; 3) suitable verses, some of which are offered as material for meditation and others full of affection for inflaming the will. Almost all these are taken from the book of Psalms. This last series supposes the habit of interior recollection and is proposed for carrying on affective conversation during the day.

---

[30] Chap. xiv of the Carmelite Rule.

[31] Ps. 118:140. Blessed John Soreth, former General of the Order, had recommended Sacred Scripture as an object of Carmelite meditation. Brandsma, "Carmes," *DSp*, II, 167.

[32] Chap. xxxii, p. 496. Chapter xiv of the Carmelite Rule urges this practise. "May the sword of the spirit, which is the word of God, dwell abundantly in your mouth and heart."

[33] Chap. xxxiii, p. 541. St. Francis of Assisi is cited as an example; also the first part of the introduction of *El símbolo de la Fé* by Louis of Granada.

[34] Chap. xxxv, p. 569.

[35] *Ibid.;* St. Teresa is quoted; *Complete Works*, II, *Interior Castle*, 2, chap. i, p. 217.

An objection to this practise immediately presents itself. The *Méthode* has continually insisted upon liberty of the spirit. How can it now justify this more or less mechanical arrangement of aspiration for all daily actions? In the first place it should be rememberd that the practise of aspirations, strictly speaking, presupposes progress in prayer and a will already disposed to love. These three series of aspirations were written for novices who as yet have not made sufficient progress in mental prayer, and hence have no material from which they can produce aspirations. By recommending these, neither the liberty of spirit nor the inspiration of the Holy Spirit is impeded, for no one is expected to follow these aspirations blindly, but should select those that appeal to the individual's disposition and which will inflame the will with love. "From all these verses we may choose those which appeal to us most, so that we may become more familiar with them. We should not fear to repeat the same verses often, even many times in an hour, if we find they increase devotion." And finally, "we should always be prepared to freely obey the graces of Our Lord, if He should desire to move us to speak with Him on some other subject." [36]

2. *Seeing God in His Creatures*. The elevation of the mind to God through visible creatures was practised greatly by the fathers of the desert and was called by some the *divina philosophia*, because all visible and sensible things spoke to them of God.[37] This exercise is comparatively easy. It is sufficient to have a firm resolution to use every occasion to lift up the heart to God. We have a wonderful example of this in the life of St. Francis of Assisi in his relation with birds and nature in general. Christ Himself practised it. In His parables He gives earthly things heavenly meaning. The *Méthode* gives twenty examples taken from common things which may easily elevate the heart affectionately to God.[38] We are warned, however, not to go outside ourselves searching for things to elevate our minds, but to elevate them when the occasion presents itself.

3. *The Sacred Humanity of Christ*. The Sacred Humanity of Christ from the beginning of the Church has always held a central position in the formation of the spiritual life. In the acquiring of virtue we should never lose sight of it, since it is necessary and useful in the spiritual progress according to the mind of all spiritual writers.

---

[36] Chap. xxxii, p. 500.
[37] This practise has a place in Carmelite tradition, Brandsma, "Carmes," *DSp*, II, 167.
[38] Chap. xxxiii, pp. 544 ff.

That is why all the spiritual writers say, following St. Dionysius, that one must never put aside the representation of the Sacred Humanity of Jesus Christ, even though it is necessary to put aside all other species and images in the state of contemplation.[39]

This representation may be made in different ways corresponding to the disposition and state of perfection of the individual.[40] Novices find it to their advantage to perform their duties in the presence of Christ, Whom they imagine to be close by watching their every action. This simple, sensible, imaginary representation does not suffice, however, for those who have made progress. These latter should form a more full affective idea of the Humanity of Christ, walking in His sight and above all imitating His holy life that soon they may be made like unto Him. The result of the practise is perfect conformity with the life of Christ which is found in perfect souls.

Inexperienced novices should not force this practise upon themselves. The advanced, however, should practise the second grade of this exercise, for it is suitable especially for those who have begun to put on Christ. In a short time they can make great progress. "If they take this exercise with a loving and faithful heart, they shall find themselves in a short time clothed with the spirit of the life and sentiment of Jesus Christ, and finally transformed into Him."[41]

4. *Exercise of Divine Providence.* The fourth exercise of the presence of God consists in this: The soul recognizes the power of God working in all things. It sees all creatures as His instruments, so that whatever happens is under the providence of God. Hence, the soul, must conform its will totally to Him. In this way the heart enjoys great peace.[42]

---

[39] Chap. xxxiv, p. 569. Cf. Truhlar, *De experientia mystica*, 98-112. The author enumerates those who would erroneously exclude the representation of the Humanity of Christ from the state of contemplation; e.g., the Beghards and the Beguines, the Illuminati, Molinos, etc.

[40] This passage of the *Méthode* needs clarification, since the Humanity of Christ is not represented in the same way in all degrees of prayer, especially in contemplative prayer. Although it is quite true that the Humanity of Christ should not be totally and permanently excluded from contemplative prayer as the quietists taught, yet it can happen that in the act of infused contemplation the mind is so drawn to the Divine Essence that *at the moment* it is unable to think of the Humanity of Christ, or is only able to think of it with difficulty and with loss to spiritual advancement. But when the soul is not so passively drawn by God, it should never willfully and *ex industria* exclude thoughts of the Humanity of Christ, although it no longer perceives the Humanity of Christ in the same way as it once did in discursive prayer. Cf. Truhlar, De *experientia mystica*, 112; also J. de Guibert, S. J., *Documenta ecclesiastica christiane perfectionis*, Rome, (1931), 267, n. 451.

[41] *Méthode* chap. xxxiv, p. 567.

[42] Chap. xxxv, p. 579.

The foundation of this practise is faith, by which we believe that nothing happens without the intercession of the divine will. For this reason this practise is called the exercise of divine providence. We receive all things as from God. Both good and evil come from God but in different ways. God only permits the evil. We have the admirable example of our Divine Savior to follow in His passion and death. "The chalice which the Father has given me, shall I not drink it?"[43] "The practise that follows from this firm belief is to take all things as coming from the hands of God and not as coming from men."[44]

This conformity to the will of God also entails a fervent act of hope by which we firmly trust that God will work out our salvation in all things. We should strive to increase our trust in Him, adoring His paternal providence by full conformity of our will with His. St. Teresa tells us: "... in this we shall find true perfection and We should not expect to find it in any other hidden and unknown mystery."[45]

Charity is the last act of this exercise and perfects it. It consists in an humble and affectionate acceptation of both good and adverse things and renunciation of ourselves.

Humble and willful acceptance of the providence of God in all things both good and bad is the consummation and essential perfection of this exercise. It is nothing else than an act of charity, by which we love all things that God does, not because they are pleasing to us in themselves, but because of our love for God, who ordains them.[46]

In this union of wills consists true love. This practise, if carried out with any amount of success, supposes great advancement in prayer. It leads to that total abandonment to God which is the end of prayer as explained in chapter nine of the *Méthode*.

A number of acts taken especially from Sacred Scripture show how charity may be practised in this exercise. We note the following: "O how good and sweet is thy spirit, O Lord, in all things."[47] "I was dumb, and I opened not my mouth, because thou hast done it."[48] It is well to observe that this exercise is intimately united with aspirations, thus forming one integral exercise which is called the presence of God.

---

[43] John 18:16.
[44] Chap. xxxv, p. 581.
[45] *Complete Works*, II, *Interior Castle*, 2, chap. i, p. 217.
[46] Chap. xxxv, pp. 591-592.
[47] Wisdom 12:1.
[48] Ps: 38:10.

IV – Counsels

The *Méthode* brings the treatise on aspirations and the exercise of the presence of God to an end by presenting eight counsels.[49] The first seven pertain to aspirations; the eighth is another way of exercising the presence of God.

1) To increase in the love of God, which is the purpose of aspirations, it is not sufficient to be disposed to elevate the heart to God; but it is necessary to actually do this. We must above all have in our hearts some good sentiments from which we are able to form ardent ejaculatory prayers.[50]

2) Although the exercise of fervent aspirations is the effect of a loving heart, and hence seems to be proper to those who have made such progress, nevertheless each one may practise it according to his ability. The beginning will be difficult, and the heart not easily inflamed, but the exercise will be none the less good and holy. If continued, one shall soon feel his heart drawn to God and shall not find peace unless he continually converses and feels himself united to God. Arrived at this state, love alone suffices, human artifices and material for aspirations are no longer necessary. By the grace of God aspirations become as natural to the soul as breathing to the body.

3) This exercise is necessary for all religious. Especially is it recommended to those who are not able meditate and to those who are continually occupied in external affairs and who need a way to compensate for the time that should be given to meditation.

Those who frequently commit voluntary imperfections will practise this exercise in vain.

4) Those who have not yet sufficient material from which they may produce any aspirations shall find it useful to use the exercises of aspirations composed by Brother John of St. Samson and Father Dominic of St. Albert.[51] They should try to produce these as though they

---

[49] Chap. xxxvi, pp. 594 ff.

[50] John of St. Samson is cited here. We remain in a state of laziness unless we have same good thoughts always in our hearts.

[51] Reference could be to *Exercice d'aspirations amoureuses, simple et unique en l'amour même, contenant les flammes amoureuses de l'amour en soi-même, propre à estre tousjour fidelement pratiqué de l'âme veritablement devenüe amour, à force d'aymer, et plus specialement dessus la Croix, tant en la vie qu'en la mort*. It is found among the manuscripts of John. Cf. Bouchereaux, *La Réforme des Carmes*, 15. Reference may also be to the *Exercitatio spiritualis* of Dominic, chaps. ii-vii; *passim*. Cf. his *Opuscula pro novitiis et professis studentibus*, in AOC, 11 (1940-1942), 25-28.

were their own. Those of a few words and of a more affectionate nature should be selected, taking into account also the state and disposition of the individual.

5. It is very useful during the day to foster the affections and reduce to aspirations the pious thoughts of the morning meditation.

6) It is also very useful to join the exercise of aspirations to the practise of the virtue which we are striving to practise during a certain week or month. (Each month a specific virtue was given to the novices to practise.) By this artifice the heart will be more drawn to the practise of the virtue and thus exterior acts will be influenced more by interior acts.

7) However, despite this preceding advice, no one should use immoderate violence in this practise. If the intellect fails to suggest motives to move the will, We should pray simply and affectionately to God, asking that He may grant us this virtue which we so ardently desire.

8) The *Méthode* comes to a close with a special way to practise the presence of God, and that is to consider God dwelling within us:[52] Why was this way not explained with the other four exercises of the presence of God? It seems the reason is that this more excellent way of living in God's presence is too advanced for novices and is meant for those already on the threshold of the mystical state. The *Méthode* describes it as follows:

> We know by faith that God is in all things by His immensity and that He is in the just by grace: After placing this act of faith the soul gathers all its powers, and withdraws within itself. The soul in this state becomes peaceful, it experiences God's presence and tastes unutterable divine operations. The soul speaks to God within itself; it is ever prepared to listen to Him; it consults God in all things. It guards itself lest anything might enter within itself to make God sad.
>
> This is the beginning of the mystical life. It is less active perhaps than the ordinary way of prayer, but it is more holy. Indeed, this simple intuition of God with a hidden desire and affection of union with Him, and of pleasing Him in all things is worth more than a thousand other acts that are made by the soul in lower states of prayer. So that what seems to be pure silence is really full of the most vital expressions and wonderful affections

---

[52] This doctrine is beautifully explained in the encyclical *Divinum illud* (*The Holy Spirit*) of Pope Leo XIII, May 9, 1897; *Acta Sanctae Sedis,* 29, 650-654. Cf. De Guibert, *Doc. eccles. christ. perf.*, 565. The *Méthode* limits it to advanced souls, but there is no reason why it cannot be practised by novices.

which Scripture and the mystics so often praise. Those who reach this state walk in most profound recollection bearing God within themselves ... possessing Him and being possessed by Him.

This high state is the end toward which every prayer should lead us. The frontier of that region toward which tend all the exercises of prayer and the presence of God of which we have spoken here.[53]

Commentary

In this chapter we have tried to present the objective teaching of the *Méthode*. However, we would like now to make the following observations. Many other spiritual writers before and after the *Méthode* have joined the exercise of the presence of God with aspirative prayer under the title, exercise of the presence of God.[54] Secondly, aspirative prayer is the most interesting way of prayer developed in the *Méthode*. Not only is it the most interesting, but it is also the central prayer toward which the others converge. Aspirative prayer in its *full sense* presupposes meditation and proceeds from it. At the same time it is the ordinary effect produced by the diligent practise of the presence of God. It presupposes imaginary and intellectual presence of God. It is the distinctive prayer of the *Méthode,* because more than meditation it expresses the particular spirit of the reform of Touraine and of the Order, which consists in continual, affective conversation and union with God. Aspirative prayer, when performed well, is a direct and eloquent application of chapters seven and fourteen of the Carmelite Rule, which exhort us to meditate (raise our hearts, says the *Méthode*) day and night on the law of God and to keep our hearts, filled with holy thoughts. At the same time we must remember that aspirative prayer is only one way to live the true spirit of Carmel. There are other forms of prayer. But aspirative prayer is a safe and short way that leads to contemplative prayer and to the heights of perfection. There is no state in which aspirative prayer cannot be practised.

Therefore, the Carmelite should have the greatest esteem for aspirative prayer, which is sometimes also called the exercise of the presence of God.

---

[53] Chap. xxxvi, pp. 609-610.
[54] E. Vansteenberghe, "Aspirations," *DSp*, I, 1017-1026.

V – Summary of the Three Ways of Prayer

We have seen in chapter two of this study, *The Spirit of Touraine*, that the spirit of the reform is a return to the true primitive spirit of the Carmelite Order, which may be expressed in the words *vacare Deo*. The true Carmelite will be a man whose whole life is occupied with God in prayer. We have seen that this thought is found in the Constitutions of Touraine, in the works of the historians and the spiritual writers of the reform, especially John of St. Samson and Dominic of St. Albert. Is this same spirit of *vacare Deo* expressed also in the three ways of prayer (meditation, mixed and aspirative prayer) that are described in the *Méthode?* Our answer can only be affirmative. The central thought of the *Méthode*, like the melody of a symphony, runs through every page. That thought is: our life is a "life of prayer." Prayer is the food of our souls. Our minds and hearts must be continually lifted up to God, engaged in loving conversation with Him. Or, as our Rule says, we must "meditate day and night on the law of God." This meditation is not the work of the intellect alone but, above all, the work of the heart which should be elevated to God so that day or night, within the monastery or outside, alone or in company, engaged in active work or left in peace, we will turn our minds to God and elevate our hearts to Him, standing like Elias in his loving presence. Methodical meditation, mixed prayer and especially aspirative prayer can lead us to this end.

VI – Prayer and Mortification

Carmelite life in the reform of Touraine, as in the reform of St. Teresa, is organized in view of prayer. Progress in prayer is progress in the spiritual life. However, for the casual reader this clear teaching of the *Méthode* might present a problem, since it is the certain teaching of the Church that advancement in the spiritual life demands mortification as a necessary means. The history of spirituality clearly teaches that a life of prayer without mortification leads eventually to quietism or something worse. What, then, can be said for the position of the *Méthode* in which we seem to find progress in perfection measured in terms of progress in prayer only?

At no time does the *Méthode* teach that progress in perfection is measured by prayer only. It is true that the *Méthode* does not explicitly consider the place of mortification in the soul's progress toward God, but this omission does not mean that it has failed to recognize the necessity of mortification. We must remember that the *Méthode* is not a complete manual of the spiritual life: It is only one of four volumes on this subject and presupposes the doctrine of the necessity of mortification, which is found in the first three volumes of the *Directoires des novices* and especially in the third volume. Therefore, although the *Méthode* measures the soul's progress in the spiritual life by its prayer, it still recognizes the necessity of mortification and of other common means, such as examination of conscience and spiritual reading, that are also means to Christian perfection.[55]

---

[55] It would be erroneous to conclude from the foregoing that a purely contemplative life of prayer is the vocation of the Carmelite friar in the reform of Touraine. A life of continual occupation with God does not exclude the active apostolate, but should be the soul of any apostolic work. Hence, the reform of Touraine was not an attempt to return to the purely contemplative life of the primitive hermits of Mount Carmel, but rather a movement to revitalize the mixed life of contemplation and the active apostolate in which contemplation would be the *pars principalior*.

SECTION THREE

THE SOURCES OF THE *MÉTHODE*

CHAPTER VII

SACRED SCRIPTURE, THE FATHERS, THE RULE AND TRADITION OF CARMEL

We have seen that the *Méthode*, edited by Mark of the Nativity, was originally the work of Bernard of St. Magdalen, who had been a novice master for fifteen consecutive years (1632-1647) prior to the publishing of the *Directoires des novices*. Throughout his whole life he was a novice master for forty years. These men collaborated in giving the novices of Touraine a manual of prayer that was truly affective and destined to lead them to interior conversation with God in the mystical state. As is stated in the preface of the *Méthode,* these ways of prayer were practised and lived in the reform of Touraine before they were finally published.

In this section it is our purpose to investigate the sources of the *Méthode*. It is a difficult task to investigate the various sources from which the methods of prayer in the reform owe their origin. It is difficult because even the authors themselves are not always aware of the tremendous influence certain people and certain books have on their spiritual formation and writing. Therefore, we cannot hope to discover every single influence. Our task is also made doubly difficult because the *Méthode* has more than one author. Indeed, as we have seen, Leo of St. John has mentioned explicitly the influence of Thibault, John of St. Samson and Dominic of St. Albert among those who had a part in the formation of all the directories for novices.[1]

Moreover, it should be remembered that all the methods of meditation of the great spiritual masters as well as the theory of aspirative

---

[1] *Delineatio*, 60.

prayer had already been written and even widely diffused throughout France when the *Méthode* was finally completed. At best, therefore, we hope to point out the spiritual writers whom we believe have had profound influence on the structural form of meditation, mixed prayer and aspirative prayer, or who have had profound influence on the spiritual doctrine contained in these three ways of prayer in the *Méthode*.

Our selection of sources is gained principally from the following facts: 1) citations of authors or their writings in the *Méthode;* 2) examination of the writings of spiritual writers and historians of the reform of Touraine, especially from a study of the writings of John of St. Samson, Dominic of St. Albert, Leo of St. John and Hugh of St. Francis, who frequently recommended the writings of others to the novices and religious of the reform; 3) comparison of the *Méthode* with other methods of prayer that were known in France at the beginning of the seventeenth century.[2]

I – Sacred Scripture

Among the sources Sacred Scripture holds a special place. The authors of the *Méthode*, according to the custom of the time, cite the Scriptures frequently, much more than modern writers are accustomed to do. The Scriptures are used in two different ways:

1) To illustrate the teachings of the *Méthode,* that is, Scripture is used as an argument of authority to confirm the doctrine of the *Méthode*. The following examples exemplify this point.

a) The ills of the world are due to a lack of reflection and meditation, as Jeremias says: "With desolation is all the land made desolate; because there is none that considereth in the heart" (Jer. 12-11).[3]

b) We must prepare carefully and diligently for mental prayer. For Scripture says: "Before prayer prepare thy soul; and be not as a man that tempteth God" (Eccli. 18:23).[4]

c) A religious should not be disturbed during the time of mental prayer. "I adjure you, O daughters of Jerusalem, by the roes and the

---

[2] We do not know what books were in the Carmelite libraries of the Touraine reform, because all these libraries were lost to the Order during the French Revolution. No catalogue has ever been found. Some of these books, no doubt, are in the public libraries of Rennes, Paris, etc.

[3] Chap. ii, p. 30.

[4] Chap. iii, p. 36.

harts of the fields, that you stir not up, nor awake my beloved, till she pleases" (Cant. 3:5).[5]

d) Our prayers should be composed of simple words. Scripture says: "For every mocker is an abomination to the Lord, and his comunication is with the simple" (Prov. 3:32).[6]

2) Scripture is also used by the *Méthode* as a prayer book and offers ready-made formulas for inexperienced novices. Verses especially from the Psalms, and suited for the different actions of the day, are gathered into groups and presented to the novices as ideal formulas that will help them to practise the presence of God and accustom them to make aspirations.[7] The following examples are found in the *Méthode*:[8]

a) On rising in the morning the novice will say: "My eyes to thee have prevented the morning: that I might meditate on thy words" (Ps. 118:148).

b) On the way to meditation: "Let my prayer come in before thee: incline thy ear to my petition" (Ps. 87:3).

c) During manual labor: "For thou shalt eat the labours of thy hands: blessed art thou, and it shall be well with thee" (Ps. 127:2).

d) In the dining room: "My meat is do the will of him who sent me, that I may perfect his work" (John 4:34).

II – THE FATHERS

The Fathers of the Church are also cited as authorities on prayer. They are quoted much less frequently than the Bible, but in much the same manner, namely, to confirm and substantiate some point of doctrine. St. Gregory Nazianzenus, St. Basil, St. John Climacus, St. Augustine, St. Dionysius, St. Bernard, St. Bonaventure and Cassian are all quoted. Examples from the *Vita Patrum* are also found here and there in the *Méthode,* usually to illustrate the great love of prayer that existed among the ancient Fathers of the Desert.[9] In citing the Fathers the exact words of the text are not given as a general rule, and the source from which they are taken is rarely cited.

---

[5] Chap. iv, p. 50.
[6] Chap. v, pp. 67-68.
[7] Chap. xxix, pp. 441-458.
[8] Chap. xxxii, pp. 496-541.
[9] *Ibid.*, chap. xx, p. 301. Heribert Rosweyde, S. J., *Vita Patrum, de vita et verbis seniorum, sive historiae eremiticae libri X* (Antwerp, 1605), in Migne, PL, 73 and 74. This is a translation from the Greek and frequently used in the seventeenth century.

The following are typical examples to show the manner in which the Fathers have been employed.

a) In order to discern true sensible consolation from that which is inspired by the devil we should follow the teaching of St. Bernard, who says that consolation from God comes rarely and passes quickly.[10]

b) Things of this world should make us raise our minds to God. For example, when we see the zeal with which men follow the vanity of the world, let us say with St. Augustine: If we were only lovers of eternal life as these are lovers of the passing things of this world."[11]

According to its custom the *Méthode* does not indicate the particular source of this quotation.

c) It is possible to impress deeply the memory of God upon the soul, so that, as St. Gregory Nazianzenus says, it becomes as natural for the soul to recall God's presence as to breathe.[12]

From these citations and many others like them we are led to believe that the authority of the Fathers was highly esteemed by the writers of the *Méthode,* although they did not make any special study of the Fathers. It seems more likely that they gathered the citations of the Fathers from secondary sources, for example, from works like the *Vitae Patrum* and from the writings of Blosius, Louis of Granada, etc., whose works were widely read in the reform of Touraine.

III – The Rule and Tradition of Carmel

One great source of the *Méthode* is the spiritual tradition of the Carmelite Order, which is found especially in the Rule and the Constitutions, and which has been faithfully interpreted down through the centuries in historical and spiritual documents of the Order.

The Rule of St. Albert, Patriarch of Jerusalem, given about 1209,[13] has undergone some changes down through the years. It is not observed in its original form any place today. But chapter seven, the essential chapter of the Rule, has never been mitigated even for the Carmelites of the Ancient Observance *as regards the precept of prayer.* It is this Rule, and especially chapter seven, that is the great motivat-

---

[10] Chap. xxii, p. 338.
[11] Chap. xxviii, p. 431.
[12] Chap. xxxi, p. 479.
[13] The Rule of the Order of the Brothers of the Most Blessed Virgin Mary of Mount Carmel, given by Albert, Patriarch of Jerusalem, and confirmed by Pope Honorius III on January 30, 1226. After adapting this eremitical Rule to the mendicant way of life Pope Innocent IV reconfirmed it on October 1, 1247.

ing principle of the reform of Touraine and the *Méthode*. This chapter says: "Let each one remain in his cell or near it, meditating day and night on the law of God, and watching in prayer, unless occupied with other just works."

Following this precept, the tradition of Carmel has always been to live a life of solitude, silence and mortification in order to be continually occupied with God. Elias, the Prophet, standing in the very sight of God, lost in adoration and loving conversation, is the ideal of every Carmelite. To be occupied with God (*vacare Deo*); this is the spirit of the Order, and it is expressed in chapter seven of the Rule. It is this spirit that St. Teresa restored to the Order. It is this spirit, as we stated above in chapter two, that the reform of Touraine brought back to the Carmel of France. It is this same spirit that we find in the *Méthode*. Time and again it returns to chapter seven to inform the novices of their vocation to a life of intense prayer.

It is this continual, actual and affective conversation with God that is principally commanded us in the Rule which says "to meditate day and night on the law of God." Not that this word *meditate* means that we must continually apply the mind to consider and reflect upon the things of God, since this is impossible because of the human weakness of the mind. But this word must be understood in relation to the affection of the heart and the ardor of the will, which not only does not become tired, and never ceases to love, as the intellect ceases to reflect, but on the contrary, the more it loves, the more attraction, desire and force it feels to love even more and more.[14]

Not only has the *Méthode* been deeply influenced by the Rule of Carmel, but it has also been influenced by the written tradition that has grown out of the Rule and left its mark on the whole Order. Among these traditions we find one in particular that is an authentic expression of Carmelite life. It is entitled: *De Institutione primorum monachorum qui in lege veteri exortorum et in nova perseverantium ad Caprasium monachum liber*. It is sometimes called the *Liber Joannis XLIV*.[15] Variously dated between the twelfth and fourteenth cen-

---

[14] Chap. xxviii, pp. 434-435. We call attention to the affective meaning given to the word "meditate." In the Bible the word meditation means a silent and prolonged reflection upon a divine truth, upon the law of God, or upon God's perfections. Some commentators would prefer this wider meaning of the word meditate to the restricted meaning given it by the *Méthode*. The Salmanticenses, for example, hold that the word *meditate* would include the study of scholastic theology and all sciences bearing upon it. Cf. A. Foulain, *The Graces of Interior Prayer*, 37-38.

turies, it was published in 1507, and thereafter was used as spiritual reading in the Order. Did it have any influence on the *Mèthode?* It is not cited in the *Méthode*, but Father Wessels, former editor of the *Analecta Ordinis Carmelitarum*, says it influenced the *Directores des novices*, though he gives no evidence for this statement.[16] One thing is certain, however, that the *Méthode* retains and passes on the same spirit of Carmel that is found in the *De Institutione*, where we read:

> The aim of this life is discovered to be twofold: the first we attain by our effort and by the practise of virtue assisted by divine grace. This means to offer God a perfect heart, free from the dross of actual sin... The second aim of this life is realized solely by a gift of God, namely, to taste with the heart and to experience in the mind in some measure at least, the power of God's presence and the intoxication of heavenly glory.[17]

Another source of inspiration to the reform, and at least indirectly to the *Méthode*, was the commentary on the Rule by Blessed John Soreth. He was elected General of the Order in 1451. He is the founder of the Carmelite nuns, and it is interesting to note that he founded them under the mitigated Rule of 1432. In his commentary he exhorts the Carmelites to silence and solitude in order to practise contemplation. He urges them to sanctify their cells, to make them silent cells in order that they can the better commune with God and live in His presence. For subjects of meditation he suggests the contemplation of nature and its beauty, the reading of Sacred Scripture and spiritual books, and finally an introspection of their lives. As models of Carmelite life he presents Our Lady and Elias the Prophet.

Blessed John Soreth is undoubtedly one of the greatest Generals in the history of the Order. His reform brought not only a rebirth of Carmelite life in the fifteenth century, but was an inspiration to Touraine. Leo of St. John, while provincial of the Touraine reform, had Soreth's commentary on the Rule published especially for the members of the province of Touraine.[18] This commentary influenced

---

[15] G. Wessels, O. Carm., "Pars ascetica regulae Joannis 44," *AOC, 3* (1914-1916), 346-347.

[16] Wessels, *op. cit.*, 346.

[17] *Ibid.*, 348.

[18] *Expositio paranaetica in regulam Carmelitarum*, auctore R.P.B. Joanne Soreth, Gallo, eiusdem Ordinis Generalis ac Reformatore an. D. 1455. Ex vetustissimo Codice manuscripto. (Paris, 1625).

the spirit of Touraine and certainly the life of prayer that flourished there.[19] At least indirectly it has influenced the *Méthode*, although it is never cited as an authority.[20]

Another commentary on the Rule, but exerting much less influence than Soreth's, was the commentary of Father Jerome Gratian, who was a very close friend of St. Teresa. He wrote his commentary, *Della disciplina regolare opera*, at the command of Father General Henry Sylvius, after he left the Discalced Carmelites and returned to the Carmelites of the Ancient Observance in 1595.[21] It is a very long and sometimes tedious book to read, but contains excellent advice on the spirit of the Order. It is cited once in the *Directoires des novices*, but not in the *Méthode* itself.[22]

Another influence that came from within the Order was the Constitutions of the reform. In the first chapter we mentioned that Thibault prepared Constitutions as early as 1615, and that they were, after some corrections, published in 1636. The *Méthode* never cites these Constitutions, but it is inconceivable that they were not a great motivating factor in the life of the veteran novice master, and an author of the *Directoires*, Father Bernard of St. Magdalen. Yet, in these Constitutions we find the contemplative ideal of the Order very well expressed, and it is this same ideal that is found in the pages of the *Méthode*.[23] We read in the Constitutions:

---

[19] Brandsma, *Carmelite Mysticism*, 60-65. Cf. Gondulphus Mesters, O. Carm., "Carmelite Spirituality According to Blessed John Soreth," *Sword*, 16 (Chicago, 1953), 323-335.

[20] It is possible that Thibault was inspired by other reforms within the Order. The reform of Mantua (1412-1783) was most influential, and produced a method of prayer anterior to that of Touraine. Cf. Peter Thomas Saraceni, *Dell'oratione mentale* (Bologna, 1636). The author says it was first published for the Mautuan Congregation in 1596. Cf. p. 50. The method has seven parts: preparation, reading, meditation, contemplation, petition, oblation, thanksgiving or epilogue. It is very much like the method of the Spanish Discalced Carmelites and like that of Jerome Gratian in *Della disciplina regolare opera* (Venice, 1600). It is difficult to say if it was known or used in the reform of Touraine.

The origin and development of meditation in common in the Carmelite Order is clearly presented in the recent article of Father Claude M. Catena, O. Carm., "La meditazione in comune nell'Ordine Carmelitano: origine e sviluppo," *Carmelus*, 2 (1955) 315-350.

[21] *BC*, I, 647.

[22] *Directoires des novices*, III, 8.

[23] The Constitutions before the reform of Touraine had the true Carmelite spirit, and therefore we should not be led to think that the Constitutions of Touraine were a startling innovation. For example, the Constitutions of 1281 say: "For we say, bearing witness to the truth, that from the time of Elias and Eliseus, the prophets, who lived piously on Mount Carmel, our fathers both of the Old and the New Testament, being true lovers of heavenly things, sought in a manner surely praiseworthy, the solitude of the same mountain for contemplation, and they dwelt continually near the fountain of Elias engaged in a life of holy penance." *AOC* 15 (1950) 208.

It is necessary that a convenient place and time be given to the newly professed so they may be more deeply imbued with the spirit of our holy Institute, and implant virtues in their minds, and transfer all their affections totally in God, so that in time they may advance in internal conversation with God and in the sweet presence of God, which beyond a doubt constitutes and makes the true Carmelite."[24]

Another influence on the *Méthode* within the Order was the reform of the Discalced Carmelites. There is no one who doubts that St. Teresa and St. John of the Cross possessed the true spirit of Carmel and manifested it in a most glorious manner both in their holiness of life and in their mystical writings. The spirit of Carmel which they strove to implant in the Order has been felt even in Touraine. It is said that the two great contemplatives of Touraine, John of St. Samson and Dominic of St. Albert, although acquainted with the writings of the Spanish Carmelite mystics, nevertheless did not seem to be influenced by them. This may be true, but it is not true of other members of the reform, especially of Thibault. He had at one time desired to join the reform of St. Teresa. He had even stayed with the Discalced Carmelites of Paris for some six weeks. And at the end of one copy of the manuscript of the Constitutions of Rennes (1615) prepared by Thibault, we read these words: "We should read often and devoutly the spiritual counsels of Blessed Mother Teresa.[25] Furthermore, we shall show in a later chapter that St. Teresa has left a marked influence on the *Méthode*.

Besides the Sacred Scriptures, the Fathers and the Rule and tradititions of the Carmelite Order, there were other sources from which the *Méthode* drew its doctrine – more immediate sources that gave the *Méthode* more precise, more definite teaching on the three ways of prayer.

To simplify our study we shall classify these sources into different groups and consider them in chronological order.

---

[24] *Constitutiones* [1636], Part I, chap., vi, p. 27.
[25] Cited by Bouchereaux, *La Réforme des Carmes,* 79, note 2. Cf. Hugh, *La véritable idée,* I, 116.

CHAPTER VIII

THE IGNATIAN SCHOOL OF PRAYER

I – St. Ignatius and the Spiritual Exercises

St. Ignatius and his *Spiritual Exercises* are so well known that they need no introduction here.[1] It is sufficient to recall that the *Exercises* contain the fundamental elements of Jesuit spirituality and have influenced practically all methods of prayer since the latter half of the sixteenth century. We must therefore examine them to see whether they have had any effect on the ways of prayer in the reform of Touraine.

We should recall here that Thibault, the father of the reform, had great admiration for the *Spiritual Exercises.* In chapter one we mentioned that Thibault studied at Pont-a-Mousson and made the *Exercises* before he began the reform. He also sent some of his first students to the Jesuit College at La Flèche in the first years of the reform. In one of his sermons he stated that he placed the *Exercises* of St. Ignatius in first place after the Sacred Scriptures. Moreover, both Bernard of St. Magdalen and Mark of the Nativity, coauthors of the *Méthode,* had studied at the Jesuit College of Rennes in their early youth. Finally, it is said that the Constitutions of the reform were prepared with the aid of the Jesuits. In view of this intimate association and collaboration would it not be surprising if Ignatian ways of prayer had no influence on the ways of prayer in the *Méthode?* Let us see if this influence actually exists.[2]

The *Méthode* makes mention of St. Ignatius only once, and then only to cite an example of how to see God in his creatures.

---

[1] *Exercitia spiritualia Sancti Ignatii de Loyola et eorum directoria* (Madrid, 1919). (Mon. hist. S.J., v. 1.)

[2] In our references to the Exercises, we shall use the English translation by L. Puhl, S.J., *The Spiritual Exercises of St. Ignatius* (Westminster, Md., 1951).

St. Ignatius of Loyola contemplating the starlit sky on a beautiful, clear night said: "How miserable the earth looks when I glance at the heavens."[3]

St. Ignatius, composed many methods of prayer.[4] We shall consider the more common ones. The first is meditation according to the three faculties: memory, intellect and will. This is the best known of all his methods and is the one understood today when we speak of the Ignatian method of meditation. It is found in the first week of the *Exercises*.

The second method is contemplation, which is an ordinary meditation on the mysteries of the life of Christ. Contemplation means to consider without exerting great effort the persons, words, and actions in some particular mystery of the life of Christ. This method insists greatly on the use of the imagination and less on intellectual activity. As is clear, St. Ignatius uses the word contemplation in a non mystical sense.

The third method is the application of the senses to the mystery. We perceive Christ and the other persons of the mystery with the eyes of the imagination, we listen to what they say, etc.

The fourth method is called the second way of prayer. Today it is sometimes called mixed prayer. It consists in taking some prayer, for example, the Our Father, and meditating on each word of the prayer, drawing from each word a thought to influence and to inflame the will, and thus passing to the next word only when a word or thought, fails to excite the will.

The fifth method is called the third way of prayer. It consists in reciting a vocal prayer slowly, so that we consider each word of the prayer for the space of a single breath.[5]

All five methods are really only parts of a large *plan* of prayer. The *plan* is the same for all methods. It includes: a preparatory prayer, two or three preludes, three or four points which make up the body of the prayer, and finally one or three colloquies. When the body of the prayer differs, the method differs. Thus, the meditation of the faculties, the contemplation and the application of the senses all pertain to the body of the prayer in the *plan* of the prayer.[6]

What is the purpose of these methods? St. Ignatus wishes to teach

... how the devout man ought to exercise himself in the purgative, illuminative and the unitive way. And how by certain exercises consisting of

---

[3] Chap. xxxiii, p. 555.
[4] For a list of commentators on the *Exercises*, confer I. Ipurraguirre, S.J., *Introduzione allo studio degli Esercizi*, (Rome, 1951), 8-9.
[5] Pourrat, *Christian Spirituality*, III, 35.
[6] Philippe, "Mental Prayer," 47-48.

meditation, prayers, and contemplation for each day of the week he shall gradually elevate himself to the possession of the desired end – union of the soul with God.[7]

Let us examine the first method of prayer, the way of the three faculties. It is composed of a preparation, preludes, the body of the prayer and the colloquy. The preparation is a preparatory prayer:

In the preparatory prayer I will beg of God our Lord that all my intentions, actions, and operations may be directed purely to the praise and service of His Divine Majesty.[8]

The first prelude consists in recalling the mystery which is the subject of the meditation, the composition of place (if this is necessary). The second prelude is a petition for a special grace to obtain from the meditation the fruit desired.

The body of the prayer is made up of the three acts of the soul. The memory places the subject before the intellect, which considers and ponders the subject, and the will moved by this consideration elicits acts which are affections.[9]

Colloquies bring the meditation to a close. They should never be omitted.

The colloquy is made by speaking exactly as one friend speaks to another, or as a servant speaks to a master, now asking him for a favor, now blaming himself for some misdeed, now making known his affairs to him and seeking advice in them.[10]

The meditation then finishes by reciting the *Pater Noster*, which is followed by an examination to determine whether it was successful or a failure. Resolutions are made to correct any failures.[11]

Let us now compare the *Méthode's* way of prayer with the above method. The *Méthode* says mental prayer should be made up of three parts: preparation, meditation and affections, which correspond to the three faculties of the soul.

In this exercise we do three things: First, we recall the matter, and then represent it to the intellect as the object of its *discursus*. Secondly, we

---

[7] H. Watrigant, "La Genèse des Exercises de Saint Ignace de Loyola," *Études religieuses*, 71 (1897), 510-529.

[8] Puhl, *The Spiritual Exercises*, the first exercise, 25.

[9] *Ibid.*, cf. meditation on the sin of angels, 26.

[10] *Ibid.*, first week, 28. Throughout the Exercises Ignatius considers God as the real director of the soul in prayer. Cf. 15th Observation, 6.

[11] *Ibid.*, first week, 36.

consider it, ruminate it and digest it. Finally, we resolve to do all those things that we are convinced should be done. Thus, the memory represents the subject, the intellect meditates, and enlightens, and the will is filled with holy affections and with good desires to practice virtue and resolutions.[12]

It is obvious that the *Méthode* follows the *Exercises* in this method. But at first sight it gives the impression that this is the only method of methodical meditation to be followed by the Carmelites. Yet such is not the case, for when we consider the various subject matter of meditation we find the *Méthode* teaching that the body of the prayer differs with the subject matter.

Thus, if we compare the contemplation of the second week of the *Exercises* with the *Méthode's* instructions for meditating on the mysteries of Christ, we shall again see that the *Méthode* follows the *Exercises*.

The contemplation of the *Exercises* contains the preparatory prayer, the preludes, the body of the prayer, the colloquies and the conclusion. Two of the preludes consider the history (general survey) of the mystery and the composition of place. The body of the prayer considers: persons, words, actions, followed by reflection in relation to self, in order to obtain the fruit of the prayer.[13]

In the *Méthode* after the immediate preparation we have a consideration of the following points in the mysteries of Christ: the history, the circumstances of place and time, persons, words, sentiments, purpose, effects, and the personal application.[14]

We notice that the *Méthode* places the history in the body of the prayer and not among the preludes. This is contrary to the mind of Ignatius, but the *Méthode* does not admit preludes as such, and chooses to make the history a point to be considered in the contemplation. We also notice that the *Méthode* considers more points in the mystery. From whence do they come? We believe they are also Ignatian and come from chapter nineteen of the *Directory* of the *Exercises*, where we read:

But although in this place [second week] only these three points are mentioned, there is no reason why others should not be added, as for instance the thoughts and interior affections of the several persons, and also their virtues and besides these, the manner and purpose of the several

---

[12] Chap. ii p, 35.
[13] Puhl, *The Spiritual Exercises,* second week, 49-51.
[14] Chap. vi, p. 80.

mysteries, their causes also and effects, the time and other circumstances in order that the deditation may be richer and its fruits more abundant.[15]

There can be no doubt that the *Exercises* either directly or indirectly have greatly influenced the *Méthode*. This influence can also be seen if one examines the ready-made meditation on the obedience of Christ to Mary and Joseph in the *Méthode*, which follows the Ignatian way of contemplation, and if one compares the meditation on hell,[16] which follows that of St. Ignatius.[17]

Other similarities with the *Exercises* can be easily pointed out. Both, for example, give affections the most important place in meditation. Both request an examen after the meditation and consider the same points. Both present mixed prayer as a separate way of prayer. In this matter we may compare the following words of Ignatius with the exposition in chapter five:

One may kneel or sit, as may be better suited to his disposition and more conducive to devotion. He should keep his eyes closed, or fixed in one position without permitting them to roam. Then let him say, "Father" and continue meditating upon this word as long as he finds various meanings, comparisons, relish, and consolation in the consideration of it. The same method should be followed with each word of the Our *Father* or of any other prayer which he wishes to use for this method.[18]

Not only do we find meditation and mixed prayer in the *Méthode* following the teaching of Ignatius, but we should mention that aspirative prayer – which is the third and last way of prayer, in the *Méthode* – is also found, but in a somewhat different manner, in the Exercises.[19] However, as we shall see, the development of aspirative prayer is not due to the influence of the *Exercises*.

It would be wrong to conclude from the above analysis that the *Méthode* has simply adopted the whole method of the *Exercises*, or at least the three methods of prayer, meditation of the three faculties, contemplation and mixed prayer. It is better to say that the *Méthode* has adapted them, taking what it wished, and rejecting what seemed unsuitable to its purpose. Thus, for example, the over-all plan of the

---

[15] W H Longridge, *The Spiritual Exercises of Saint Ignatius of Loyola*, 4th ed. (London, 1950), 313-314.

[16] Chap. vii, p. 100. This is not an exact reproduction of Ignatian meditation, but it it composed almost entirely *of the application of the senses* to the horrors of Hell.

[17] Puhl, *The Spiritual Exercises*, first week, fifth exercise, 32.

[18] *Ibid.*, three methods of prayer, 110.

[19] *Ibid.*, 112. This is the third method of prayer.

meditation is different from the *Exercises*. As we shall see, the plan (the different parts of the meditation, e.g., remote, proximate, immediate preparation, etc.) has been gathered from diffrent sources. Furthermore, the *Méthode* uses the prayer of the faculties in a wide sense, that is, to include all subjects of meditation.

Moreover, the colloquies so essential to the *Exercises* do not end the meditation in the *Méthode*. The *Méthode*, as can be seen from the outline in chapter four, closes its prayer with general affections, which recall the method of Louis of Granada, as we shall see. However, the *Méthode* gives the greatest attention to colloquies during the whole prayer, both during the *discursus* and the eliciting of all affections. This insistence on colloquies or conversation during the meditation is most characteristic of the *Méthode*. It is at the same time in harmony with the *Exercises*.[20]

There is a difference, too, when we consider the proper use of the imagination, intellect and will. The *Exercises* give much more importance to the imagination, especially in the consideration of the mysteries of Christ. It advocates the representation of the mystery as actually taking place during the time of meditation.[21] It encourages even a fictitious representation or image of a spiritual subject.

The *Méthode* encourages the use of the imagination for beginners, but it neither encourages or discourages the representation of the mystery in the present time. It leaves the religious free to choose his own way. However, it does not encourage the fictitious images for an intellectual subject.[22] In contemplating the mysteries of Christ it gives much less freedom to the imagination than the *Exercises*. It says:

> If you meditate on the birth of the Savior, recall the stable, the crib, the straw, but then quickly pass to the consideration of the merit of the One who is born, of His love for us, of the reasons for His birth, etc.[23]

There is no appreciable difference between the *Exercises* and the *Méthode* on the use of the intellect in prayer. Both subordinate it to the will. Both see the necessity of being convinced and moved by the truth before eliciting affections. There is no need to defend the intellectual element in the *Exercises*, But we might ask, does not the

---

[20] Puhl, *The Spiritual Exercises*, third Observation, 2. St. Ignatius cautions great reverence in the colloquies.
[21] *Ibid.*, second week, first day, 52.
[22] Chap. vi, p. 75.
[23] Chap. xxiv, pp. 375-376.

Méthode, which tends to affective prayer, diminish the role of the intellect? We do not believe this is true. We have abready mentioned in chapter four the role of the intellect, but it is well to cite here the words of the *Méthode:*

> We ought to advance more and more each day in love and knowledge, but this will not ordinarily follow unless we meditate on many different subjects that will more and more enlighten the mind.[24]

The will is of the greatest importance in all methods of prayer. Both the memory and the intellect are used in prayer to move the will. Meditation without affections of the will is sterile. Both the *Exercises* and the *Méthode* give great emphasis to affections and resolutions. But we do not think that the *Méthode* is under the influence of the *Exercises* here. First all, the *Méthode* distinguishes between particular and general affections. Speaking of the general affection of petition it cites Louis of Granada. Moreover, it makes resolutions a distinct part of prayer, that is, one of the general affections. This division of general affections is not from the *Exercises*. It also calls the will the queen of the faculties and speaks of affective meditation. It speaks of love as "the inexhaustible source of lights and of holy thoughts."[25] In other words, love will produce deeper knowledge. It admits, of course, that the operation of the intellect precedes that of the will, but also holds that once the will is inflamed with love it can increase our understanding of God and divine things. For proof of this statement it appeals to Dominic of St. Albert and other members of the reform who have experienced this action in their own souls. When speaking of the affections, therefore, the *Méthode* is not so much under the influence of the *Exercises* as of other sources, some within the reform itself.

For these reasons we also believe the *Méthode* presents a more affective method than the Exercises. This is not surprising when we consider the different purposes they intend to accomplish. The *Méthode* presupposes the election of the Carmelite life which is *vacare Deo*, and orientates the novices toward affective conversation with God. Ignatius wrote his *Exercises* for all Christians.[26] For him prayer is only a means to apostolic service. In the formation of his disciples he places abnegation before prayer, and this abnegation is expressed primarily in

---

[24] Chap. xxiv, p. 374.
[25] Chap. xxiv, p. 368.
[26] Puhl, *The Spiritual Exercises*, second Observation, 1-2.

perfect obedience. However, we should bear in mind that the methods of prayer proposed by Ignatius, lead the soul to infused contemplation. But all prayer, even infused prayer, was for him a means to apostolic service, the *effective* glory of God.

From these observations it is evident that the *Méthode* does not follow the meditations of the Exercises exactly. It cannot be said that the *Méthode* has taken over or adopted the methods of St. Ignatius.

From these observations it is evident that the *Methode* does not follow the meditations of the Exercises exactly. It cannot be said that the *Méthode* has taken over or adopted the methods of St. Ignatius. Yet it is evident that the *Méthode* has taken many things from the *Exercises* and has been deeply influenced by them, especially in regard to the body of the prayer (meditation in the strict sense). It receives from the *Exercises* especially the prayer of the three faculties, the contemplation on the mysteries of Christ and the examen after meditation. But has this influence been direct? Or has it come rather from the disciples of St. Ignatius, for example, from de la Puente, or Francis Arias, etc., who follow the *Exercises* in their meditations? We cannot say with certainty, for the authors of the *Méthode* may have obtained the Ignatian methods of prayer from the disciples of the Saint. Therefore, we shall examine the writings of the disciples of St. Ignatius to see whether they may have influenced the *Méthode*.

II – Francis Arias, S.J.

Francis Arias, S.J., was born at Seville in 1533. He was ordained a priest before he entered the Society of Jesus in 1561. He was a professor of theology, a preacher and religious superior. He was considered a very holy man, but often difficult to live with because of his extreme rigorism and stubbornness. He died in 1605.[27]

Arias is best known for his spiritual books that were translated into many languages.[28]

---

[27] J. de Guibert, S.J., "Francis Arias", *DSp*, I, 844-845.

[28] His writings were edited separately and collectively. They have been translated into French, Italian, English, etc. In 1588 he published at Valencia *Approvechamiento espiritual*, which contained a series of treatises on Spiritual Progress, Self-Denial, A Rosary of 50 Mysteries, Imitation of the Blessed Virgin, Mental Prayer, Mortification, The Use of the Sacraments, An Exercise on the Presence of God. At Seville, 1599, he published his best work, *Libro de la imitaction de Christo nuestro Señor*. It is very sound and clear, but diffuse and monotonous. The treatises in his first work are more concise and enjoyable. His treatise on mental prayer was translated into French and edited separately: *Traicté de l'orairon*

Were the spiritual works of Francis Arias known in the reform of Touraine? They were not only known, but, some at least were highly recommended by John of St. Samson to the novices.[29] Furthermore, Hugh of St. Francis, historian and propagandist of the reform, says that the meditations of Arias, Bellintani, Granada, Molina, etc., should be placed in the hands of novices to help them meditate.[30] The *Méthode* does not at any time refer to Arias, so that the only way we can be certain that the *Méthode* depends upon him is by examination of their respective methods of prayer.

Francis Arias followed St. Ignatius in his method of meditation. Arias was also acquainted with the works of Granada, Bellintani, Ruysbroeck, Harphius, etc.[31]

He divides his treatise into three parts: 1) the remote and proximate preparation, 2) immediate preparation, considerations, and affections, 3) counsels and examen after meditation, and a division of the subject matter according to the three grades of perfection.

There is nothing new in this general plan. It simply is a development of the plan of prayer in the *Exercises*.

---

mentale (Lyon, 1598; Douay, 1603; Rouen, 1614). The Exercise of the Presence of God was also translated into French (Paris, 1608; Lyon, 1609).

[29] *Oeuvres*, I, *La conduite des novices*, 915.

[30] Hugh, *La Véritable idée*, II, 71-74.

Bellintani, Matthias de Salo, O.F.M. Cap., *Pratica dell'orazione mentale*. This is the most remarkable work of Bellintani (1534-1611). It contains four parts, but not all parts appear in every edition. It was translated into French from the Italian in 1593, and published at Lyon and many times after that. St. Francis de Sales recommended it to Philothea.

Bellintani proposes a method of meditation and a number of subjects for meditation. He divides prayer into three parts: preparation, meditation and action. By action he means. acts of the will. The will produces two effects: affections and actions. The book is characterized by its affective nature. A critical edition. is being prepared by Umile da Genova, O.F.M. Cap., in the Bibliotheca Seraphica Capuccina. It is difficult to say whether this method had any influence on the *Méthode*, but we do notice the prominent place that both Bellintani and the *Méthode* give to resolutions, making them an important part of prayer. Resolutions, oblation, thanksgiving, etc., are *actions*, or effects of the will for Bellintani.

Anthony Molina, O. Carth. (c. 1550-1617), *Exercicios spirituales de las excelencias provecho y necessitad de la oracion mental reducidos a doctrina y meditaciones, sacado de los santos padres y doctores de la Iglesia* (Burgos, 1613).This was translated by René Gaultier into French, Paris, 1621. In his meditations Molina has nothing new. One sees the influence of the Ignatian school and of Granada. In his treatise on the presence of God and aspirations, he follows the well-known authors of the time, especially Blosius. He teaches prayer in a spirit that is conformable to that of the reform of Touraine. But we see no reason to admit any dependence of the *Méthode* upon Molina.

[31] *Traicté de l'oraison mentale*, preface, ed. of 1598. The preface is lacking in the ed. of 1614. All subsequent citations are from the ed. of 1614.

However, there is such a striking similarity between the methodical structure as well as the doctrine of meditation presented by Arias and that of the *Méthode* that we shall cite his teaching in more detailed form, and compare it with that of the *Méthode*.

Both Arias and the *Méthode* divide the remote preparation into two points and suggest the same acts for the immediate preparation.

Let us consider the remote preparation. It consist says Arias, of 1) a life free from sin – a pure conscience, 2) avoidance of vain and inordinate occupation, 3) a heart that is strong against scruples and vain fears, 4) interior recollection.[32]

The proximate preparation consists of two parts: the reading and a strong desire to perform mental prayer. The *Méthode* presents the same division.[33] One should choose a good book, says Arias, for example, the Meditations of Granada. The reading should be moderate, prepared in the evening for the morning. It is good to read to avoid distractions. One who is well acquainted with the subject need not read.

Arias next explains the place and the time of prayer and the position to take while praying. The best time to pray is at night after midnight, or early in the morning.[34] While praying we should kneel or stand.[35] The *Méthode* follows the same order as Arias in discussing these subjects but in a much shorter manner. There is no evidence of textual dependence here. The *Méthode* also suggests that the novices darken their cell during the day to pray better.[36]

One also sees similarity in their presentation of the immediate preparation. Arias describes it as follows: Arrived at the place of prayer, one should make the sign of the cross, place oneself in the presence of God, examine one's conscience, make an act of humility, ask pardon for one's sins, offer the prayer for the greater glory of God, and implore the help of the Blessed Virgin and the saints to pray well. This preparation should be brief, but if affections arise here, one should utilize them as long as possible.[37] The *Méthode* offers the same immediate preparation, with the same acts.[38]

---

[32] *Oraison mentale,* chap. i-iii, pp. 1-35; *Méthode,* chap. iii, nos. 1-4, pp. 38-41. The *Méthode* differs only on the third point. It does not mention scruples. Its third point is on the detachment of the heart from creatures.

[33] *Méthode,* chap. iii, pp. 41-46.

[34] *Oraison mentale,* chaps. v and vi, pp. 42-61.

[35] *Ibid.,* chap. viii, p. 75.

[36] *Méthode,* chap. iv, p. 48.

[37] *Oraison mentale,* Part II, chap. i, pp. 94-102. We shall see that Granada presents the first three of these acts prior to Arias.

[38] *Méthode,* chap. iii, p. 54. Cf. outline on p. 43.

Following the preparation Arias presents the points that are to be considered in the body of the prayer, together with the affections that are to be drawn from these points. Arias, however, does not give a detailed discussion on the nature of the meditation, but simply presents the following points that should occupy us in meditating on the life of Christ: 1) Consider the history and substance of the mystery, 2) the circumstances of the persons, 3) the causes, that is, the reasons Our Lord did this, 4) the great pain and sorrow both internal and external of Our Lord, and the fruits we derive from them, 5) the virtues of Our Lord.[39] The *Méthode* includes, these points, at least the first three, in its method of meditation.[40]

Arias next considers the affections. The following generally, but not always, are produced: love of God, hope, contrition, admiration, compassion, thanksgiving, joy. Finally, one should draw from meditation a strong determination to imitate the virtues of Christ. This would include resolutions. The *Méthode* presents similar doctrine, but in much more concise form.[41]

However, there is nothing in the *Méthode* comparable to the description of each affection that is given by Arias. So well has he described the affections that St. Francis de Sales recommended this part of his treatise to Philothea.[42]

We note briefly the peculiar position taken by Arias in regard to petition. He would consider it an act of the intellect and not an affection of the will.[43] It is indeed a part of the meditation, but not the principal part. According to Arias the principal part of meditation is to love and produce other affections and acts of virtue. Indeed, petition may be made within or outside of meditation.[44] The affections which have the character of receiving rather than petitioning are the principal parts of prayer, and meditation is composed of four parts according to St. Paul: *oratio, obsecratio, gratiarum actio* and *postulatio*.

The *Méthode* differs definitely on this point with Arias. Petition is considered an affection. The *Méthode* would reject the opinion of those who would call petition an intellectual act. "Some think," it says, "that petition is an act of the intellect, but really it is an act of the will, that is expressed through the intellect."[45]

---

[39] *Oraison mentale*, Part II, chap. ii, pp 102-115.
[40] *Méthode*, chap. vi. p. 80.
[41] *Oraison mentale*, Part II, chap. ii, pp. 102-115; *Méthode*, chaps. vi, p. 84; xi, pp. 144 ff.
[42] *Oeuvres*, III, Part II, chap. vi, p. 81.
[43] *Oraison mentale*, Part II, chap. xxi, pp. 276-285.
[44] *Ibid.*, p. 283.
[45] *Méthode*, chap. xiii, p. 164 (in margin).

The third part of the treatise on mental prayer by Arias contains advice on the defects to be avoided and other counsels on how to pray well.[46] His advice on the use of the intellect and will merits our consideration. We may sum it up in the following points:

1) Do not look for subtle considerations which exercise only the intellect.

2) Many considerations are not necessary. One will suffice, if it is strong enough to move and occupy the will.

3) If one point does not inflame the will, pass to the next point. When the affections arise, prolong them as long as possible. When they grow weak, pass to the next point.

4) If point after point fails to arouse the acts of the will, be patient and resigned to the will of God. But do not look for consolation or spiritual joys. Spiritual consolations are a gift of God and are very helpful, if they are used well.[47]

Arias considers the three grades of perfection. The division of subjects in meditation is in harmony with the three grades of perfection, and again affords us ample material for comparison with the *Méthode*.

Subject matter for beginners is generally on sin, death, judgment, hell. The advanced consider the life and passion of Our Lord, the lives of saints, divine gifts. The perfect contemplate divinity, infinite beauty, and the attributes of God. The life and passion of Our Lord, however, is recommended to all three grades of the spiritual life. Then, too, this division is not to be taken too strictly. Sometimes it may be useful to take subject matter without respect to one's grade in perfection. The *Méthode* gives identical advice, but does not mention the passion of Our Lord.[48]

Both Arias and the *Méthode* close their meditatian with an examen.[49] From the above outline and comparison we can perceive the similarity of the two methods at a glance. But can we therefore say that the *Méthode* depends upon Arias? Before answering we must first admit that many of the points of similarity are common parts of meditation and common doctrine that is found in methods of prayer before

---

[46] *Oraison mentale,* Part III, pp. 297-485.

[47] *Ibid:*, chap. vii, pp. 364-333; *Méthode,* chap: xxiv, p. 376: We shall see in chap. ix, infra, that the *Méthode* and Arias both are in agreement on these counsels with Granada, who preceded them.

[48] *Osaison mentale,* Part III. chap. xx, p. 469; *Méthode,* chap. vii, pp. 90-92.

[49] *Oraison mentale,* Part III, chap. xxi, p. 480; *Méthode,* chap. xxiv, no. 12, pp. 394-395.

the time of Arias. Both St. Ignatius, and, as we shall see, Louis of Granada, who preceded Arias, have all the fundamental points of doctrine that Arias teaches. At the same time they do not have all the parts of the form or plan of meditation that Arias has given us. And it seems that this form or plan, at least the threefold preparation, was borrowed by the *Méthode* from Arias. We have noted the almost absolute identity of the remote, proximate and immediate preparation; and the similarity of points to be considered in the meditation.

The doctrine on affections is generally the same in both, but the *Méthode* does not depend upon Arias for its division and doctrine on the general affections.[50] They differ especially on the nature of petition. Could it not be that the *Méthode* had Arias in mind when it says that some authors would consider petition as an act of the intellect rather than an act of the will?[51]

In the light of this evidence we are of the opinion that the *Méthode* owes much to Arias, even though it never cites him explicitly. We believe it borrowed from him the form and instructions for remote, proximate and immediate preparation. Furthermore, it found in Arias a method of prayer modeled on the *Exercises* of St. Ignatius that was well known in the reform of Touraine and could hardly have escaped the attention of the veteran novice master, Bernard of St. Magdalen. At the same time we admit that we have found no textual dependence. Arias develops the parts of meditation at great length, whereas the *Méthode* in a few lines is very concise, especially in regard to the parts of preparation. Arias has developed an exact explanation of the affections that are the fruit of reflection on the mysteries of Christ. Such a clear profound explanation is found in few books.

The Presence of God. – In the *Exercicio de la presencia de Dios,* composed of twelve chapters, Arias teaches the common doctrine found among authors of his time. There is no reason to believe that the *Méthode.* depends upon him here. Arias placed this treatise last in his *Aprovechamiento espiritual* because he believed it was the epilogue and compendium of all other means of spiritual advancement, namely, meditation, mortification, the use of the sacraments, that he had already treated. Therefore, he calls it the principal exercise and the most excellent for spiritual progress.

The exercise of the presence of God is not limited to imaginary or intellectual presence. It includes acts of the will, that is, aspirations and

---

[50] The *Méthode* quotes Granada on petition, chap. xiii, p. 168.
[51] *Ibid.*, p. 164.

colloquies. It is an exercise of the virtues of faith, hope and charity. It is an exercise for all purposes and for all times.

It produces excellent effects. Through it, the soul becomes purified of all stain of sin, it conquers temptations, and helps the soul to acquire virtue and exterior modesty. It gives joy and peace to the heart.[52]

He places great stress on the part of the will in producing aspirations. He quotes the *Mystica theologia* of St. Bonaventure (actually the work of Hugh of Balma) and calls the aspirations "vehement desires, burning affections," because they lift the heart up to God. He says that these burning affections of the soul are expressed sometimes in short prayers that are called ejaculations, because like darts they ascend to God. He calls them also colloquies, because just as the soul speaks with God, so God speaks to the soul, answering aspirations with inspirations and interior sentiments which He infuses into the soul, which then turns with greater desires and insatiable sighs to God.

Arias recommends aspirations for all three stages of the spiritual life. He gives many examples of aspirations.[53]

Finally, he presents different ways to practise the presence of God: 1) ask God for this gift; 2) use signs (bells, signs in your room) to remind you to raise your heart to God; 3) make this the subject of your particular examen; 4) the best way is to have true love of God. Loving God makes you think of Him often. "Where your heart is, there your treasure lies." [54]

This very clear teaching has many things in common with the *Méthode*, but there is nothing here that the *Méthode* could not have gotten elsewhere. There is no reason, therefore, to believe that this particular treatise had any influence on the *Méthode;* it is the *Traicté de l'oraison mentale* that has left its imprint on the methodical meditation of the reform of Touraine.

III – Alphonsus Rodriguez, S. J.

Rodriguez, Alphonsus, S. J., (1538-1616), *Exercicio de perfeccion y virtudes christianas* (1609). (This Rodriguez is not to be confused with the Brother Coadjutor, St. Alphonsus Rodriguez.) His works are of great ascetical value. They had great influence and were translated into some twenty languages. At least six French translations appeared

---

[52] Chaps. iv to vi, pp. 872-880.
[53] Chap. viii to x, pp. 882-887.
[54] Chap. xi to xii, pp. 887-892.

in the seventeenth century, the first at Paris in 1621.⁵⁵ Rodriguez was recommended by Leo of St. John, and therefore was known and esteemed in Touraine.⁵⁶ For Leo of St. John was, as we have mentioned elsewhere, one of the most important men in the reform of Touraine. From what Rodriguez has written on prayer it is impossible to say whether he exerted any influence on the *Méthode*. His teaching on meditation, which he calls ordinary mental prayer, and his exposition on the exercise of the presence of God are in accord with the *Méthode*. However, we should mention that because of the anti-mystical times in which he lived he shows little desire to write of higher prayer, although admitting that meditation tends to contemplation.

Rodriguez follows the Exercises of St. Ignatius without mentioning all the parts of mental prayer. He dwells with profit on the relation of the considerations to the affections. The hour of prayer should not be passed in reflections, but the reflections should serve to inflame the will and the desire to practise virtues. To bring out the futility of those who pass all their time in reflections and end their prayer without any affections he employs the example (which he says is not his own) of a hungry man at a table loaded with food that he is not permitted to take, but must be content to look at. The *Méthode* uses a similar example, the servant unable to eat the food on the table of the master.⁵⁷ Rodriguez also insists on resolutions. He says prayer should be practical; it should always tend to the virtue we aspire to. If resolutions are not afterwards put into practise, then take care to examine these resolutions to see whether they were not mere desires instead of firm promises.⁵⁸

His teaching on the presence of God is even more interesting.⁵⁹ He unites the exercise of the presence of God with aspirations and ejaculations. He speaks of the imaginary and intellectual presence of God, but also of the affective presence of God that dominates the prayer of aspirations in the *Méthode*. But he does not use the term affective presence. He cautions strongly against too much use of the imaginary presence of God. He says it is not expedient, and urges the intellectual presence of

---

⁵⁵ J. P. Grausem, "Rodriguez (Alphonse)," *DTC*, XIII, 2758-2761

⁵⁶ Leo of St. John, *Studium Sapientiae universalis* (Lyon, 1664), III, 219. "Caput lege ex libro ad instructionem destinato. Eiusmodi sunt Thauleri Institutiones, Patrum et Sanctorum vitae Elogia praesertim in singulas anni dies concinne distributa: opera Granatensis, Teresiae, Salesii, Alvaris, Roderici, Joannis a Cruce, a Sancto Sampsone, et similia."

⁵⁷ Chap. ix, p. 119.

⁵⁸ *The Practice of Christian and Religious Perfection* (3 vols., New York, n. d.) I, Treatise V, chap. xxvii, p. 323.

⁵⁹ *Ibid.*, I. Treatise VI, chap. ii, pp. 334-348.

God by an act of faith. The *Méthode* has no such warning to the novices. It urges each one to practise the way he finds more suitable. He encourages the practise of thinking often of God, Who dwells within us. But the prayer of aspiration, i.e., in its full sense, and which presupposes the acquired habit of meditating well, is not developed by Rodriguez.

He proposes different ways of living in God's presence: 1) the constant use of aspirations;[60] 2) the use of all creatures to elevate the mind to God; [61] 3) doing all things, every action to please God.[62] We should perform these actions by first recalling that God is within us. He also has a long treatise on conformity to the will of God, which is really another way of remaining in God's presence, although he does not treat the subject in his treatise on the presence of God.[63]

In spite of these points of similarity we do not find so intimate a connection between the *Méthode* and the teaching of Rodriguez as we do, for example, between Arias and the *Méthode*. It is difficult to say that the *Méthode* in any way depends upon Rodriguez, because their similarity could have been drawn from other sources that present the same teaching.

IV – Luis de la Puente, S. J.

Luis de la Puente (Du Pont in French and de Ponte in Latin) was a well-known Spanish ascetical writer, who was born at Valladolid on November 11, 1554. He entered the Society of Jesus on December 2, 1574. He taught philosophy and theology, and later was placed in charge of the spiritual formation of novices and young religious of the Society. Poor health prohibited him from taking part in other apostolic work. His ascetical writings were universally accepted and praised. They were translated into many languages and have seen many editions. They were all written in Spanish with the exception of a commentary on the Canticle of Canticles which was written in Latin. Luis de la Puente died on February 16, 1624, at Valladolid. His cause of beatificatton was introduced by Pope Benedict XIV. He is now known as Venerable since Pope Clement XIII in 1759 declared that during life he had practised heroic virtue.[64]

---

[60] *Ibid.*, I, Treatise VI, chap. iii, p. 342.
[61] *Ibid.*, I, Treatise VI, chap. iii, p. 343.
[62] *Ibid.*, I, Treatise VI, chap. iv, pp. 345-346.
[63] *Ibid.*, I, Treatise VIII, chap. i, pp. 386-390.
[64] A. Fonck, "Puente (Louis de la)," *DTC*, XIII, 1159-1161. See also *DTC*, IV, 1961.

His works have been published singly and collectively. The first edition of his collected works appeared at Madrid in 1690 and bears the title: *Obras espirituales del V.P. Luis de la Puente, S.J., natural de la ciudad de Valladolid, en cinco tomos.*[65]

De la Puente was above all an ascetical writer, but he also entered the field of mysticism. There can be no doubt that his writings, especially his *Méditations,* were well known and esteemed. Father Ugarte, S.J., in an introduction to a recent French edition, says of their influence:

> We find them in nearly all European languages and even in Arabic. Some have made extracts, abridgements or adaptations, and we may say without fear of error that all the books of meditations that have appeared after him are more or less inspired by the work of de la Puente.[66]

These *Méditations* were well known in the reform of Touraine. Dominic of St. Albert in his *Exercitatio spiritualis* recommended them to novices.

> In order to make meditation easier for beginners and the inexperienced, let them be given the full, ready-made meditations, such as the meditations of Granada and de la Puente, etc. which have abundant material.[67]

The *Méthode* makes no explicit mention of de la Puente, but in the light of the above facts we believe his meditations and teaching on mental prayer are worth studying.

De la Puente obviously follows the order and method of St. Ignatius in his *Méditations.* He refers to three ways of prayer taught by St. Ignatius, that is, meditation, mixed prayer and aspirative prayer.[68]

---

[65] Vol. I: *Meditaciones* (preceded by an epitome of the author's life by P. Cachúpin.) Vols. II-III: *De la perfección en el estado de Cristiano; De la perfección de Cristiano en los estados y oficios de la republica seglar, eclesiastica y religiosa.* Vol. IV: *Guía espiritual.* Vol. V: *Directorio espiritual; Tesoro escondido; Vida del Padre Baltasar Alvarez; Cartas.*

French and Latin editions of some of these works also appeared. The *Meditaciones* in Latin (4 vols., Cologne, 1611-1614; the *Guía espiritual* (Cologne, 1613); *De la perfección de Cristiano* (Cologne, 1614). A French translation of the following works done by René Gaultier also appeared in the early part of the 17th century: *Meditaciones.* (2 vols., Paris, 1614); *De la perfección de Cristiano* (2 vols., 1613-1614); *Guía espiritual* (Paris, 1613-1614).

[66] *Meditations sur les mystères de notre sainte foi avec la pratique de l'oraison mentale.* Trans. by P. Jennesseau, S.J., (6 vols., Paris, 1932-1933), I, xxii-xxiii. We shall cite this edititon.

[67] *AOC,* 11 (1940), chap. ii; p. 28.

[68] *Méditations,* I, 32-33. "Our Father Ignatius places in his little book on *Exercises* not only a variety of subjects for meditation, but various ways of prayer – the way of examinatian of conscience, the way of application of the interior senses of the soul, the way of various analogies and parables, and particularly three very helpful ways of prayer; accommodated to those who walk in the three above mentioned ways (purgative,

He divides mental prayer (meditation) into four parts: exercise of the memory, intellect, will, and in the end an act of petition for our needs, which is made in the form of a colloquy to the Trinity or to one of the divine Persons.[69]

The entrance to mental prayer contains the following acts: act of the presence of God, an act of humility (reverence), kneeling, making the sign of the cross, invocation of the Trinity, and, if one wishes, the recitation of the *confiteor*. These are followed by offering the meditation for the greater glory of God and a petition for grace to pray well.[70] The meditation proceeds according to the plan of prayer in the *Exercises*, although de la Puente does not speak of preludes. The *discursus* proceeds in orderly fashion. The subject is considered according to its *causes, effects* and *circumstances:* For example, the Incarnation may be proposed to the mind. Then the motives, the end or purpose, and finally the circumstances of place, time and manner of the Incarnation are considered.[71]

The prayer (meditation) should consist especially of colloquies. The colloquies are made to express love, admiration, joy, thanks and petitions for favors. In making our petition we should act like a child to his father, or a sick man before the doctor, or a pupil before his teacher, or a bride with the beloved, but must always remember that our first and principal teacher in prayer is the Holy Spirit, Whose impulses we should follow. Moreover, the colloquies may be made with the saints.[72]

De la Puente, following St. Ignatius, presents three ordinary ways of mental prayer: ordinary meditation (*discursus*), mixed prayer, and a form of ejaculatory prayer.[73] He realizes that the action of the intellect and will differs with the individual. Some have much *discursus* and few affections, others have little *discursus* and many affections. Still others have no *discursus* but a simple intuition of the truth from which the affections immediately come, and this is contemplation.[74] The subject matter of mental prayer is all revealed truths and may be divided according to the three ages of the spiritual life.[75] The meditations that fol-

---

illuminative, unitive), although all three ways can be of great help to all." He then gives an explanation of aspiration or affective prayer. He refers to it again in pp. 50-52, where he says aspirations or ejaculations should be used throughout the day to insure the good effect of meditation, that is *devotion*, in all our actions.

[69] *Ibid.*, 3-5.
[70] *Ibid.*, 19-20.
[71] *Ibid.*, 23-28.
[72] *Ibid.*, 12.
[73] *Ibid.*, 32-35.
[74] *Ibid.*, 35-39.
[75] *Ibid.*, 15-19.

low this introduction to prayer are divided according to these three states. The meditations in the first two parts of the book pertain to the purgative way (sin, the four last things, the infancy of Christ); the third and fourth parts pertain to the illuminative way (public life of Christ and His passion); the fifth and sixth parts pertain to the unitive way (glorified life of Christ, the Trinity and the divine perfections).

An examen of the meditation should always follow. It concludes with a resolution to put into practise what we know from the meditation should be done immediately to advance toward unton with God.[76] A reformation of our way of life or a greater imitation of Christ should be the fruit of our meditations.

De la Puente also discusses various ways of extraordinary or mystical prayer, but they have no relation to our investigation.[77]

From the above analysis it is obvious that the method of mental prayer explained by de la Puente is similar in many parts to the method of meditation in the *Méthode*. One might say this similarity is due to the fact that both depend upon the *Exercises* of St. Ignatius. But we see more than similarity. Both methods speak at length about colloquies during the meditation, and when we compare the following two passages it seems to us that the *Méthode* has borrowed directly from the method of de la Puente.

Speaking of the manner of making colloquies de la Puente says:

La seconde fin pour laquelle nous devons nous entretenir avec Dieu Notre Seigneur, est d'obtenir de nouvelles grâces, de nouveaux dons célestes en vue de notre salut et de notre perfection, pour la gloire de Dieu. La demande peut se faire de diverses manières, selon les dispositions differentes de la personne qui prie et traite avec Dieu.

Nous pouvons converser avec Dieu de la même manière qu'un fils converse avec son père, en lui demandant avec amour et avec confiance tout ce qu'un bon fils peut demander au meilleur des pères... Nous pouvons aussi traiter avec Dieu comme un homme pauvre et délaissé traite avec un homme riche et compatissant, à qui il demande d'aumône... Dans d'autres moments nous traitererons avec Dieu comme un malade traite avec un médecin, à qui il declare ses infirmités pour en obtenir la guérison; ou comme un accusé traite avec son juge, lui exposant sa cause, sollicitant une sentence favorable ou le pardon de son crime: Dans ce cas, l'entretien doit être accompagne du sentiment de l'humiliation, de la douleur d'avoir péché, de la resolution de satisfaire et de se corriger.

---

[76] *Ibid.*, 30-32. 1) Was it made with proper preparation? 2) Was it successful? 3) What affections and inspirations were obtained from it? 4) What resolutions were made? 5) What fruits obtained?

[77] *Ibid.*, 39-47.

> D'autres fois enfin, nous poussons converser avec Dieu comme fait un disciple avec son maître, le priant de nous éclairer et de nous enseigner ce que nous ignorons; ou comme un ami converse avec un ami, lorsqu'il traite avec lui une affaire sérieuse et lui demande conseil, aide et direction. Si la confiance et l'amour nous en donnent la hardiesse notre âme pourra s'entretenir avec Dieu comme une épouse s'entretient avec un époux, et lui adresser les diverses paroles qui remplissent le livre des Cantiques...
>
> Quant au succès de nos demandes, il dépend principalement du Saint-Esprit qui, comme dit Saint Paul, prie pour nous avec des gémissements ineffables. Ses inspirations nous instruisent et nous excitent à prier; il nous dicte nos demandes, et il nous communique les sentiments convenables.[78]

Likewise, when speaking of how to prolong the *discursus* by the use of colloquies or conversations, the *Méthode* says:

> Il leur sera aussi fort utile de se presenter devant Nostre Seigneur, quel que fois comme des criminels devant leur juge, duquel ils attendent leur condamnation, ou leur absolution; dans laquelle disposition ils parleront à sa Maiesté avec grande crainte, humilité et reverence. Une autre fois ils s'y presenteront comme des malades devant un charitable médecin, lui decouvrans leurs playes et leur maladies. D'autrefois, comme de pauvres mendians devant un seigneur riche, et plein de compassion. D'autrefois encore, comme des disciples devant leur maistre, auquel ils demandent lumiere et instruction. Tantost comme enfans bien aimez ils parleront à leur père celeste, avec une amour filial, plein de respecte et de confiance. Tantost enfin comme avec le plus sincere et le meilleur ami qu'ils ayent au monde, lui decourans leurs doutes pour avoir son conseil; leur bons desirs, pour obtenir son assistance, et tous leur besoins, pour en recevoir le soulagement, suivant les dispositions interieures, dans lesquelles chacun se trouvera. Car nous supposons tousjours dans les preceptes que nous donnons ici, que le sainct Esprit est le principal maistre de ce divin exercice.[79]

This idea is also found in more concise form in the *Exercises* of St. Ignatius. But we believe that the *Méthode* has taken it directly from de la Puente.

Furthermore, a comparison of the following two texts on mixed prayer seem to indicate dependence, although not as clearly as in the preceding example. De la Puente says:

> La seconde manière consiste à se proposer, comme matière de méditation, certaines paroles, par exemple, un psaume de David, un discours ou une sentence de Notre-Seigneur, une prière, une hymne de l'Église. On s'ar-

---

[78] *Ibid.*, 9-11.
[79] *Méthode*, chap. vi, pp. 85-89.

rêtera à chaque mot, afin d'en exprimer tout ce qu'il contient de pensée et de sentiment... Quant à la forme à observer, on considérera, sur chaque parole, de qu'elle est, à qui elle s'adresse, à quelle fine, de quelle manière, et dans quel esprit elle a été dite, et ce qu'elle signifie, exprime-t-elle un ordre, un conseil, une menace, prière: on tirera les sentiments qui en sortiront naturellement...

Cette seconde manière de prier convient surtout à ceux qui marchent dans la voie illuminative, et désirent connaître et sentir les vérités de la foi, afin de croître en esprit. Nous en montrerons la pratique dans la seconde partie et dans la troisième où nous ferons voir comment on peut méditer sur la salutation angelique, sur le cantique de la Saint Vierge, sur l'oraison dominicale, sur diverses maximes de prières de Notre-Seigneur, dont il faut peser toutes les paroles avec une attention particulière.[80]

The *Méthode* says:

On choisira quelque psalme, verset, ou autre oraison vocale, qui soit affective, ou bien à laquelle on aye desia queque attrait de devotion; afin de n'estre pas frustré de son dessein, si on prenoit un suiect, sur lequel on ne se pourroit occuper, pour estre sterile de lui mesme, ou pour n'y avoir aucun goust.

On doit prendre tous les mots, ou tous les versets les uns apres les autres, les considerer attentivement, et les peser d'un sens rassis, et d'un esprit tranquille, taschant de s'en toucher. Mais si quelque mot ou verset ne fournist aucune pensée, apres s'y estre quelque peu arresté, on passera à un autre, sans en vouloir tirer par force des conceptions. D'autant qu'il faut tenir l'esprit en grande liberté durant l'oraison, et une bonne pensée, qui vient comme d'elle mesme, est beaucoup plus profitable, que toutes celles qu'on voudroit avoir par force.[81]

The *Méthode* then presents the Our Father and the Hail Mary as models of mixed prayer. It will be noticed that the *Mèthode* presents mixed prayer in a more affective manner than Louis de la Puente, in keeping with the affective nature of prayer that characterizes the reform of Touraine.

It seems, therefore, that the *Méditations* of de la Puente were not only used in the reform of Touraine by the religious, but that his instructions on how to make mental prayer were studied, and in part influenced the composition of the method of prayer in the reform. At the same time the method of Touraine seems to be much more affective than the

---

[80] *Méditations*, I, 33-34.
[81] Chap. xxv, pp. 397-398.

method proposed by de la Puente. It teaches not only colloquies to be made at the end of meditation, but recommends that even the points to be considered, as well as the affections, be carried out in the form of conversations with God. In fact, the models of meditations proposed in chapters seventeen to nineteen are all in the form of conversations with God. Yet, despite these differences, we believe that the *Méthode* has borrowed some inspiration and direction from Louis de la Puente.

V – Alvarez de Paz, S.J.

James Alvarez de Paz was born at Toledo in 1560 and entered the Society of Jesus in 1560. He taught philosophy and theology at Lima, Peru. Later he became the provincial of Peru, and died at Pofosi in 1620. He had a great reputation for sanctity among the Peruvians.[82]

He was the author of a complete treatise of the spiritual life, and his work is characterized by a methodical spirit, clarity and tender piety.[83]

His writings were available in various editions, and we find that they were recommended reading in the reform of Touraine.[84] Leo of St. John says the meditations of Alvarez should be used as ordinary material for spiritual reading and meditation. [85]

Since Alvarez de Paz is a follower of the *Exercises,* we deem it necessary to mention only the remarkable points of his teaching on ordinary mental prayer. Mental prayer has a highly affective nature in the writings of Alvarez de Paz. So much so, that some have erroneously said he is the first to employ the term affective prayer, which refers to that state of ordinary prayer which follows discursive prayer.[86] In his *De inquisitione pacis* he divides the subject of meditation according to the three common grades of perfection. In each grade one should examine

---

[82] A. Poulain, "Alvarez de Paz," *DTC,* I, 929.

[83] The best edition: *Opera Jacobi Alvarez de Paz* (6 vols., Paris, 1875-1876). We shall refer to this edition.

[84] *De vita spirituali ejusque perfectione* (Lyon, 1608 and 1611; Mainz, 1614; Pozen, 1618). *De exterminatione mali et promotione boni* (Lyon, 1613 and 1623; Mainz, 1614). *De inquisitione pacis sive studio orationis* (Lyon, 1617, 1619, 1623; Mainz, 1619; Cologne, 1620, 1628). This last volume is of particular interest to us, especially the first three books which bear the titles: *De oratione tum vocali, tum mentali; De his quae procedunt, comitantur, et sequntur orationem mentalem; De materia orationis mentalis.* This third book is a collection of meditations following the plan of the Exercises of St. Ignatius. A partial edition in French appeared under the title: *Méditations,* translated by J. du Jardin (Douay, 1626).

[85] *Studium sapientiae,* III, 219.

[86] Father Philippe, O.P., states that the term affective prayer received its name from the Spanish Jesuit, Antonto Cordeses, in 1574. Cf. Philippe, "Mental Prayer," 51.

the nature, the causes, the effects, the properties of the subject matter which is either human miseries, the works and mercy of God, life of Christ, His mysteries, the divine nature and divine perfections.[87] In the same chapter he introduces the colloquy as a means to aid meditation.[88] The colloquy is twofold: 1) to express the affections, 2) to form the reasoning *discursus* of the meditation. This second device is not a mutual colloquy. However, it is called a colloquy, because God always gives some answer to our prayers. Here one speaks not only to God, but to the Blessed Virgin, the saints, creatures and even inanimate creatures, "*Benedicite sol et luna Domino.*" This method is common to all spiritual men. Some in each point use many colloquies to express affections. This is a very good practise. Others wait until the end of meditation before eliciting the colloquy.

In book three of the *De inquisitione pacis* Alvarez de Paz presents a group of meditations according to the method of St. Ignatius. With the exception of the first one they are in the form of colloquies with God, Jesus Christ, the Blessed Virgin, etc.

In the light of the above description we may ask what influence, if any, did Alvarez de Paz have on the *Méthode?* The division of the subject matter of meditation according to the three grades of perfection, the points to be considered in each subject (e.g., the nature, the cause, the effects, the properties, etc.), the colloquies for the *discursus* as well as for the affections, the reference to affective prayer are characteristics of the method of Alvarez de Paz that are also found in the *Méthode*. But at no time have we been able to find any direct dependence upon Aivarez de Paz. Yet, a writer of such renown whose works underwent so many editions in the early years of the seventeenth century could hardly have escaped the attention of the Carmelites of Touraine who helped write the directories. At the same time, it seems his influence in general does not equal that of Luis de la Puente.

Conclusion

In conclusion we note that the *Méthode is* not only similar in many things to the manner of meditation in the *Exercises,* but even retains similarity with that same method exposed and enlarged upon by the spiritual sons of the founder of the Society of Jesus. Many of these points of similarity, however, are common to all mental prayer, but the

---

[87] *Opera,* V, Bk. II, Part II, chap. xi, p. 416.
[88] *Ibid.,* 418.

particular psychological development and additions to mental prayer offered by St. Ignatius and his school (presence of God, colloquies during and after meditation, examen after meditation) have also found their way into the reform of Touraine just as in practically every system of meditation after St. Ignatius. Without any exaggeration, then, we may safely say that the *Méthode* owes its threefold diviston of prayer (mental, mixed, aspirative), the exercise of the memory, intellect and will in meditation, the remote and proximate preparations, entrance to prayer (presence of God, act of humility, petition before prayer, which is called direction), and development of colloquies to the Jesuit influence. It is also our opinton that the treatise of Arias on mental prayer as well as that of de la Puente were used, and are the sources of the similarity of methods.

However, the school of St. Ignatius has not contributed to the *Méthode* the doctrine on affections, especially the division of general affections. Finally, it is not, as we shall see, to the Ignatian school that the *Méthode* owes its aspirative prayer.

CHAPTER IX

LOUIS OF GRANADA

We turn now to the writings of Louis of Granada, one of the most profound writers on prayer in the entire history of Christian spirituality.[1] After St. Ignatius he was one of the first to formulate a method of prayer intended for all Christians. A number of works on prayer had been written before his time for the faithful in Spain, but none of these was as complete or as successful as the *Libro de la oración y meditación* of Granada.

Louis de Sarria was born at Granada in 1505. He joined the Dominican Order in his youth and after his ordination to the priesthood he became a renowned preacher. In 1534, while preaching at Granada, his fame reached the court of Lisbon, and it was not long before he was summoned to appear there. Besides becoming the official court preacher, he also acted as the spiritual director of Catherine, Regent of Portugal. While at court he was held in the highest esteem and as a reward for his labors was offered the archbishopric of Braga, which he refused in order not to interrupt his apostolate of preaching and writing, that continued until his death at Lisbon in 1588.

Louis of Granada began to write comparatively late in life, the greater number of his works being printed after he had reached the age of sixty. Apart from his many sermons he has written four masterpieces of spiritual theology. The first is the *Libro della oración y meditación*, which appeared in 1554 in two parts and went into eleven edi-

---

[1] A. Huerga, O.P., in the *Summa of the Christian Life* (St. Louis, 1954), I, lxv. This is the first of two volumes of selections from the writings of Louis of Granada, translated and adapted by Jardan Aumann, O.P., from *Suma de la vida cristiana*. The general introduction in the first volume by Father Huerga is an excellent summary of the life, works and influence of Louis of Granada.

tions in five years. Then came the *Memorial de la vida cristiana* in 1566 with the *Adiciones* in 1674. His best-known work, the *Guía de pecadores,* appeared in a corrected edition in 1567. This was followed by the *Introducción* del *símbolo de la fe* in 1583-1584.[2]

The ascetical writings of Granada enjoyed great success throughout Europe. They were translated into more than twenty-five languages, and from 1572 to 1615 numerous editions of his works appeared in France both in French and Latin.[3]

The theme of his ascetical works is ever the same: That the Christian lives the life of Christ and is identified with Him through the grace that He merited for us by the redemption and is communicated to us through the sacraments.[4]

Louis of Granada, besides being an ascetical writer, was a humanist and a nature lover. He reminds one of St. Bonaventure as he leads the soul from the beauty and mystery of the created universe to the infinite beauty and mystery of God. He had more than a nodding acquaintance with St. Augustine and the great medieval mystics, and citations from their works abound in his pages. He possessed a high literary skill, and his influence upon sixteenth and seventeenth century spiritual life cannot be overestimated.[5]

The method of prayer proposed by the learned Dominican is not entirely original. It is said that it was inspired by the *L'Ecerjitatorio* of the Benedictine, Garcia de Cisneros, probably by the *Spiritual Exercises* of St. Ignatius, the *Tratado de la oración* of Antonio Porras, and also by the *Trattato della vita spirituale* of the Italian Serafino de Fermo.[6]

Granada presents a method that simplifies the Ignatian method of the three faculties. St. Francis de Sales shows some dependence upon it. Other authors have extracted small treatises from his works. Still others copied it *ad litteram,* as St. Peter of Alcantara in his *Tratado de la oración.*[7]

It seems that we have not yet fully estimated the great influence of Louis of Granada in his own time and in succeeding centuries. Some of his contemporaries, however, recognized his genius. St. Charles

---

[2] The critical edition of his works was made by Justo Cuervo, O.P., *Obras de Fray Luis de Granada* (14 vols., Madrid, 1906-1927).

[3] H. Bremond, *Histoire ... du sentiment religieux*, II, 5.

[4] Huerga, in the *Summa of the Christian Life,* I, lxii.

[5] M. H. Lavocat, "Louis de Granade," *DTC*, IX, 957.

[6] *Ibid.,* 958.

[7] P. Dudon. "Dans son *Traité de l'oraison,* St. Pierre d'Alcantaca a-t-il démarqué Louis de Grenade?" *RAM,* 2 (1921), 384-401.

Borromeo, St. Teresa, St. Ignatius, St. Peter of Alcantara and St. Francis de Sales all acclaimed his writings.[8] Today historians are in agreement that for many centuries Granada was the recognized master of the spiritual life.

In view of all these words of praise it would be surprising and even lamentable if the influence of this great Dominican had not left its mark on the Carmelites of the reform of Touraine. The two foremost contemplatives of Touraine, Brother John of St. Samson and Father Dominic of St. Albert, both recognized the merits of Louis of Granada and recommended most highly his writings to the novices. They had great admiration for his *Guía de pecadores* as well as for his meditations for each day of the week.[9] Finally, in the *Méthode* itself we find two explicit references to Granada that need no comment. At one time he is called "an excellent author,"[10] and again "this great religious and true father of the spiritual life."[11]

In this chapter we shall endeavor to determine more exactly the influence of Granada on the *Méthode*. We shall begin by examining the *Libro de la oración y meditación,* a book which is concerned with prayer and devotion. Its purpose is to instruct in ordinary prayer and meditation, but on occasion the author does not hesitate to direct his aspirants to a higher state, the prayer of quiet. Writing for all Christians and not just for priests and religious, Granada unfolds the following plan: He begins with a long explanation on the utility and necessity of thought and reflection. This is followed by subjects of meditation for each day of the week, and by his method of meditation. Following his method he points out the difficulties in prayer, and gives the means of overcoming them. In the first part of the *Libro de la oración* he presents fourteen meditations, one for each morning and evening of the week. The morning meditations treat of the passion, death and resurrection of Christ. The evening meditations deal with life, death, judgment, hell and heaven. These latter meditations are to facilitate conversion for beginners.[12]

---

[8] Lavocat, "Louis de Grenade," *DTC*, IX, 953-959.

[9] John of St. Samson, *Oeuvres*, II, *La Conduite des novices,* 904. Dominic of St. Albert, *Exercitatio spiritualis,* in *AOC*, II (1940), 28. Cf. Hugh of St. Francis, *La Véritable idée,* li 74.

[10] Chap. xiii, p. 163.

[11] Chap. xxxiii, p. 550.

[12] We have used the French translation of Simon Martin, *Les Oeuvres spirituelles du R. P. Grennade* (8th ed., Lyon, 1686, first published in 1645), Part I, pp. 480-554. This edition is probably the translation used by Mark of the Nativity in composing the *Directoires*. We shall cite the various books in this edition of 1686 by the following abbreviations:

Then comes the way of methodical meditation which they should follow, if they are inexperienced in this manner of prayer. He proposes five parts of prayer: preparation, reading, meditation, thanksgiving and petition.[13] Later in his *Memorial de la vida cristiana*[14] he again proposes five parts but with a slight modification. Here we find the reading included in meditation, and oblation is added as a distinct part preceding petition. All these parts are not necessary in every meditation, but are recommended to beginners.[15] He closes the explanation of his method in the *Libro de la oración* with seven counsels that explain the essence of mental prayer as he conceived it.

But, someone may ask, where is the method of Louis of Granada today? Strange as it may seem, it is not a living method, that is, it is no longer used in the way that it came from the pen of Granada. It has not had the same success as the methods of St. Ignatius. It is little appreciated today. Even the Dominicans have not embraced it. For example, Father Cormier, O.P., has adopted the method of St. Francis de Sales in his manual for novices.[16] However, the Discalced Carmelites, more than any other Order or Institution, have borrowed the method of Granada and have reproduced its essential elements, if not the details, in the method which they presented to their novices in the seventeenth century and which they still use and recommend to all devout souls today.[17] Hence, the method of Granada in its essential lines has been preserved by the followers of St. Teresa.

But what of the method of prayer in the reform of Touraine, which is still the form of prayer for the Carmelites of the Ancient Observance? Has it also taken over the method of Granada? We have already seen that the Ignatian school has left a profound influence on the *Méthode*. It cannot be said, therefore, that Touraine has adopted the method of Granada. Nor can it be said that it has remained as faithful to the parts of prayer in Granada as the Discalced Carmelites have. Yet, we must admit more than a general concordance of doctrine, and in some points the method of Granada is the source of the *Méthode*.

Oración for *Libro de la oración et meditación*; *Memorial* for *Memorial de la vida cristiana*; *El Símbolo* for *El Símbolo de la fe*.

[13] *Oración*, Part I, p. 415, and chap. iv, pp. 577-578.
[14] Part II, chap, iii, pp. 302-310.
[15] *Memorial*, Part II, chap: ii, p. 308.
[16] H. M. Cormier, O.P., *L'Instruction des novices à l'usage des Frères Préheur... composé sur d'anciens manuscrits* (1882), 324-327.
[17] G. Lercaro, *Metodi*, 197.

Let us compare their teaching. Both authors define prayer as elevation of the *heart* to God.[18] Generally prayer is called an elevation of the *mind* or the *soul* or the *intellect* to God.[19]

On the necessity of mental prayer we see an agreement of thought and, probably, a dependence of the *Méthode* on Granada.

The Dominican writes:

> One of the principal causes of all evils in the world is the lack of consideration. As St. Jeremias testified when he said: "With desolation is all the land made desolate; because there is none that considereth in the heart:"[20] Hence, it seems that the cause of our evil is not so much the lack of faith as a lack of the consideration of the mysteries of the faith.[21]

The *Méthode* echoes this same thought.

> All evils of the world come from a lack of consideration, as St. Jeremias testifies: "With desolation is all the land made desolate; because there is none that considereth in the heart."
> It is the opinion of some that all the miseries and sins of life come from a lack of faith. This is true in one sense, but if we look deeper, it is equally, true that the source of all these evils is a lack of meditation and consideration.[22]

There is harmony of thought and even of expression when both authors speak of the correct approach to prayer. "Meditation is not for our pleasure," says Granada, "but to do the will of God and to seek His grace."[23] The *Méthode* says, "we do not pray for our own pleasure, but to please God."[24]

In comparing the parts of prayer, we again find some similarity. Preparation for the *Méthode* is threefold: remote, proximate and immediate. Granada speaks only of immediate preparation, but it would include the three special acts proposed in the Carmelite method, namely, act of the presence of God, acts of humility and reverence and a short examination of conscience. The *Méthode*, however, would also add the offering of the meditation to the honor and glory of God and the petition to pray well.[25] These latter two points show the influence of the Ignatian School.

---

[18] *Oración*, in preface. *Méthode*, chap. i, p. 14.
[19] De Guibert, *Theologia spiritualis*, 204-205.
[20] Jeremias, 12: 11.
[21] *Oración*, preface.
[22] Chap. ii, pp. 30-32.
[23] *Oración*, preface.
[24] Chap. xix, p. 294.
[25] *Oración*, Part. I, chap. v. p. 578; *Méthode*, chap. iv, p. 59.

The *reading* that precedes the act of meditation, according to both authors, is not only an attentive act of the intellect, but also an act of the will. The will should desire to benefit from the reading and to taste its substance.[26] The *Méthode,* more lengthy than Granada, gives eight rules for good reading, and includes all that Granada has to say on this subject.[27]

The subject of meditation should be either sensible (imaginative) or intellectual.[28] The *Méthode* says the same.[29] If the subject is imaginative (Granada gives much attention to the use of the imagination in his meditations), we should represent the mystery in the place in which we are or within our hearts according to our disposition. It is a difficult practise, however, and may even cause a headache if we were to imagine ourselves in the place where the mystery, took place, e.g., in Jerusalem or in the holy places.[30] The *Méthode* would differ on this last point, believing it is indifferent whether one represent the subject near or far from oneself or within or outside oneself.[31] Both agree that the imagination should never be fixed on the subject. It may cause one to believe that he sees what he only imagines.[32]

Meditation on the life, passion and gifts of Our Lord is the foundation of this exercise. The principal circumstances to be considered, if we meditate on the passion, are four: Who suffers? For whom does He suffer? Why does He suffer? In what manner does He suffer?[33] We have seen in chapter eight that the *Méthode* follows the Ignatian contemplation of the mysteries of Christ rather than this brief and more simple outline of Granada.

Yet, if we consider the function of meditation, or the body of prayer, we shall see the influence of Granada on the *Méthode. Meditation,* the body of the prayer, is not a mere intellectual act for Granada.

It contains acts of the will. In fact, the will should, as soon as possible, become inflamed. In prayer the will should predominate. We pray not to learn, but to love and prepare ourselves to do the will of God. In prayer the intellect and will act as a balance to one another. If too much time is given to the operation of the intellect, the operation of

---

[26] *Oración,* Part I, chap. v, pp. 581-582.
[27] Chap. iii, pp. 41 ff.
[28] *Oración,* Part I, chap. vii, pp. 582-583.
[29] Chap. vi, p. 73.
[30] *Oración,* Part I, chap. vii, p. 583.
[31] Chap. v, p. 78.
[32] *Oración,* Part I, chap. vii, p. 583; *Méthode,* chap. v, pp. 77-78.
[33] *Memorial,* Part II, Bk. VI, chap. iii, p. 305.

the will is weakened. On the other hand, if the operation of the will is given more time in prayer, then the reflections of the intellect are lessened, but the prayer will be better. Now, just as the hunting dog does not devour the wounded rabbit which it has tracked down, but simply finds it and guards it for the hunter, so the intellect does not consume all the time given to prayer in the enjoyment of the truth which it has discovered, but simply presents it to the will.

If we insist on this point it is because Granada has sometimes been accused of neglecting the true affections in prayer, because of his insistence on a discursive method. Nothing could be farther from the truth. Listen to the words of the great Dominican spiritual writer as he extols the predominance of affections in meditation:

> Seek less to have speculations dominate in prayer than the affections and sentiments of the will... Reflection revives the flame of prayer when it is exercised with due measure; it extinguishes prayer when it becomes excessive... Does a soul which tastes God wish to meditate? It will not be slow in feeling devotion no longer... Let us be content with a rapid knowledge of divine things; then the soul will reunite all its forces, and it will be able to consecrate them to loving with all its heart and honoring Supreme Beauty... To speak little; to love much, to come to the aid of the will in order that it may bear itself towards God with all its energy, that is the way to profit well from prayer.[34]

We believe the *Méthode* presents this same affective tendency in prayer. Besides referring the reader to chapter four of this study to verify our position, we cite here a few short texts. "Too much time should not be given to the intellect."[35] "We meditate in order to love."[36] The intellect and the will are related to one another in meditation as the hunting dog to its prey.

> The dog chases the animal, but once it captures it, it stops running and stands guard. So also the intellect, once it finds the truth, ceases to reason, and allows the will to produce affections.[37]

Here we find not only the same affective tendency in meditation. that we have found in Granada, but we find the *Méthode* using the identical example presented by the great Dominican master of affective prayer.

---

[34] *Oración,* Part I, chap, ix, pp. 587-588; also *Memorial,* Part II, Bk. VI, chap. iii, p. 305.
[35] Chap. ix, p. 120
[36] *Ibid.*
[37] *Ibid.*

But Granada is keenly aware that beginners in prayer will find it difficult to produce affections. In order that they may not give all their time to reflection or to distractions, he presents for them the affections of thanksgiving, oblation and petition. These acts of the will can come at the end of prayer or even during it. They are merely helps to pray well, and are not always necessary. Granada places them at the end of his method, because affections usually come at the end of prayer.

Those who find these acts too methodical or artificial should recall that Granada wishes the hour of meditation to excite devotion in the souls of Christians, and that it matters little whether they use all six parts in prayer, provided the end is gained.[38] However, he writes from long years of experience, and knows that novices without a method will not pray well.

If you only praise prayer in general to a novice who is beginning to pray mentally, and do not show him the way, and fail to assign the particular subject of his prayer and the manner of exercising it, he will begin to meditate with a wandering and distracted heart, without firmness or any stability.[39]

Petition above all should receive our attention. One may pass the whole hour of meditation in this one part.[40] The petition may be twofold. First, prayer for one's neighbor, for the Church, religious Orders, priests, etc., and secondly for oneself. Granada understands petition as a colloquy with God. It is most fruitful when it is a loving colloquy in which the soul asks God for more and more love. "Try," he says, "to converse with God especially about things of love and in the exercise of aspiration."[41]

The *Méthode* follows Granada in this explanation, and explicitly refers to him.

An excellent author [the name of Louis of Granada is placed in the margin] believes that one praying and seeking something should place himself in His presence in the same manner as a little dog in the presence of his master sitting at the table. For this poor little animal makes all sorts of gestures and takes up different poses to obtain a morsel of food, and although repulsed on one day he returns the next, taking up the same position and going through the same antics.[42]

---

[38] *Memorial*, Part II, Bk. VI, chap. iii, p. 308.
[39] *Ibid.*
[40] *Oración*, Part I, chap. ix, p. 587.
[41] *Ibid.*
[42] Chap. xiii, p. 168.

Granada closes his treatise on prayer with seven warnings or counsels. Here is where we especially see similarity of doctrine, although the *Méthode* at no time refers here to Granada. These seven counsels, which we shall paraphrase, are concerned with the meditation, or body of prayer, and express the exact mind of Louis of Granada on the importance of affections in mental prayer.

1) If while following a set of meditations for the days of the week, new thoughts foreign to the subject offer themselves in which one finds more joy and usefulness, they should be fostered. Because these come from the Holy Spirit, and it would be irrational to forsake true devotion of divine things and to look for it elsewhere.[43]

2) One should avoid too much intellectual discourse and give place to the affections of the will.[44]

Curious speculation should be avoided. One should be content with a look and the simple understanding of divine things in order that the soul may move more swiftly and profoundly to the love of God.[45]

They err who meditate as if they were studying to preach. They go outside themselves rather than within themselves. In prayer we should esteem more the act of listening than of speaking.[46] For this reason we should speak little and love much. The relation between the intellect and the will is demonstrated by many examples. One of which is the hunting dog and its prey that we have already mentioned.[47]

3) The exercise of the will should be controlled, so that we must never use force to produce affections.[48] It is foolish, while meditating on the sorrows of Christ's passion, to force ourselves into the state of sadness. We should accept tears, if God wills, but force should not be used.

Sensible devotion is often a gift of God to beginners. If it passes away, this is not a sign that meditation is worse. Often one loves more without sensible consolation.[49]

4) Our attention during meditation should be moderate; neither forced nor too remissive. Lack of due attention is often the reason of

---

[43] *Oración*, Part I, chap. x, p. 590; *Méthode*, chap. xxiv, p. 378. All seven counsels are found pp. 590-598. In the notes that follow we refer only to the *Méthode*.

[44] *Méthode*, chap. ix, p. 120.

[45] *Méthode*, chap. xxiv, p. 378.

[46] *Méthode*, chap. v, p. 64, and especially chap. xxiv, p. 380, where we read: "It often happens that we do not hear His voice, because we speak too much."

[47] *Méthode*, chap. v, p. 65. Both give the same example.

[48] *Méthode*, chap. xxiv, p. 386.

[49] *Méthode*, chap. xxii, p. 329.

little or no progress in prayer.[50] One must make a strong, serious effort to apply his mind to the subject matter.

5) The most important counsel is to persevere in prayer.[51] For those who have difficulty, reading should be mixed with prayer.[52]

6) We should not leave the considerations for any kind of pleasure or affections that we feel in prayer, but we should consider the subject well. For a small flame improperly nourished dies quickly.[53] Therefore, the time of prayer should be long, that is, about one and one-half hours or two hours, because it takes some time to quiet the imagination before the soul can meditate well.

7) When God visits the soul this grace should not be allowed to pass without good results. In an hour we can sail farther with this wind, which is a special grace, than we could in many days without it.[54]

After this comparison we are in a position now to draw up points of similarity and dissimilarity between the two methods of meditation.

1) The immediate preparation contains the same three acts, although the *Méthode* adds offering and petition.

2) It is obvious from the seven counsels *alone* that the *Méthode* recommends the same use of the intellect and will in meditation as Louis of Granada. Both consider meditation or mental prayer a work of love – an exercise in which affections predominate. The *Méthode* uses the same example as Granada to demonstrate the relation of the intellect to the will in meditation.

3) Almost all the seven counsels proposed by Granada are found in some manner in the *Méthode,* which, however, gives some twenty-eight counsels.

4) Thanksgiving, oblation and petition are the three last parts of prayer. The *Méthode* quotes Granada on the nature of petition.

5) The parts of prayer in both methods should be followed by beginners, but may be discarded by one who has made progress in prayer, or when the Holy Spirit sends special graces.

The following are points of dissimilarity:

1) Granada, like St. Ignatius, wrote for all Christians and places the object of prayer in the acquisition of devotion, that is, in the attain-

---

[50] *Méthode,* chap. v, p. 63.
[51] *Méthode,* chap. xxiv, p. 384.
[52] *Méthode,* chap. xxiv, p. 380.
[53] *Méthode,* chap. v, pp. 63 ff.
[54] *Méthode,* chap. xxiv, p. 380.

ment of a ready will to serve God in all things. The *Méthode* was primarily written for Carmelite novices and directs the novice toward introversion and interior loving conversation with God. Although both methods would lead ultimately to the same end, it is obvious that the choice of language and thought differs. The *Méthode*, following the Rule of the Order and the spirit of Touraine, continually holds habitual, loving conversation with God before the novices as their end. These expressions are not so pronounced in the works of Granada, who is intent on directing the Christian to a perfect observance of God's commandments.

2) Granada admits six parts in prayer: preparation, reading, meditation, thanksgiving, oblation and petition. The *Méthode* admits three parts: preparation, meditation and affections. It divides the affections into particular and general and considers resolutions as a part of the general affections. Granada does not give as much importance to resolutions, and places them as a part of the general affection of petition.

3) Fourteen meditations, two for each day of the week, are proposed by Granada in the *Libro de oración*. The *Méthode* proposes meditations according to the grade of perfection or the age of the spiritual life.

4) Although both recognize the Holy Spirit as the master of the soul in prayer, the *Méthode* emphasizes this truth much more than Granada. Perhaps the difference may be explained by the fact that Granada, although he has his eyes on higher prayer, rarely tells us what it is. He does not describe in detail the soul's progress beyond the point where meditation ceases and gives place to higher prayer. This no doubt is due to the age in which he lived. In Granada's time mystical prayer was held in suspicion even in orthodox circles because of the *Alumbrados* or false mystics.[55] The *Méthode*, on the contrary, orientates meditation toward more advanced prayer, and prepares the soul for the inner work of the Holy Spirit. It explicitly unfolds descriptions of that state that transcends the efforts of man, wherein the soul by the simple intuition of truth is drawn to greater quiet, and being led by this divine attraction stands before God, conversing with Him in the innermost part of its being.[56]

---

[55] M. Lavocat, "Louis de Grenade," *DTC*, IX, 958.
[56] *Méthode*, chap. xxiv, pp. 376-377.

The Presence of God

Aspirative prayer, as it is developed in the *Méthode,* is not found in the writings of Granada. But he does recommend the practise of the presence of God and ejaculatory prayer. These exercises are presented as two distinct exercises by Granada. Both have the same purpose, namely, to keep the soul recollected in God, to prepare it well for the hour of meditation.[57] The Dominican master recommends the thought of the humanity of Christ as a great means to remain throughout the day in the presence of God. And he uses all things in the world as an aid to elevate the heart to God in ejaculatory prayer. The *Méthóde* refers to the first part of Granada's *El Símbolo de la fe* as containing excellent material to show the novice how to find God in all creatures.[58]

However, it does not seem that Granada had any substantial influence on aspirative prayer in the *Méthode*. He considers ejaculatory prayer as a common exercise that will help souls acquire devotion and prepare them for meditation. He cites St. Augustine, Cassian and the Fathers of the Desert to show the efficacy of ejaculations in our daily life. He presents a few examples of ejaculatory prayer taken from the Psalms. The *Méthode* has the same doctrine but much more enlarged and much more advanced. Aspirative prayer in the Carmelite manual is a transport of love that leads to the threshold of the mystical life. It is not so much a preparation for meditation as a result of meditation that has been practised for some time by one who is in the illuminative way. It is evident that Granada is not the source of the *Méthode's* sublime doctrine on aspirative prayer.

In concluding our study of Granada as a source of the *Méthode* we recall that it has referred to him as "an excellent author" and has quoted him as an authority, "a true father of the spiritual life." These expressions of praise alone are a witness to the influence of Granada on the *Méthóde*. His influence was indeed great in the whole reform, for his book of meditations as well as his other works were highly recommended by Venerable John of St. Samson, the blind mystic, whose special ministry consisted in forming the novices in the ways of the spiritual life. Indeed, Louis of Granada was a favorite author in the novitiate of Touraine. How, then, shall we explain the similarity of doctrine that we have just compared? In many cases it may be due to

---

[57] *Oración*, Part I, chap. ii, pp. 628-633.
[58] Chap. xxxiii, p. 549.

fundamental truths of mental prayer taught by the best spiritual writers, or it may be due to the mutual dependence of Granada and the *Méthode* on certain writers, among them St. Ignatius. But from the evidence it is certain that, just as the *Méthode* depends on the Ignatian School for its teaching on the body of prayer in meditation and the examen after meditation, so also it is influenced directly by Granada, whom it cites (although not necessarily by Granada alone) for its teaching on the predominance of the will in meditation and for its general affections of thanksgiving, oblation and petition.

The dependence upon Granada is not so profound, however, in the section of the *Méthode* given to the presence of God and aspirative prayer. It is necessary to look elsewhere for the sources of aspirative prayer, which is in a special way the prayer of the Carmelite. Nevertheless, it must be said that apart from the authors and traditions of the Carmelite Order itself no single spiritual writer has had as much direct influence on the *Méthode* as Louis of Granada.

CHAPTER X

LOUIS DE BLOIS (BLOSIUS)

Louis de Blois, commonly known as Blosius, was a Benedictine abbot of Liessies (1506-1566). Through his writings he helped to reform not only the spiritual lives of his own monks, but had great influence outside of his own Order. His books were often edited and translated into many languages.[1]

There can be no doubt that he was one of the better-known spiritual writers in the reform of Touraine. John of St. Samson in his letters recommends especially the *Institutio spiritualis*.[2] Bouchereaux thinks that John has also read the *Psychologia* of Blois, a collection of the writings of some of the Fathers.[3] Dominic of St. Albert also recommended the writings of Blois to the young religious because they are written in the form of colloquies and dialogues and are excellent examples of how to converse with God.[4] All the writings of Blosius were easily obtainable. They were edited separately and collectively. A definitive edition of all his works was published in Antwerp in 1632.[5]

We have already seen that John of St. Samson and Dominic of St. Albert had much to say in the preparation of the *Directoires*. We do not doubt that both Bernard and Mark were also familiar with and in some way influenced by Blois. They teach practises that are

---

[1] P. de Puniet, "Blois Louis de," *DSp*, I, 1730-1738. Blois was greatly influenced by John Tauler, O.P. He wrote a defense of Tauler against the injurious attacks of Eck. Moreover, the first appendix to his *Institutio spiritualis* is drawn almost entirely from the writings of Tauler. Cf. B. Wilberforce, O.P., in his preface to the English translation of *Institutio spiritualis*, that is, *A Book of Spiritual Instruction* (London, 1925).
[2] *Oeuvres*, II, 641; 655, 666.
[3] *La Réforme des Carmes*, 159.
[4] *Regulae exteriores, AOC*, 11 (1940), 69-70.
[5] *Lud. Blosii Opera omnia* (Antwerp, 1632).

very similar to the ones he recommends on the presence of God and aspirations.

In his *Institutio spiritualis* Blois joins the exercise of the presence of God with aspirations. He makes no distinction between aspirations and ejaculations, and uses both words indiscriminately.

Blois presents three means to acquire union with God: self-denial, introversion and aspirations. All spiritual writers insist on self-denial as a means to perfection. Since the fall of Adam self-denial is necessary for every man born in original sin and weighed down by the burden of concupiscence.

This great Benedictine author is much more interesting when he speaks of introversion. We should recall here that John of St. Samson used this word frequently in his writings, and the *Méthode* explains that the ways of prayer it presents are necessary "to acquire introversion and interior conversation with God."[6]

What is introversion? For Blois it is the practise of the presence of God, not any practise of the presence of God, but that whereby we withdraw from all outside distractions and become recollected in God Who dwells in the inmost sanctuary of our soul. He writes:

> Therefore should he "introvert" himself – that is, should turn himself into "his own soul, and dwell there in his own heart – for there will he be able to find God. For God, who indeed is everywhere, dwells in the simple basis, or inner sanctuary, of the soul in a very special manner. There he dwells in His own image, and never departs.[7]

We should recall that the *Méthode* mentions this kind of presence of God, but considers it too far advanced for novices, although the best way that leads quickly to the mystical state.[8]

This divine presence is the great principle of unity in our life, says Blois. Even though our life is filled with many varied occupations, we should try to be conscious of God in all these actions. We should learn to converse with Him as a child converses with its father.[9]

Blosius distinguishes, as the *Méthode* does, between three kinds of presence of God: imaginary, intellectual and affective. He does not

---

[6] Chap. i, pp. 19-20. Cf. L. Reypens, "Ame," *DSp*, I, 458. The writer says that John of St. Samson was greatly influenced by Ruysbroeck in his doctrine on the faculties of the soul and the nature of introversion. We believe Blosius also influenced him.

[7] Chap. iii, p. 36. Pagination is from the English translation of *Institutio spiritalis* by B. Wilbeforce, O.P., *A Book of Spiritual Instruction* (London, 1925).

[8] Chap. xxxvi, pp. 607-608.

[9] Chap. iii, pp. 38-39.

make this threefold distinction explicitly, but an examination of his writings shows that he admits all three. For example, speaking of the humanity of Christ as a means to practise the presence of God, he proposes first the beautiful image of Christ which in time will become a formless image.

> Therefore should the servant of God impress the beautiful image of the crucified Manhood of Christ on the powers of his soul and the senses of his body, and betake himself wholly to it. For after a time this will in a wonderful way lift him up into the superessential and formless image, to the eternal Word and Wisdom of the Father, into the most high Godhead of Christ.[10]

Blois also speaks of intellectual and affective presence of God.

> He ought, I repeat, to consider that God is always present to him in every place, and thus try to direct his interior eyes to Him not indeed with any violent effort, but quietly and simply, stretching forth his spirit lovingly into the Godhead.[11]

When he speaks of introversion Blois refers to affective presence of God, as becomes quite clear if we compare chapters three and five. He recommends different ways of practising this presence: 1) by using a collection of aspirations, 2) representation of the manhood of Christ, 3) thinking of God dwelling in the inmost sanctuary of the soul. These three ways are recommended in the *Méthode,* but the last way is considered a little too advanced for novices.

Blois also recommends aspirations for all three stages of the spiritual life. He gives many examples, especially in chapter four. He finds that aspirative prayer together with self-denial is the shortest way to perfection.

> The diligent darting forth of aspirations and prayers of ejaculation and fervent desires to God, joined with true mortification and self-denial, is the most certain as well as the shortest way by which a soul can easily and quickly come to perfection – that is, to the wisdom of mystical theology.[12]

In like manner the *Méthode* teaches us that we should strive

> ... to have a great desire for God which we make known to God by frequent and fervent ejaculations. This will bring us in a short time and by a short way to affective and continual union with God.[13]

---

[10] Chap. vi, p. 56.
[11] Chap: vi, p. 35.
[12] Chap. vi, p. 48.
[13] Chap. xxviii, p. 438.

The *Méthode* constantly speaks of acquiring loving conversation with God. We can find a good description of conversation with God in the *Institutio spiritualis* of Blois. In Appendix II he presents ten different conversations with God and the saints. These are excellent examples to teach novices the meaning of loving conversation with God. It seems these are the exercises that Dominic of St. Albert recommended to the novices and young professed.

It is obvious that the *Méthode* reflects the spiritual teaching of Blois on the value of aspirative prayer. Much that Blois says is found in the *Méthode,* which has much more to say than Blois about aspirative prayer and the presence of God. Thus, they present the same fundamental doctrine. John of St. Samson and Dominic of St. Albert seem to have undergone the influence of Louis de Blois. When we shall treat more explicitly of these two contemplatives of Touraine, we shall see their profound influence on the *Méthode*. In concluding our study of Blois we are forced to admit a similarity of doctrine, but we have not found his direct influence in the *Méthode*. Even so, a Carmelite will find in Blois the spirit of prayer that his Order desires him to attain.

CHAPTER XI

ST. TERESA AND THE DISCALCED CARMELITE SCHOOL

I – St. Teresa

We have seen the influence of the Ignatian School and of Louis of Granada on the ways of prayer taught to the novices in the reform of Touraine. Has the reform of St. Teresa and of St. John of the Cross had any influence on the methods of prayer in the reform of Touraine? The fame of St. John of the Cross had not spread to France as rapidly as that of St. Teresa; so that in the first years of the seventeenth century he was not well known in France.[1]

John of St. Samson knew of John of the Cross and was probably acquainted with some of his writings.[2] But neither John of St. Samson nor Dominic of St. Albert depend upon him for their mystical doctrine, nor do they recommend him in their writings. With the passing of time all the writings of John of the Cross were translated into French, so that by the time Mark of the Nativity took up the completion of the *Directoires des novices* in 1647 John of the Cross was much better known in France and in the reform.[3] There is no mention of John of the Cross in the *Méthode*, but the *Directoires des novices* mentions him elsewhere twice.[4] From

---

[1] John of St. Samson died in 1636. He could have known the following work: John of the Cross, *Cantique d'amour divin entre Jesus-Christ et l'âme devote*, translated by René Gaultier (Paris, 1622).

[2] Bouchereaux, *La Réforme des Carmes;* 270.

[3] The following translations were known in France: St. John of the Cross, *Opera mystica,* trans. into Latin by Andrew of Jesus, O.C.D. (Cologne, 1639). *Oeuvres spirituelles du B.P. Jean de la Croix,* trans. by Cyprian of the Nativity of the Virgin (2 vols., Paris, 1641).

[4] *Spiritus actionum religionis,* 631. It is a compendium of vol. III of the *Directoires des novices,* translated into Latin. It is found in the second part of the *Methodus clara et facilis*

these citations we believe that he was held in high esteem in the reform. At the same time we do not believe the *Méthode* was influenced by him. First of all, John of the Cross had little to say about the ordinary ways of prayer. His mystical writings would have been too difficult for young novices to understand. Secondly, there is no evidence of his influence.

When we come to St. Teresa, however, the story is completely different. Her works were known in France at the time the *Méthode* was begun by Bernard of St. Magdalen in 1634. Her reputation as a spiritual writer had greatly increased when the *Méthode* was taken over to be completed by Mark of the Nativity some thirteen years later.

The first French translation of St. Teresa's writings appeared at Paris in 1601. The translator was Jean de Quinanodoine de Bretigny. It was a work composed of three volumes and contained the *Vida* with the *Addiciones,* the *Camino* with the *Avisos, Las Moradas* and the *Exclamaciones.* Other translations followed: in 1630 the edition of Father Eliseus of St. Bernard, O. C. D.; in 1644 the edition at Paris of Father Cyprian of the Nativity of the Virgin, O.C.D. A translation of the *Vida* from Latin into French was made by I.D.B.P.E.LP. and published at Douay in 1629. Many other translations and complete editions appeared in France in the succeeding centuries.[5]

It is quite evident that the writings of St. Teresa were available to the reformers of Touraine. However, there is no indication of her influence on John of St. Samson and on Dominic of St. Albert.[6] We know, nevertheless, that she was an inspiration to Thibault. We have already mentioned in chapter seven that he recommended the frequent reading of her spiritual counsels. We are not surprised, then, to find St. Teresa quoted often as a great authority on prayer in the *Méthode*. On six different occasions she is quoted, which is more often than any other single authority, if we except the Holy Scriptures.[7] Hence, we may ask: To what extent did the writings of St. Teresa influence the *Méthode?*

---

vacandi orationi mentali (Cologne, 1687). The *Spiritus* refers to Blessed John of the Cross as an exalted Carmelite mystic. There are other references to Blessed John of the Cross in *Direttorio spirituale de' Carmelitani,* 2nd ed. I, 306, 311.

[5] P. Pourrat, "Thérèse, Sainte," *DTC,* XV, 571-572.

[6] Eugene Tonna, O. Carm., *De doctrina spirituali Ven. Dominici* (unpublished dissertation), 115.

[7] Chap. ii, p. 22; chap. ii, pp. 33-34; chap. xix, p. 293; chap. xxii, p. 330 (exact words of St. Tereaa are given); chap. xxiv, p. 382 (exact words of St. Teresa are given); chap. xxiv, p. 392.

St. Teresa's Concept of Prayer

We shall try briefly to summarize St. Teresa's teaching on meditation and mental prayer for beginners without entering the field of mystical prayer. St. Teresa's definition of mental prayer is well known. "And mental prayer in my view is nothing but friendly intercourse, and frequent solitary converse with Him Whom we know loves us."[8] For St. Teresa prayer is a work of love. The intimacy of love grows with the progress in prayer. "The soul's profit, then, consists not in thinking much but in loving much."[9] She declares prayer is necessary for all, but that there are many ways of doing it.

So practise mental prayer, sisters, or, if any of you cannot do that, vocal prayer, reading and colloquies with God, as I shall explain to you later. Do not neglect the hours of prayer which are observed by all the nuns; you never know when the Spouse will call you (do not let what happened to the foolish virgins happen to you) and if He will give you, fresh trials under the disguise of consolations.[10]

What ways of prayer does St. Teresa suggest? We limit our investigation to ways of prayer for beginners, since these alone pertain to our task. First of all, she suggests ordinary meditation or methodical meditation. She never wrote a treatise on this subject, but esteems very highly the method proposed by Father Louis of Granada and St. Peter of Alcantara, although she does not mention them by name.[11] However, in her *Constitutions* she does recommend the books of Granada and St. Peter of Alcantara.[12]

The humanity of Christ, she says, should occupy a central place in our prayer, even in the prayer of beginners.

Returning to what I was saying – the meditation upon Christ bound to the column – it is well to reflect for a time and to think of the pains which He bore there, why He bore them, Who He is that bore them and with what love He suffered them. But we must not always tire ourselves by going in search of such ideas; we must sometimes remain by His side with our minds hushed in silence.[13]

---

[8] *Complete Works*, I, *Life*, p. 50.

[9] *Ibid.*, III, *Foundations*, chap. v, p. 20; II, *Interior Castle*, chap i, p. 233.

[10] *Ibid.*, II, *Way of Perfection*, chap xviii, p. 73.

[11] *Ibid.*, chap. xix, pp. 76-77. Cf. P. Gabriel of St. Mary Magdalen, O.C.D., *La mística teresiana* (Fiesole, 1935), 52.

[12] Gabriel of St. Mary Magdalen, *La mística teresiana*, 52.

[13] *Complete Works*, I, *Life*, chap. xiii, pp. 82-83.

We recognize the plan of meditation of Granada. Who has suffered, for whom, why, how? [14]

St. Teresa fully realized that all beginners are not capable of practicing ordinary meditation. So she suggests using a book during meditation to aid recollection.

> It is also a great help to have a good book, written in the vernacular simply as an aid to recollection. With this aid you will learn to say your vocal prayers well – I mean, as they ought to be said – and little by little persuasively and methodically, you will get your soul used to this, so that it will no longer be afraid of it.[15]

Another simple way of recollecting the thoughts is suggested by St. Teresa.

> I am not asking you now to think of Him or to form numerous conceptions of Him, or to make long and subtle meditations with your understanding. I am asking you only to look at Him. For who can prevent you from turning the eyes of your soul (just for a moment, if you can do no more) upon this Lord? Look upon Him bound to the column, full of pain, His flesh all torn to pieces by His great love for you. How much He suffered, persecuted by some, spat upon by others, denied by his friends, and even deserted by them with none to take His part, frozen with the cold and left so completely alone that you may well comfort each other! [16]

Finally, we find in St. Teresa a method of mixed prayer, which she recommends to those who have difficulty with meditation. We have remarked elsewhere that St. Ignatius proposed this as the second way of prayer.[17] St. Teresa, however, has presented it in a new light, and given it her own personal affective touch. These pages on mixed prayer concern the *Pater Noster* and are some of the best known pages of St. Teresa. She writes here especially of the prayer of quiet and the prayer of union, and also of the prayer of recollection that leads to the prayer of quiet.[18] It is evident from these quotations that St. Teresa knew and recommended methodical meditation. At the same time we cannot but admire the liberty she grants to her nuns, even beginners, in choosing other ways of prayer, that are more conducive to their nature and the grace of God.

We would like now to compare this teaching of St. Teresa with the doctrine found in the *Méthode*. In the first place, St. Teresa is never

---

[14] *Memorial de la vida cristiana*, Part II, Bk. vi, chap. xiii, p. 305.
[15] *Complete Works*, II, *Way of Perfection*, chap. xxvi, pp. 109-110.
[16] *Ibid.*
[17] *Exercises*, 4th week, "Three Ways of Praying."
[18] *Complete Works*, II, *Way of Perfection*, chaps. xxvii, xxviii, xxx, pp. 110-126.

quoted in the *Méthode* as an authority on methodical meditation, mixed prayer or aspirative prayer, *as such*. Whenever she is cited, it is always in reference to prayer in general, that is, the importance of prayer, the necessity of prayer, the difficulties (aridity) in prayer. She is generally referred to as St. Teresa, but once she is called the Holy Virgin and Mother Teresa.[19] She is quoted, so we are told, because she possessed the genuine and true spirit of the Carmelite Order.[20]

The *Méthode* does not give a definition of prayer from St. Teresa, but its description of it harmonizes perfectly with those of the Saint of Avila. The Carmelite Rule, according to the *Méthode* prescribes affective prayer wherein the heart is continually united to God.[21] Again, meditation is necessary to acquire internal conversation with God.[22] This conversation should be a loving, continual colloquy.[23] It is quite evident that, like St. Teresa, the *Méthode* teaches that prayer is above all a work of love.

And the Carmelite should have the greatest esteem for this work of love. "St. Teresa," says the *Méthode,* "whom God had inspired most copiously and abundantly with the true and genuine spirit of our holy Carmelite Order, recognized in prayer a great abundance of spiritual goods, and tasted in it such wonderful sweetness that she was accustomed to say that she did not care where or in what state she would be, as long as she would be able to pray, and for this reason she did not fear purgatory."[24]

The *Méthode* also calls to mind the difficulties that St. Teresa experienced in prayer before her total conversion, and how she often wished her hour of prayer were over. The exact words of the Saint are not quoted, but the passage referred to is from chapter eight of her *Life*.

The *Méthode* also refers to St. Teresa when speaking of perseverance in prayer.[25]

The basis of all prayer, even the most sublime acts of pure love, is humility, says the *Méthode,* as it again quotes the authority of St. Teresa.[26] The *Méthode* does not cite the book or the chapter, but this idea is found in St. Teresa's *Life*.

---

[19] Chap. xxiv, p. 382.
[20] Chap. ii, p. 22.
[21] Chap. i, p. 15.
[22] Chap. i, pp. 19-20.
[23] Chap. xxviii, p. 434.
[24] Chap. ii, p. 22.
[25] Chap. xix, p. 293. *Complete Works,* I, *Way of Perfection,* chap. iv, pp. 15-16.
[26] Chap. xxiv, p. 392.

What I have learned is this: that the entire foundation of prayer must be established in humility, and that, the more a soul abases itself in prayer, the higher God raises it. I do not rememher that He has ever granted me any of the outstanding favors of which I shall speak later save when I have been consumed with shame by realizing my own wickedness.[27]

It is very clear that St. Teresa, to use a modern expression, was considered by the *Méthode* as the "mistress of prayer."

Did St. Teresa have any influence on the methodical meditation of the *Méthode?* St. Teresa is never quoted on this particular subject. And, as we have seen, the body of this prayer depends on the Ignatian School, whereas the general affections go back to Granada. There is no reason to see Teresian influence here, even though St. Teresa presents a short method which is similar to that of Granada.[28]

St. Teresa found that all could not use methodical meditation, so she suggests a book with which they might do meditative reading. The *Méthode*, gives the same advice granting the same liberty to its novices. Ordinarily there would be no reason to believe that St. Teresa is the source for this teaching in the *Méthode*, since it is given by many other spiritual writers; however, it is quite probable that she is the source in this particular case. It is true that the *Méthode* does not cite St. Teresa, but in the same counsel in which meditative reading is advocated, the *Méthode* presents another way of prayer for those having difficulty with mental prayer (the simple gazing on the sufferings of Christ without penetrating the mystery), and this time St. Teresa is quoted at length. Moreover, the citation is from the *Way of Perfection*, chapter twenty-six, the same chapter that contains the counsel on using a book to aid mental prayer.[29]

Finally, a word should be said on mixed prayer in the reform. The second part of the *Méthode,* which is very short (it contains three chapters), is given over to this form of prayer. Essentially it does not differ from meditation. A vocal prayer is used to bring about reflection that the mind itself does not feel capable of doing by itself. It seems, as we said before, that the *Méthode* could be influenced here by the Ignatian School, but it is probable that St. Teresa had some influence also. Now, St. Teresa had developed this form of prayer, and although she develops it even in the mystical state, still what she says, especially in

---

[27] *Complete Works,* I, *Life,* chap. xxii, p. 141.
[28] *Ibid.,* chap. xiii, pp. 82-83.
[29] *Méthode,* chap. xxiv, p. 382.

the *Way of Perfection*, can be used by beginners.[30] Although the models of mixed prayer developed in the *Méthode* contain neither the beauty nor sublimity of doctrine expressed by St. Teresa, the purpose is the same, namely, to lead the novices to more affective prayer that will dispose them to the prayer of contemplation. Mixed prayer is especially affective prayer.[31]

In presenting other ways of prayer to help those who cannot meditate, the *Méthode* presents the prayer of simply gazing at God (simple regard) and allowing the will to remain inclined toward Him. This we believe is similar to the prayer that St. Teresa recommends in the *Way of Perfection* when she tells her sisters: "I am not asking you to make long and subtle meditations... I am asking you to only look at Him."[32]

In the light of the above study we believe we are justified in concluding that St. Teresa and her teaching on prayer was an inspiration to the authors of the *Méthode*. They not only venerated this great saint, but assimilated her doctrine on prayer, in so far as it was instructive to beginners. They did not bind the novices to a rigid, formal method of meditation, but like St. Teresa granted them the greatest freedom, recognizing that the Holy Spirit is the first director of souls and leads them the way He wills. A method is only an aid to more perfect affective prayer. Influenced, no doubt, by St. Ignatius and his school, the authors of the *Méthode* also found in the writings of St. Teresa a guide for the ways of prayer in the reform. In this great "mistress of prayer" they found the true and genuine spirit of Carmel.

II – Spanish Discalced Carmelites

Besides St. Teresa's works there are other writers of the Discalced Carmelites who followed in the footsteps of St. Teresa and St. John, and who could have easily influenced the ways of prayer in the reform of Touraine. The first document of the Teresian reform in which we find a method of mental prayer is the *Instruccion de novicios Descalzos de la Virgen Maria del Monte Carmelo conforme a las costumbres de la misma Orden*.[33] It was published by the supreme council of

---

[30] *Complete Works*, II, chaps. xxvii to xxix, pp. 110-123.
[31] *Méthode*, chap. xxv, pp. 397-398.
[32] *Complete Works*, II, chap. xxvi, p. 107.
[33] Madrid, 1591. New edition by Fr. Evarist of the Virgin of Carmel (Toledo, 1925).

the Order. The signature of St. John of the Cross is among those who approved it.[34]

This method contains seven parts: preparation, reading, meditation, contemplation, thanksgiving, petition, epilogue. Among the authors was Father Aravalles (John of Jesus and Mary), who has also written a treatise on prayer in which he enumerates seven parts corresponding to the above.[35]

Father Jerome Gracian of the Mother of God, a close friend of St. Teresa, has also left us a small treatise on prayer in which he, too, divides meditation into seven parts.[36]

Father Gabriel of St. Mary Magdalen in his excellent book on Teresian prayer, from which we have derived these facts, believes that this septenary division may owe its origin to St. John of the Cross.[37] This method is original in that it presents *contemplation* as an ordinary part of meditation. For these Carmelites it consists in an affective colloquy between God and the soul. It is an application of the will to the conclusion of the reasoning and a prolonged delay on the known subject.[38] It is not to be identified with infused contemplation.

We shall pass over these treatises on mental prayer since there is no reason to believe they had any influence an the *Méthode*. In the first place, they were not popular in France in the first part of the seventeenth century, and most probably were not known or at least did not influence the reform of Touraine. In fact, we are inclined to believe that these treatises of the Spanish Discalced Carmelites had little influence at the beginning of the seventeenth century outside of Spain.

III – John of Jesus and mary of Calahorra (1564-1615)

Among the probable sources of the *Méthode* from the Discalced reform are the writings of Venerable John of Jesus and Mary of Calahorra (not to be confused with Aravalles), who was one of the

---

[34] It is difficult to know the concrete idea John of the Cross had on meditation other than it was indispensable for beginners. In his books he teaches only the moment when one should cease meditation in order to pass to contemplative prayer. Cf. Gabriel of St. Mary Magdalen, "L'École d'oraison carmelitaine," *Études carmélitaines*, 17 (Oct., 1932), 8.

[35] *Tratado de oración* (1587), edited by Fr. Evarist of the Virgin of Carmel (Toledo, 1926; second edition, Madrid, 1952).

[36] *De la oración mental y de sus partes y condiciones. Obras de P. Jerónimo Gracián de la Madre de Dios*, edit. by Silverio de S. Teresa (Burgos, 1932), I, 333-372.

[37] "Orazione e metodo" *La mística teresiana* (Fiesole, 1935), 61.

[38] Aravalles, *Tratado de oración*, ed. by Fr. Evarist, chap. vi, p. 28.

four great authorities of the Teresian reform, and the soul of the Italian Congregation. In 1611 he became the preposite-general of the Italian Congregation, and was instrumental in introducing the reform into France, Poland and Belgium. His spiritual formation began at Pastrana, Spain, where he made his novitiate in 1582 under the guidance of the immediate disciples of St. John of the Cross. Shortly after finishing the novitiate at the age of eighteen, he left for Genoa, Italy. Strangely enough, in his spiritual writings and even in his mystical doctrine he does not reflect any special influence of John of the Cross. On the other hand, he is a fervent and authoritative disciple of St. Teresa as well as an excellent theologian.[39] So well does his spirit typify the spirit of the Teresian reform that even today his *Instructio novitiorum* is used in the spiritual formation of the young friars.[40]

Venerable John of Jesus and Mary composed his spiritual works in Latin and for this reason many of them were well known in the reform of Touraine. John of St. Samson recommended to the novices the *Stimulus compunctionis* and the *Schola Jesu Christi*.[41] Father Dominic of St. Albert recommended these same works because they were written in the style of colloquies and dialogues.[42] Hugh of St. Francis also advises the novices to read and study the *Stimulus compunctionis*.[43] Perhaps the best-known work of John of Jesus and Mary is the *Instructio novitiorum*, which was first published in Latin at Rome as early as 1605. Still another work which we shall have occasion to mention, the *Schola in qua de oratione, contemplatione*, written originally in Italian, appeared in Latin in 1622. There is also the *Instructio magistri novitiorum*, published in Latin at Naples, 1608; Paris, 1612; Cologne, 1614.[44] The *Instructio novitiorum* attained great popularity and was translated into many modern languages. It is divided into four parts. The third part is on prayer.[45]

---

[39] For an accurate and brief biography of John of Jesus and Mary read Pier Giorgio del S. Cuore, O.C.D., *La Contemplazione secondo il Ven. P. Giovanni di Gesù Maria Carmelitano Scalzo* (Cremona [1950]), 15-19. See also Florencio del Niño Jesús, O.C.D., *El V.P. Fr. Juan de Jesús María, prepósito general de los Carmelitas Descalzos, 1564-1615; su vida sus escritos y sus virtudes* (Burgos, 1919), Both works contain a bibliography of his works.

[40] Théodore de Saint-Joseph, O.C.D., *L'Oraison d'apres l'école carmélitaine* (2nd edit., Bruges, 1929), 35.

[41] *Oeuvres*, I, *La Conduite des novices*, 915.

[42] *Exercitatio spiritualis*, in *AOC*, 11 (1940), 69.

[43] Hugh, *La Véritable idée*, II, 74.

[44] John of Jesus and Mary, *Opera omnia* (3 vols., Florence, 1771-1774), II, 502. We shall cite the *Opera omnia* in our references.

[45] English translation: *Instruction for Novices* (New York, 1925).

Venerable John departed from the primitive Spanish tradition of the reform on the parts of methodical prayer. He admitted only six, and refused to consider contemplation as the seventh. "There are certain spiritual writers," says John, "who enumerate contemplation among the parts of prayer, but this is an obstacle for beginners – because forcing themselves to contemplate they lose time and often the whole fruit of prayer."[46] It seems at first glance that John differs from the traditional Carmelite School, but actually there is no doctrinal difference. There is only a difference of terminology. John of Jesus and Mary, following St. Teresa, considered contemplation in its strict sense as a mystical prayer and, therefore, could not list it among the parts of methodical prayer. On the other hand, the traditional Carmelite method in Spain used the term contemplation in a wide sense, that is, to mean the affective colloquy which flows normally from reflection or meditation, and which pertains necessarily to the very essence of methodical prayer. Consequently, it may truly be said that John of Jesus and Mary presented in six parts the same method of prayer that traditionally was presented in seven parts to the novices of the Teresian reform.

But what did Venerable John of Jesus and Mary teach concerning methodical prayer? He divided it into six parts: the preparation, reading, meditation, thanksgiving, oblation and petition. He explains meditation with minute precision; he multiplies counsels, warnings and rules. Although his method is precise and methodical, he recognized that prayer is above all a work of grace, and that the method must be adapted to suit each individual. His method is predominantly affective. In this he is a faithful disciple of St. Teresa, for whom progress in prayer is not to think much but to love much. This affective prayer still characterizes the whole Discalced Carmelite School, for whom ways of prayer are only means to sublime contemplation.

Did the method of Venerable John of Jesus and Mary have any influence on the methodical meditation of the reform of Touraine? Let us compare the methods of prayer found in the *Instructio novitiorum* and the *Méthode*. But before doing so, let us recall that Philip Thibault is said to have spent two years at the monastery of S. Maria della Scala in Rome, were he learned the methods of prayer taught to Discalced Carmelite novices. It is said also that he spent six weeks in the novitiate of the Discalced in Paris in 1616. If this is true, then Philip certainly learned of the method of prayer of Venerable John of

---

[46] *Opera omnia*, II, *Schola de oratione*, 509.

Jesus and Mary, since it was taught to the novices. Later, he would hardly be silent about such matters when the reform of Touraine under his leadership would begin to prepare instructions for its own novices.[47]

Prayer, which is the elevation of the soul to God, says Ven. John of Jesus and Mary, has three parts: the preparation, the body (meditation) and the conclusion (affections). These are again subdivided into the six parts enumerated above. The *Méthode* proposes the same three parts, but adds resolutions among the affections.[48]

The preparation is remote and proximate. The former consists in avoiding the occasion of distractions, the renunciation of all inordinate solicitude about things.[49] The *Méthode* proposes substantially the same doctrine in four points.[50]

The proximate preparation and the reading are separate parts. This preparation consists of a twofold consideration. First, a consideration of the divine majesty and, secondly, of our own vileness, which awakens humility and contrition for our sins.[51] Then follows the reading which may come before or after the proximate preparation. It should not be made for the sake of learning, but to excite the will to the love of God.[52] The *Méthode* makes the reading part of the proximate preparation, and adds an immediate preparation which contains the acts of the Venerable John's proximate preparation.[53]

The second part of prayer, meditation, is an act of the intellect.

Meditation is nothing else than a process of reasoning on the part of the intellect by which it impels the will to good or turns it from evil. For this reason, meditation... should be used as a means by which the will may attach itself to good. One ought to avoid with equal care making it too long or too short, but should subordinate it entirely to the particular needs of the heart, so that when the will becomes inflamed it may be interrupted and resumed again when the affections grow weak.[54]

Substantially the same doctrine may be read in the *Méthode*, where this subject is more developed. "Meditation is a *discursus*

---

[47] See above, p. 9, note 29.
[48] Chap. ii, p. 35; chap. xi, p. 144.
[49] *Opera omnia*, III, *Instructio novitiorum*, 205.
[50] Chap. iii, pp. 40-41.
[51] *Ibid., Instructio novitiorum*, 206.
[52] *Ibid.*
[53] Chap: III, pp. 42 ff.
[54] *Opera omnia*, III, *Instructio novitiorum*, 206.

formed by the intellect... from which are elicited practical conclusions and by which the will is impelled efficaciously to embrace the known good and flee evil."[55] And again, "... the *discursus* should terminate as quickly as possible in affections. The general rule is to cease the *discursus* as soon as the will is *surely* inflamed."[56]

The affections follow from the meditation.

More time and attention should be given to eliciting the affections than to the meditation. This is so true that, generally speaking, the more excellent will the prayer be, on account of the numerous affections with which it is enriched.[57]

The *Méthode* would lead to the same conclusion. Speaking of those who are not able to make *discursus*, it proposes a way of eliciting affections without this reasoning process, and then adds: "The best prayer is not that which fills the intellect with a great number of thoughts and ideas, but rather that which proceeds from a perfect will, followed by greater fidelity in overcoming bad habits and in exercising the virtues."[58] And again we are warned to elicit affections immediately when we feel the will inflamed, even if the will is aroused by a simple glance of the truth without any *discursus*.[59] Finally, "if the heart has been gained to God, then everything has been gained, because knowledge is not as necessary as love."[60] Indeed, "too much emphasis must not be given to the intellect."[61]

The *Instructio novitiorum* next considers the subject matter of meditation.

Meditation is made in two ways: Either on sensible things that the mind may represent to itself under corporal images, such as the circumstances of Our Lord's passion; or on intellectual subjects such as the goodness and beauty of God. The latter may also be conceived under corporal images; it is not however strictly necessary...[62]

The *Méthode* presents the same division, although it makes no mention of an artificial corporeal image for spiritual subjects.[63]

---

[55] Chap. v, p. 63.
[56] Chap. xxiv, p. 376.
[57] *Opera omnia*, III, *Instructio novitiorum*, 206.
[58] Chap. xxiv, no. 9, p. 382.
[59] Chap. ix, p. 120; chap. xxiv, pp. 376-377.
[60] Chap. xxiv, no. 1, p. 372.
[61] Chap. ix, p. 120.
[62] *Opera omnia*, III, 206.
[63] Chap. vi, p. 73.

The conclusion of the meditation, according to John of Jesus and Mary, should contain acts of thanksgiving, oblation and petition. Thanksgiving may be an act of gratitude or praise. Then follows the offering.

As the heart which is animated by the spirit seeks to do all in its power for the benefactor, so the offering by which we strive to fulfill this task follows the thanksgiving in natural order The petition very appropriately comes last, for it is but just to demand that for which the price has been offered.

We should ask first for ourselves and then for the whole Church and mankind. We should petition absolutely for graces that pertain to sanctity, but ask only conditionally for temporal things.[64]

We have seen above in a previous chapter that the *Méthode* gives these same general affections that usually have part in every meditation. There is, however, one important difference. The *Méthode* gives four general affections, adding resolutions to the other three. "The whole fruit of the affections consists in eliciting good and efficacious resolutions.[65] The *Instructio novitiorum* does not give much emphasis to resolutions. However, elsewhere we read:

Resolutions should be made when one is moved to acts of virtue. It is, necessary to make many resolutions to perform the works necessary for the acquisition of virtue, and to use much effort to overcome difficulties. In these affections we should delay as long as possible.[66]

Affections in the method of John of Jesus and Mary are the predominant acts of meditation. He recognizes the necessity of resolutions, but does not accentuate their importance with the same finality that we find in the *Méthode*. Nor would he make them one of the parts of methodical meditation. He places them as an integral part of the examination of conscience which is performed twice each day.[67]

In completing his treatise on methodical meditation John of Jesus and Mary proposed sixteen counsels in the *Instructio novitiorum*.[68] Many of these are repeated in his other works.[69] A comparison of these counsels with the *dubia circa meditationem* in the *Méthode* shows a striking similarity. They both caution a moderate use of the imagina-

---

[64] *Opera omnia*, II, *Schola de oratione*, 521.
[65] Chap. xi, p. 144.
[66] *Opera omnia*, II, *Schola de oratione*, 512.
[67] Théodore of St. Joseph, *L'Oraison d'après l'école carmélitaine*, 5.
[68] *Opera omnia*, III, 206-207.
[69] *Opera omnia*, II, *Schola de oratione*, 509-521.

tion in prayer; the inspiration of the Holy Spirit should be followed in eliciting affections, even if they differ from the subject prepared; reasoning should cease when the will is inflamed; too ardent affections should be moderated; all parts of methodical meditation should be used, but this is not necessary if the will is occupied with affections; those who suffer great distractions should recollect their souls before prayer; it is also useful to use a book or practise mixed prayer; it is not necessary to converse with God in the second person when eliciting affections; we may also speak to our soul, to the saints, to creatures.

These are some of the more important counsels in which both methods are in agreement. There is no great or major discordance or difference in their teaching. Both are affective methods, although the *Méthode* has given greater emphasis to the part of resolutions in prayer. Secondly, the *Méthode* teaches the novices how to prolong the points of meditation, an artifice which is not found in the *Instructio novitiorurn*.

The obvious similarity of these methods, both of which are long and perfectly developed, raises the question as to the dependence of the *Méthode* upon the *Instructio novitiorum*. The latter work was published in 1605. It could have easily been, like some of John's other writings, in the hands of the reformers of the province of Touraine. However, we have not been able to find any proof of this. And the similarity of doctrine on meditation does not warrant a conclusion of dependency. All the parts of meditation and the doctrine on methodical prayer existed before the *Instructio novitiorum* and the *Méthode*. John of Jesus and Mary received his teaching not only from St. Teresa but from Louis of Granada, whom he highly esteemed. For he recommended the writings of Granada to novice masters.[70] Like Granada, John of Jesus and Mary divides meditation into the same six parts, and follows the same affective method. The *Méthode*, too, as we have seen, was influenced both by St. Teresa and Louis of Granada. Hence, even though we cannot say that the *Méthode* depends upon the writings of John of Jesus and Mary for its teaching on meditation, we can at least say that the similary and concordance of their methods especially in regard to the affections may be explained by the fact that they used the same common sourees – St. Teresa and Louis of Granada.

---

[70] *Instructio magistri novitiorum*, editio critica by Anastasius of St. Paul, O.C.D. (Rome, 1929), chap. vi, p. 24. Florencio del Niño Jesús, O.C.D., *El V. P. Fr. Juan de Jesús Maria* (Burgos, 1919), 58. John of Jesus and Mary also recommended the treatises of Francis Arias on prayer and mortification to the novice masters (*Instructio magistri novitiorum*, 24). Cardinal Lercaro clearly states that the Discalced Carmelites have taken Granada's method in its essential elements. Cf. *Metodi*, 197.

The Presence of God

In the *Instructio novitiorum* John of Jesus and Mary speaks of the exercise of the presence of God in our daily actions.[71] It is a short chapter composed of seven counsels which are full of wisdom.

He recommends an imaginary or intellectual act of the presence of God. He does not mention an affective presence of God after the manner of the *Méthode*. But he does join aspirations and ejaculatory prayers with this exercise as the normal and best way to practise it.

He desires that all things, especially our fellowmen in whom we should see the brothers of Christ, be used as a means to elevate the mind to God. He ends this short chapter with the words: "Finally, let them be fully convinced that nearly all the science of the spiritual life is contained in the few counsels given in this chapter, so that if they neglect these they can never hope to become spiritual men."[72]

In these short counsels John of Jesus and Mary gives the fundamental principles of the practise of the presence of God that are found in many authors, and are enlarged and greatly developed in the *Méthode*. The latter, however, develops especially the affective presence of God. It develops many ways of living in God's presence that do not seem to be developed in the works of the Venerable John of Jesus and Mary.

Aspirative Prayer

John of Jesus and Mary treats aspirative prayer separately from the exercise of the presence of God, although he does not separate them in practice. He writes of aspirative prayer in his *Theologia mystica* and therefore does not consider it an ordinary practise for beginners or novices.[73] His procedure is understandable, for he considers aspirative prayer as an advanced prayer and an easy and short way that leads to mystical theology, that is, contemplation. He is not original in this opinion, and says all the authors that he read agree that aspirative prayer elevates the soul to the deepest knowledge, sense and experience of God.

Aspirative prayer, therefore, is not for all. It presupposes some progress in mental prayer, as well as progress in virtue. Those who are so advanced should join imaginative and intellectual presence of God

---

[71] *Opera omnia*, III, 214.
[72] *Ibid.*, 215.
[73] *Ibid.*, II, 446-447.

with aspirations and anagogical motions. This kind of prayer is not for lazy people. It demands an energetic soul; but all types of people, even the most simple, will find it helpful to live in intimate familiarity with God. They should try to inflame their souls at all times, that is, wherever they are, in public or private, while eating, while speaking, etc. It is a prayer for all times, and should be interspersed throughout the actions of the day. He gives many very fine examples of aspirations that he invites his readers to imitate.

In this short exposition we do not find anything new on aspirative prayer. John, as he himself tells us, follows the general teaching. He recommends practically the same teaching as in the *Méthode*. But it is not as long or as instructive. There is no reason to believe that the *Méthode* depends upon John for its doctrine on aspirative prayer.

In conclusion, it is evident that the reform of Touraine and the Discalced Carmelites of the Congregation of Italy proposed similar methods of prayer for their novices – methods above all affective and perfectly designed to lead to higher, contemplative prayer. This is especially true of their methods of meditation. Both these methods are being used today. The Carmelites of the Ancient Observance still instruct their novices with the method of Touraine, which has been reproduced almost to the letter in the new *Directorium carmelitanum*. Likewise, the Discalced Carmelite Friars still use the method of Venerable John of Jesus and Mary in the spiritual formation of their novices.[74]

---

[74] Théodore of St. Joseph, *L'Oraison d'après l'école carmélitaine*, 35.

Chapter XII

ST. FRANCIS DE SALES

St. Francis de Sales (1567-1672) was one of the greatest men in the seventeenth century in France, and one of the most lovable saints in the Church. His influence on the spiritual writers of his own time as well as in subsequent centuries is a generally conceded fact. Our particular interest is to find whether he had any influence in the spiritual formation of Touraine and especially on the ways of prayer taught in the reform.

This great saint published his famous book *Introduction à la vie dévote (Philothea) in* 1608 and it became immensely popular. It was followed by *Traité de l'amour de Dieu (Theotimus)*, 1616.

Were these books known and used in the reform of Touraine? We know that St. Francis de Sales was a close friend of the Carmelite Robert Berthelot, of the Carmel of Lyon, who became the titular bishop of Damascus and the suffragan bishop of Lyon. It was this same Robert Berthelot who assisted St. Francis de Sales on his death bed. Berthelot never took an actual part in the reform of Touraine, but he favored it and before his death in 1630 he had corresponded often with Thibault, the father of the reform, and had given him encouragement and advice.[1]

John of St. Samson makes no mention of Francis de Sales. Yet he must have held him in high esteem. John often gave counsel to the bishop of Dol, Most Reverend Anthony de Revol, who was a close friend of Francis de Sales.[2] It is hardly possible that Revol never talked of his good friend, whose reputation for sanctity was well known in France before his death in 1622. Dominic of St. Albert is also silent concerning Francis de Sales. It is true that Father Simpli-

---

[1] *BC*, I, col. 687. Hugh, *La Véritable idée*, I, 231.
[2] Bouchereaux, *La Réforme des Carmes,* 163.

cianus of St. Francis (died 1710), translator into French of Dominic's *Exercitatio spiritualis* and other works, includes the writings of Francis de Sales among the books recommended by Dominic for students.[3] However, this citation seems to be an interpolation, because the original Latin text of the *Directio spiritualis pro studentibus*, although it mentions the *Imitatio Christi*, is silent concerning St. Francis de Sales.[4]

Hugh of St. Francis, an historian of the reform, who often cites books read by the novices, likewise makes no mention of St. Francis de Sales. Neither does the *Méthode* refer to the Saint of Geneva. However, Leo of St. John, disciple of John of St. Samson and a leader in the reform, whom we mentioned in chapter one, has written a panegyric of St. Francis de Sales that contains these amusing words:

> Theotimus is food for stronger and learned men. Philothea is sweet honey for the weaker and devout sex. I urge you again, and I insist: Are you a man? Read Theotimus. Are you a woman? Read Philothea.[5]

Elsewhere, without making the above distinction, he recommends the works of de Sales for meditative reading, which Leo calls mixed prayer because it is prayer composed with study.[6]

Our inability to find other writers of Touraine who cite St. Francis de Sales is, of course, only a weak argument against the spiritual influence the Saint of Geneva may have had on the ways of prayer in the reform. It remains for us to compare the ordinary ways of prayer taught by St. Francis with the ways of prayer in the *Méthode*.

St. Francis de Sales wrote his *Philothea* for every rank and class of society, for the religious, the priest, the nun, the artisan, the widow, the bride. Among other things it includes a simple method of mental prayer[7] and an exercise on the presence of God.[8]

He divides the exercise of mental prayer into preparation, meditation, affections and resolutions, conclusion. The preparation consists of an act of the presence of God.[9] Four different ways of making this act are presented. This is followed by an invocation which contains an

---

[3] Manuscript Orleans 1430, 196 ff. 221. This text is used by Bouchereaux, *La Réforme des Carmes*, 336

[4] Chap. xiii, *AOC*, 11 (1940), p. 69.

[5] See *BC*, I, col. 239.

[6] *Studium sapientiae*, III, 219.

[7] *Oeuvres*, III, Part II, chaps. ii-vii, pp. 73-83.

[8] *Ibid.*, chaps. xii-iii, pp. 91-100.

[9] *Ibid,.* chap. ii, p. 74.

act of humility and a petition to pray well. The saints may also be invoked.[10] Then comes the *compositio loci*,[11] if this is necessary.

This preparation is followed by the act of meditation, which is a reflection on truths and is ordered toward affections.[12] The affections follow, which are the fruit of reflection. These affections are love of God and neighbor, zeal, joy, compassion, sorrow, etc. They should be converted into specific resolutions which are the special fruit of meditation.[13]

The whole exercise concludes with the special acts of thanksgiving, oblation and petition.[14] These acts may be made in the form of colloquies with God, the saints, etc.

The hour meditation concludes with the Our Father and the Hail Mary. From the meditation we should gather a nosegay, that is, collect a few striking thoughts from the meditation to think about during the day.

The Saint recognized that not all can meditate. So, like St. Teresa, he recommends reading and vocal prayer for these souls.

It takes but a glance to see the harmony of this method both as to form and doctrine with the *Méthode*. One sees in this method an affective tendency that leads meditation toward the contemplative way. Indeed, Francis calls his method "prayer of the heart."[15] It is reminiscent of Granada and his method of prayer: One also sees the influence of the *Exercises* of St. Ignatius. Of all the methods we have found prior to the *Méthode* this one of St. Francis de Sales emphasizes more than the others the necessity of resolutions in meditation.[16] His special emphasis on this point together with the expression that resolutions are the fruit of meditation is more like the doctrine of the *Méthode* than the other methods previously proposed. Could it be that the *Méthode* depends upon St. Francis de Sales for this practical doctrine? We are unable to answer this question.

The nosegay of thoughts taken from the meditation and to beconsidered by many as unique in the Salesian method. Yet, we find in the *Méthode* something similar, but explained in less delightful and picturesque language.

---

[10] *Ibid.*, chap. iii, p. 77.
[11] *Ibid.*, chap. iv, p. 78.
[12] *Ibid.*, chap. v, pp. 79-80.
[13] *Ibid.*, chap. viii, p. 83.
[14] *Ibid.*, chaps. vii and viii, pp. 82-86.
[15] *Ibid.*, chap. viii, p. 84.
[16] *Ibid.*, chap. viii; pp. 83-84.

Let us compare the texts. St. Francis writes:

> To this I would add that we should gather a little nosegay of devotion. When we walk in a beautiful garden, we usually gather some few choice flowers, inhale their fragrance, and carry them away with us; retaining and enjoying them through the day. So when our mind has fed upon some mystery by meditation, we should select some few points which especially strike us and are most calculated to benefit us, and dwell upon them, inhaling their spiritual fragrance. And this we should strive to do in the place in which we have been engaged in meditation, or in solitude afterwards.[17]

We read in the *Méthode:*

> One should try to be recollected all day long by using ejaculatory prayers and by recalling the good affections that one has felt in meditation. Avoid curiosity and too much talking. It is also good to recall the good resolutions [of the meditation] and renew them during the day.[18]

The Presence of God

When we come to the exercise of the presence of God in the writings of St. Francis we again see a great likeness between his teaching and that of the *Méthode*, a likeness that bespeaks more than merely agreement on fundamental principles.

The presence of God is imaginary or intellectual, and there are many ways to practise it. 1) Think of God as everywhere. 2) Think of God within you. 3) Imagine Christ in his sacred humanity present in heaven looking down at you. 4) Imagine the same Christ near you or really present in the Eucharist.[19]

This presence of God is joined with aspirations:

> The whole world, says St. Augustine, following St. Anthony, speaks to them in silent but intelligible language of their love, everything excites them to holy thoughts, whence arise countless and elevating aspirations after God.[20]

In chapter twelve of the second part of the *Philothea* St. Francis exhorts us to the pactise of the presence of God by any of the four ways mentioned above. Attention, however, is first given to being near Jesus or with Him in whom we find repose, far from the cares of the

---

[17] *Ibid.*, chap. vii, p. 82-83.
[18] *Méthode*, chap. xxiv, pp. 394-395.
[19] *Oeuvres*, III, *Philothea*, Part II, chap. ii, pp. 74-76.
[20] *Ibid.*, chap. xiii, p. 96.

world. The second way is to think of Him within us. We should make the heart an oratory, where we turn to God even when greatly occupied. Ejaculations flow from this exercise.

In the next chapter St. Francis presents two other ways of practising the presence of God.[21] The first is to collect holy thoughts and ejaculations which we use during our daily actions to keep close to God, although it is best to use ejaculations that arise freely from within our own souls. There are," he says, "many useful collections of vocal aspirations, but I would advise you not to confine yourself to any formal words; rather use those which are prompted by the feelings of your heart, as you need them: they will never fail you."

We do not find in St. Francis the threefold division of imaginary, intellectual and affective presence of God, in the way it is found in the *Méthode*. The affective presence of God is really for advanced souls. However, the exercises of the presence of God taught by the saintly bishop of Geneva are all found in the *Méthode*, namely, the use of a collection of ejaculations, the elevation of the mind to God through creatures, thinking of the humanity of Christ and thinking of God within us. The *Méthode* also adds another distinct exercise, namely, seeing God operating in all things and accepting everything from the hands of divine providence. But St. Francis includes this in the exercise of finding God in all creatures. It is also worth observing that both speak of making the heart an oratory where we think of God indwelling. St. Francis presents this to Philothea as an ordinary practise. The *Méthode* is more cautious and considers it a sublime practise for advanced souls that are on the threshold of the mystical life.[22] It is difficult to understand why the *Méthode* restricts this practise to only spiritually advanced souls.[23]

Aside from this difference the exercise of the presence of God is substantially the same in both authors, although the *Méthode* tends always most explicitly toward a more affective prayer that leads to contemplation, which is the goal of every prayer.

Aspirative prayer as explained and developed in the *Méthode* (where it is considered the effect of meditation that has been long and well practised) is not touched upon by St. Francis. He speaks of aspi-

---

[21] *Ibid.*, chap. xiii, pp. 94-100.

[22] Chap. xxxvi, p. 607.

[23] However, it could be following here the theory of introversion explained by the mystical writers of the sixteenth and seventeenth centuries, and which John of St. Samson, following the writers like Ruysbroeck, Harphius, Blosius and Barbanson, explains as a very advanced way of prayer beyond the grasp of the ordinary young novices.

rations and ejaculations as necessary for every spiritual state of life, but he does not develop or explain the nature of aspirative prayer as an affective prayer that leads to contemplative prayer. We shall see in the next chapter that the *Méthode* depends upon John of St. Samson for its explanation of aspirative prayer.

What shall we conclude? The similarity of teaching on the fundamental points of meditation and the exercise of the presence of God does not allow us to conclude that the *Philothea* was definitely a source of the *Méthode*. It is quite probable that both works depend on a mutual source, i.e., St. Ignatius, his disciples, Granada and St. Teresa. Yet we do feel that the teaching of St. Francis on resolutions in meditation is more strongly emphasized than in other earlier methods. In this point especially we see a likeness of the *Philothea* with the *Méthode*.

CHAPTER XIII

THE CARMELITES OF THE TOURAINE REFORM

I – VEN. JOHN OF ST. SAMSON

Venerable John of St. Samson, Carmelite of the province of Tours, was one of the greatest spiritual men of seventeenth century France. Like his predecessors in Spain, St. Teresa and St. John of the Cross, he wrote of the higher states of the mystical life, which he actually experienced. However, his writings lack the clarity and the charm of the Spanish mystics. Just as St. Teresa became the mother of the spiritual revival among the Discalced Carmelites of Spain, so John of St. Samson was the soul of the new spiritual movement that came to life in the reformed province of Touraine.

In this chapter we propose to determine more definitely the influence of John of St. Samson on the ways of prayer in the *Méthode*. How great was his influence? Did his ideas on prayer and the mystical life, to which he believed all are called, extend to the simple methods of prayer that were taught to the novice? Before answering these questions we shall say something about the man himself.[1]

John of St. Samson was baptized Jean de Moulin. Stricken with a serious illness at the age of three, he became totally blind. Yet his blindness did not hinder him from a life of study. He became in time a skilled organist, and often played in the Carmelite church in Paris. He

---

[1] Bouchereaux, *La Réforme des Carmes*. This contains the most recent and the best critical life of John of St. Samson. Cf. also Brenninger, O. Carm.: "De Ven. Joanne a S. Samsone," in *AOC*, 7 (1930-1931), 224-258. This is a short life and explanation of his mystical doctrine and a bibliography of those who have written on his life and works. H. Bremond, *Histoire du sentiment religieux*, 11, 372, refers to John as one of France's exalted mystics.

was intensely pious, perhaps even a mystic, before he sought entrance into the Order at the age of thirty-five. He first confessed his desire to became a religious to young Father Matthew Pinault, who was finishing his studies in Paris, and was about to return to his monastery in Dol. John entered the unreformed monastery of Dol in 1606, but later was transferred in 1612 to the cradle of the reform at Rennes. Here, according to the statutes of the reform, he made a second novitiate and began soon to edify all by his sincere love of the interior life. His knowledge and his experience of the higher ways of prayer so impressed his superiors that they ordered him not only to instruct the novices and young clerics, but also to put in writing his doctrine of the spiritual life. John did not relish the task of teaching the young religious, since his lack of theological training made him feel unqualified. Nevertheless, he complied with the wishes of his superiors and for twenty years instructed the novices at Rennes. During this time he left Rennes for one year only to help start the reform at Dol. His spiritual doctrine soon attracted attention outside the Order. Frequently distinguished visitors, such as Anthony Revol, Bishop of Dol, came to consult him. When death finally came to John in 1636 the Carmelites realized that they had lost a saint, the very soul of the reform, who had been sent by God to restore the contemplative spirit of Carmel to France.

Some of the writings of Brother John were first published in French in 1651 at Paris and again in 1656 by Father Donatian of St. Nicholas, one of John's many secretaries, under the title: *La Vie, les maximes et partie des oeuvres du trés excellent contemplatif, le V.F. Jean de S. Samson, aveugle des le berceau et religieux laic de l'ordre des Carmes reformes*. In 1654 Father Mathurin of St. Anne published at Lyon the Latin version of Father Donatian's work: *Vita, theoremata et opuscula insignis mystae, V.F. Joannis a S. Samsone coeci ab incunabulis, laici Ordinis Carmelitarum Reformatorum, provinciae Turoniae*. Finally, in 1658 and 1659 Father Donatian collected many of the writings of Brother John in two tomes which he prefaced with a compendium of the life and spiritual principles of the author. This edition, which we frequently cited in the course of this study, has many imperfections. It is not always easy to distinguish the thought of the author from that of the editor. A critical edition of all the known works, in so far as this is possible, is now under consideration. A list of the writings of John, both printed and manuscript, that are known today can be found in the frequently quoted work of Miss Bouchereaux.[2]

---

[2] Bouchereaux, *La Réforme des Carmes*, 12-15.

It is quite evident that the published works of John were not available when the *Méthode* was being prepared. However, the manuscripts were in the hands of various members of the province. We know, for example, that Bernard of St. Magdalen possessed a few, because after the death of Brother John, Father Joseph of Jesus and Father Boniface of St. Euphrasia made inventories of all the manuscripts of Brother John, and complained that Bernard had some that he was reluctant to relinquish.[3]

Turning to the blind brother's teaching on ordinary mental prayer,[4] we find that he recommends the three ways of prayer, that is, meditation, mixed prayer and aspirative prayer, that form the three principal divisions of the *Méthode*.[5] He also recognizes the traditional division of the three ages of the spiritual life that are also found in the *Méthode*.[6]

Moreover, certain patented expressions, such as "internal loving conversatian with God" and "introversion," which are found in the *Méthode* to explain the goal to be obtained by using methods of prayer, are found frequently in the writings of John of St. Samson. In fact, the phrase "internal loving conversation with God" is found in almost all the spiritual documents of Touraine. It is a phrase that was burnt into the minds of the reformers by their master, the blind brother of Rennes.

Brother John does not give us, as far as we know, a detailed method of meditation. Yet, he does give some instructions that we shall see are in perfect harmony with the teachings of the *Méthode*. He called meditation the daily bread of religious and composed a set of meditations for a ten-day retreat.[7] In these he proposes a method beginning with immediate preparation, followed by meditation, affections and resolutions, and at the end, the prayer of petition. He seems to indicate that the meditation be made according to a method already known to the religious.

It is necessary to place yourself in the presence of God in a lively manner by a very brief and affectionate colloquy according to the ardor of your desire. Then enter into the matter. Digest it well and in an orderly manner. Then make resolutions according to the prescribed form. When you feel

---

[3] *Ibid.*, 12.

[4] Like St. John of the Cross, John of St. Samson is best known for his mystical doctrine. For studies on his mystical doctrine we refer the reader to the above-mentioned works of Miss Bouchereaux and Father Brenninger.

[5] Bouchereaux, *La Réforme des Carmes*, 212, 215.

[6] *Ibid.*, 211.

[7] John Brenninger, O. Carm., "Joannes a S. Samsone de animo et ingenio Ordinis Carmelitarum," *AOC*, 8 (1932), 22.

yourself entirely dry in prayer, take the subject matter in hand and read it so as to receive some light and then return to pray. Ordinarily you should pass one hour each evening in prayer... Remember to pray for all those who have been recommended to your prayers at the end of each exercise.[8]

Following this prologue the blind brother introduces thirty meditations. The first ten consider creation and the fall, sin and the four last things. Then follow meditations on the vows, true devotion, simplicity, modesty, the love of God under different aspects and finally zeal. In each meditation four or five considerations are presented followed by affections and resolutions.[9]

From the foregoing it is obvious that the blind brother's writings on meditation are brief and concise. At no time does he take great pains to teach a method. He seems to follow principles and practises common to all spiritual writers of the time.

But a difficulty presents itself. In the preface of the *Méthode* we read that the method contained therein is the traditional practise of the reform. "This was the practise and method which was taught and observed and always practised in our observance from the beginning to the present time." How then can we reconcile the teaching of Ven. John of St. Samson with this method?

The difference in methods is only apparent. In the first place, John of St. Samson had no intention of writing a complete method of prayer for novices. In his meditations for the ten-day retreat he does not even mention the passion of Christ, which elsewhere he tells us should be the principal subject of prayer. "The more ordinary subject of prayer should be the holy passion of Our Lord."[10] Furthermore, in these same meditations he was not concerned with the theory of prayer for the novices, but with the practise for all religious, even the perfect. "I am sure these exercises will be helpful not only to pious souls, who are good people, but even in general to all souls, even the perfect."[11] It seems, then, that the prologue to these meditations was not an attempt to outline a method for the religious, but simply to recall to their minds some of the salient steps of a method already known and practised by them.

Moreover, in the *Conduite des novices* that the blind brother wrote for novice masters we fail to find a method, but his suggestion of au-

---

[8] *Oeuvres*, I, *Méditations pour les retraites*, 530.
[9] *Ibid.*, 529-586.
[10] *Ibid.*, II, *La Conduite des novice*, 912.
[11] *Ibid.*, I, *Méditations pour les retraites*, 530.

thors who have written on this subject enlightens us as to the method he preferred. Among others he seems to have an attraction to Granada. Concerning Granada, whose works were popular in many countries of Europe, he says: "... the directors shall place in their hands some books that treat fully of these matters, as for example, the *Week of Granada*, assigning to them the meditation he has composed on sin and human miseries."[12]

John also had the highest admiration for Granada's *Guía de pecadores* and recognized it as the source of many other treatises on sin.[13]

John also recommended his own writings to the novice masters as well as certain selections from Constantine of Barbanson.

And if the director [of novices] is the kind I expect him to be, then he will use our exercises, and a good part of our writings, omitting that which is of no help to himself or to anyone else. He should also use the first part of the Direction of Barbanson [*Sentiers secrets*]. But he should be imbued with his spirit, because the book is not at all organized and divided, as Granada's book, and others. It will be very helpful to him, if he can use the theory and the simple and mystical wisdom it contains. For those who make progress it is very expedient that the director leads them according to this practise, since it is very like to my spirit and has the true order of perfect wisdom.[14]

---

[12] *Ibid.*, II, 904: The *Méthode* warns the novices not to use other books of meditation. However, as we bave seen, it also esteemed the writings of Granada, teaches the same doctrine, and offers the novices a similar method with meditations that are very similar to those of Granada.

[13] *Ibid.*, 902. The *Méthode* has some meditations on the horror of sin that echo the thought of Granada.

[14] *Ibid.* Fr. Constantine of Barbanson (1582-1631) was a Belgian Capuchin of the province of Cologne. He wrote two spiritual works. His *Sentiers secrets de l'amour divin* was printed in Latin the first time in 1623 at Cologne and again in 1634, 1636 and 1639. German and Latin translations followed. The text of the original French edition (probably edited in 1617) was reedited in 1932 with a preface of the editor and with notes. An English translation is *The Secret Paths of Divine Love*, abridged and edited by Dom Justin McCann (New York, 1928). His second work is less known: *L'Anatomie de l'âme et des opérations divines en icelle, qui est une addition, au livre des Secrets sentiers de l'amour divin.* Editions in 1635 and 1638. Barbanson was influenced by the trend of his times. The spiritual writers of the 16th and 17th centuries have a special word to explain union with God in the depths of the soul. This word is "introversion" and is found often in the *Sentiers secrets.* Barbanson teaches us not to go outside ourselves in search of God, but to find Him within ourselves. It is this introversion that appealed to John of St. Samson in the writings of Barbanson. The latter treats all the degrees of prayer beginning with meditation and ending with the unitive way. He does not, however, present a method of prayer for beginners, but suggests the following works: *Pratique de l'oraison mentale ou contemplative* by Matthias Bellintani de Salo, Capuchin; *Traicté de l'oraison mentale* of Francis Arias, S.J., and *La Mystère de la flagellation de N.S.J.C. mis en forme de méditation pour chacque jour de la*

A further study of his writings shows that the blind brother teaches that the *discursus* is always subordinate to the affections. The *discursus* should not be long, since meditation is an affective exercise. Meditation should become an affective meditation as soon as possible. Affective and brief colloquies are recommended.[15] This is the same advice that we have found in the *Méthode* when it speaks of affective prayer.[16]

John of St. Samson explains the subordination of the intellect to the will by the example of the dog that hunts its prey. John, it is true, uses this example when he explains the nature of aspirations, but from all his writings there is no doubt that the will is the supreme faculty in prayer. We have found the same example of the hunting dog used in the *Méthode* to explain this same subordination of the intellect to the will. Both John and the *Méthode* depend upon Granada for this example. The blind mystic writes:

It is necessary that the continual practise and exercise of aspirations follow from meditation and affective, easy prayer. It is not necessary that here the understanding is again filled up with thoughts of divine things, for having seen and known them sufficiently well, it ought to give them to the will to inflame it and nourish it. Because just as a hunter uses a dog to track down the prey, but does not allow the dog to devour it, so the intellect should not extend its service other than to give light and discover truth. The intellect should not be allowed to have its own way, but when it has penetrated the truth sufficiently, the will ought to take it for its own supernatural food, and try to move and inflame itself as well as it can. I should have more to say on this subject, but it is too ordinary and too detailed. The mystics,

---

semaine by Bernardine of Balbano, Capuchin. These, he says, are well known and solid authors. Hence, he adds only a little advice: "Livres tres connus et necessaires a tout vrai amateur de l'oraison mentale, sont clairs et si exacts en ce fait, enseignant le tout si particulierment, qu'il n'est besoin de rien ajouter. Seulement donc je toucherai ici quelques points brevement" (*Sentiers secrets,* Part II, p. 118, quoted from the edition of 1932). We may take it for granted that the works of Barbanson were well known to the authors of the *Méthode,* because they would be expected to follow John's advice. Whether they used the Capuchin's works as a source is not easy to say. Probably not, since they were not written for beginners. One notices, however, the word "introversion" in the *Méthode,* and also a practise of the presence of God according to the three theological virtues that is similar, but on a much lower level, to a practise recommended by Barbanson to those in the mystical state. Barbanson also considers meditation as the foundation and the support of aspirations. These points of similarity were common in the 17th century to many spiritual writers, and are found in John's writings too; hence, there is no reason to say that Barbanson had any direct influence on the writing of the *Méthode.*

[15] Bouchereaux, *La Réforme des Carmes,* 215-216.
[16] Chap. xviii, p. 290.

among them Granada, have written enough on this subject, and have deduced the first and principal means of this divine science. Let us only say here that it is the will that has everything to do, so to speak, in this exercise [aspirations]. However, it is most suitable that considerations precede aspirations for a long time. That is to say, the affections need the preceding movement of the intellect and of its enlightening representation, after which it may take immediately this knowledge, being moved and inflamed with love of God.[17]

Finally, John recognized that all cannot use the same method of meditation. For those who have difficulties he recommends reading when distracted.[18] In time of dryness he recommends ejaculations, vocal prayer, or a change of subject. Above all he advises perseverance in prayer.[19] All this advice we find in the *Méthode,* as we have previously seen.

From these four observations we can see that there is perfect harmony between the teaching of John of St. Samson and the *Méthode* on the essentials of meditation. If they differ on numbering the parts of meditation (a matter that is difficult to decide) it would be of little importance, since the division is of secondary concern. It seems most likely, too, that Venerable John's esteem for Granada has influenced his disciple to use the writings of Granada in composing the *Méthode.* Finally, it is clear that the authors of the *Méthode* followed in essential matters the *teaching, spirit* and at times the *language* of their spiritual father, Brother John of St. Samson. This fact becomes even more evident when we compare their teaching on aspirative prayer.

Aspirative Prayer

Aspirative prayer forms one of the most interesting aspects of the teaching of John of St. Samson. It is a way of living in God's presence which for him is the true spirit of Carmel.

Among the religious orders founded to practise perfect love of God, it is our lot as successors and legitimate sons of the great prophet Elias in the Order of Our Lady of Mount Carmel... not to necessarily dwell on Mt. Carmel, but to live in our homes, with purity of soul and body, practising fervent, actual continual presence of God, so that we live more by this exercise than our bodies live by our souls. This is the true spirit of the Order.[20]

---

[17] *Oeuvres,* I, *Le Miroir et les fiammes de l'amour divin,* 321.
[18] Bouchereaux, *La Réforme des Carmes,* 216.
[19] *Ibid.*
[20] *Oeuvres,* I, *Meditations pour les retraites,* 580.

Aspirative prayer is really an affective exercise of the presence of God. It is for souls advanced in prayer, and presupposes meditation and affective prayer. It is ordinarily above the power of novices. It has many degrees and is most sublime in the mystical states. Nevertheless, much of what Brother John says can be explained to novices, and in fact the *Méthode* does this.

John of St. Samson distinguishes between aspirative prayer and ejaculatory prayer. He recommends the latter for those little advanced in prayer and who labor with meditation.[21] Affective colloquies are also different from aspirations. They are really a preparation for the simplified prayer of aspirations, which John defines as a loving, inflamed impulse of the heart and the spirit which elevates the soul above itself and all created things to unite it directly with God by the action of this loving expression."[22]

Aspirative prayer is proper to those who are of an affective nature and who are not given much to speculation. However, it is not for sensual natures who seek sensible consolation and their own pleasure. It is for generous souls who give themselves earnestly to prayer and desire to be directly united with God. Aspirative prayer is a soaring to God, the bursting forth of a flame from a loving heart. It is an impulse of the soul to lose itself in God. God takes it to Himself and fills it with His spirit. This exercise should be practised not only during the hours of prayer but during other occupations as well, so that the soul remains recollected in God, not only in times of fervor, but in times of aridity and temptation. We should try to keep the soul always turned toward God.[23]

As in all forms of prayer there are certain dangers to be avoided. The Holy Ghost is the supreme guide, and there is no need to force the mind or the heart to breathe forth artificial aspirations that only cause distress to the mind and body.

Aspirative prayer is founded on the intellect and the will which tend toward union with God. Various degrees, therefore, can be found in this exercise that lifts the soul to God. John of St. Samson speaks of four degrees in the mystical order (therefore not expected of novices)

---

[21] Bouchereaux, *La Réforme des Carmes*, 218, note 6; Brenninger, "Joannes a S. Samsone de animo et ingenio Ordinis Carmelitarum," *AOC*, 8 (1932), 32.

[22] *Oeuvres*, I, *Le Miroir et les flammanes de l'amour divin*, 321. "C'est élancement amoureux et enflammé du coeur et de l'esprit, par lequel l'Ame se surpassant et toute chose crée, va s'unir étroitement à Dieu en la vivacité de son expression amoureuse."

[23] *Ibid.*, *Le Vray esprit du Carmel*, 88.

which differ according to the ardor of love that burns in the soul: offering, petition, conformity and union.[24]

The effects of aspirative prayer are many. Acts of the intellect and the will are simplified and seek to unite the soul directly with divine simplicity. The soul acquires a deep knowledge of itself, of its sins, of its many imperfections, which are clear to it in the light of God. It becomes filled with compunction and deep humility. The spirit of God fills the soul with love and joy and makes it see the great degree of perfection that God desires for it. The soul seeks to respond to the divine love that consumes it.

These spiritual joys are followed by a period of pain, darkness and abandonment which tend to purify the soul. The soul continues to love, but without light or joy. The fidelity of the soul in this trial is the measure of its love.

Purified by these trials the soul is free from images and created things and seeks attachment to God alone. It is attached to the will of God alone and seeks to be one in union with its beloved. It becomes, as it were, buried and lost in the essence of Jesus Christ, its love and spouse.[25] In this perfect union of love we find the full meaning of the prayer of aspiration which is:

Aspiration is not only an affectionate colloquy, which is a good exercise in itself, but it is born of and proceeds from the exercise of colloquies. It is, then, a loving and inflamed transport of the whole heart and spirit by which the soul surpasses itself and every created thing to unite itself directly with God in the swiftness of its loving expression. This loving expression surpasses all sensible,

---

[24] *Ibid.*, 81-82. Father Brandsma describes this exercise as follows: "The first step is the sacrifice (offering) of oneself and all creation to God. In doing this it is best to focus the offering all in one idea: that all is His, without drawing special attention to one particular work of His hands. We are to see God, not the creature; the creature only in so far as is needed to mount up to God. The second step is a request for His gifts, that He Who is able to give them may give them; that He Who is so rich and mighty may diffuse this splendor. The third step is the making of oneself similar to God, by loving Him fervently and by desiring all to accept this love and incite it in themselves. The last step is the union, of oneself perfectly with God. This includes all the previous steps, but on a higher plan.

"All this is far from easy, therefore the Brother quite understands that success does not come at once, but he wishes us to take great pains. Gradually we shall proceed. The exercise can, as it were, be ever more intensified, till at length it grows into something like an immediate seeing or grasping of God and grows so familiar that it becomes second nature. All images disappear; we pass above everything immediately to God. Only we should not push this so far that we should want to exclude Christ's humanity from our upward flight to God. His is ever to remain our intercessor, our Mediator." (*Carmelite Mysticism Historical Sketches* (Chicago, 1936), 99).

[25] Bouchereaux, *La Réforme des Carmes*, 220.

reasonable, intellectual and comprehensible love, arriving by the impetuosity of the Spirit of God and of its own effort to union with God—not to any kind of union, but to a sudden transformation of the spirit into God. The spirit, I say, surpasses all knowable and intelligible love, to arrive at the abundant and ineffable sweetness of God Himself, in Whom it is lovingly absorbed.[26]

Aspirative prayer as explained and developed by John of St. Samson is not meant for beginners, but is a simplified way of prayer for those who are advanced. Yet, much of John's teaching can be found in the *Méthode,* which has adapted aspirative prayer to beginners in the spiritual life. The *Méthode* uses the words aspiration and ejaculation indiscriminately. On the other hand, John of St. Samson considers aspiration as a higher degree of prayer than ejaculation.[27] The *Methode*, however, does acknowledge the sublime degree to which this prayer of the heart can ascend, and directs its novices to that end.

The Mèthode cites John of St. Samson on aspirative prayer in the three following incidents: Besides recommending to the novices an exercise of aspiration composed by the blind mystic,[28] it recalls his advice always to have some holy thoughts in the heart from which aspirations can be formed, otherwise spiritual laziness will result.[29] Then the *Méthode* encourages them to persevere in the prayer of aspirations, because only in this way will they find themselves continually drawn to God in their heart and feel themselves united to His divine majesty, where love alone suffices.[30] That is, in this state they will no longer need rules and artifices to guide them, because aspiratians will become as natural to the soul as breathing to the lungs.

Even where John of St. Samson is not quoted in the *Méthode* we often see his thought. For example, the definition of aspiration given in the *Méthode* [31] is traditional among spiritual writers, but the explanation of this definition follows the mind of Brother John of St. Samson. We read in the *Méthode* that aspirations sent to God awaken a response in Him, Who answers each ejaculation a hundredfold. A combat of love arises in which God is the victor to the great advantage of the soul. This *"combat d'amour"* is a special theme in the writings of Brother John of St. Samson.[32]

---

[26] *Oeuvres,* I, *Le Miroir et les flammes de l'amour divin,* 321.
[27] Brenninger, "Joannes a S. Samsone," *AOC,* 8 (1932), 32.
[28] Chap. xxxvi, p. 597.
[29] *Ibid.,* 595.
[30] *Ibid.,* 596.
[31] Chap. xxviii, p. 426.
[32] Bouchereaux, *La Réforme des Carmes,* 293; John of St. Samson, *Oeuures,* I, *Le Miroir et les flammes de l'amour divin,* 326.

The teaching in the *Méthode* [33] that aspirations belong especially and more properly to those advanced in prayer is also the teaching of John, who says: "When he shall find them [novices] disposed by the practise of prolonged affections, he shall make known to them and give them the theory of remote aspirations, explaining the meaning of them in proportion to their ability to practise them."[34]

Again we see the *Méthode* expressing the teaching of John of St. Samson when it advises aspirations for beginners as a preparation for the more perfect prayer of aspirations.[35] John says:

> However, aspirative prayer in a remote sense ought to be the entrance of this exercise for those who are more disposed to illumination. And it is true that this exercise is practised even in the active life, although at intervals and very painfully.[36]

Finally, the *Méthode* proposes to the novices the same high, noble effect of aspirations that John had proposed in his writings, namely, God is a consuming fire, so that the more we elevate our hearts to God through transports of burning love the more shall we be consumed by the burning love of God.[37] God "a consuming fire" is another of the more pronounced themes in the works of John of St. Samson.[38]

The *Méthode* owes much of its doctrine and expression on aspirative prayer to John of St. Samson. John, however, is not entirely original in his teaching. He has given his own peculiar touch to aspirative prayer, since he writes not so much from speculative knowledge as from experience. Yet he owes much of his doctrine and its expression to Henry van Herp (Harphius).[39] He praises and recommends the great Flemish writer to his fellow Carmelites. Harphius, in turn, is indebted to the Carthusian, Hugh of Balma, author of *Theologia mystica*, for his doctrine on aspirative prayer.[40] It is interesting to note that the *Méthode* cites once the *Theologia mystica* (calls it *Liber de theologia mystica* of St. Bonaventure) when it speaks of the effects of aspiration.[41]

---

[33] Chap. xxviii, p. 426.
[34] *Oeuvres*, I, *La Conduite des novices*, 911.
[35] Chap. xxviii, p. 428.
[36] *Oeuvres*, I, *La Conduite des novices*, 911.
[37] Chap. xxviii, pp. 427-428.
[38] Boucher eaux, *La Réforme des Carmes*, 289-291.
[39] *Ibid.*, 292-293. For the writings of Harphius on aspirations: *Spieghel der Volcomenheit*, ed by L. Verschueren, O.F.M. (Antwerp, 1931), II, 184-188.
[40] S. Autore, "Hugues de Balma," *DTC*, VII, 215-220.
[41] *Méthode*, 291. Hugh de Balma, *Mystica theologia*. Falsely attributed to St. Bonaventure in *Seraphici Doctoris Bonaventurae opusculorum theologicorum Tomus Secundus* (Venice, 1634).

Did the authors of the *Méthode* draw directly from Harphius and Hugh of Balma? There seems to be good reason to believe that the authors were acquainted with the writings of these men, since they were easily accessible and widely read in the first half of the seventeenth century.[42] At the same time there is no reason to believe that these writers were the primary and direct sources for the doctrine on aspirations in the *Méthode*. In the first place, the writings of Harphius and Hugh of Balma were too advanced for novices and, in the second place, the novices had no real need of their works since they had substantially the same doctrine developed in their own reform by their master, John of St. Samson, who both by his example and his teaching made it abundantly clear that the prayer of aspirations embodies the true spirit of Carmel. He who practises it stands, like the prophet Elias, with his soul turned with love toward the ever present God. To stand continually in God's presence is an admonition that John never tires of repeating in his writings. Time and again he says: "It is necessary for the soul, that desires God to adhere faithfully and continually to this practise [presence of God], as if there were no one else except God and itself in the world."[43]

The *Méthode* wished to teach the novices the true spirit of Carmel, the contemplative spirit, which manifests itself in the practise of continual prayer that remains uninterupted even in the active apostolate. The authors of the *Méthode* found this spirit embodied in the practise of the presence of God and aspirative prayer, which their own master, John of St. Samson, eloquently described in his writings and faithfully practised in his daily life. Whatever the relative merits of John of St. Samson and the writers of the *Méthode* may be in the history of French spirituality, it will always remain true that they have bequeathed to future Carmelites a way of contemplative life that bears with it the warning that no Carmelite is worthy of the name unless he strives sincerely to live each moment of his life in the loving presence of God.

---

[42] The writings of John Lansperge (Lanspergius), O. Carth., Bavarian (1489-1539), were also recommended together with the works of Blosius to the religious of Touraine by Dominic of St. Albert in chap. xiii of his " Regulae exteriores," *AOC*, 11 (1940-1942), 68-69. Lansperge has many exercises of aspirations for recollecting the soul. *DTC*, VIII, 2606-2607. His complete works were published in five volumes at Cologne by John Kreps in 1630.

[43] *Oeuvres*, I, *Le Miroir et les flammes de d'amour divin*, 306.

II – Venerable Dominic of St. Albert

Father Dominic of St. Albert was known in the world as Vincent Eschard.[44] He was born in Fougères in lower Brittany on April 14, 1596. Before receiving the Carmelite habit in Rennes in 1613 at the age of seventeen, he had studied at the Jesuit college in that same city. His first prior was Philip Thibault, and his novice master was Matthew Pinault. He pronounced his vows on May 14, 1614. Nothing definite is known about his years of study. But it was during that time that he became the beloved disciple of Brother John of St. Samson and learned from him the ways of the mystical life. Even after his ordination Dominic remained the disciple of the blind mystic.

Dominic was a learned man, and despite his desire to give more time to prayer he was forced to teach theology. He was also a novice master for a few years, and perhaps it was during this time that he composed some of his spiritual works.

In 1630 at the annual congregation of the province held at Nantes, Dominic was elected vicar provincial of the reformed houses of the province. Father Bernard of St. Magdalen was then provincial. In 1632 he was elected prior of Nantes. During this three-year period he suffered intense physical pain which he bore heroically. He was afflicted with an ulcer of the colon, which he concealed from others because of a peculiar sense of modesty. This infection, unfortunately, brought him to a premature death. He died in the odor of sanctity on January 24, 1634, at the age of thirty-eight.

Much of the sublime mystical doctrine of Dominic came from his director, Venerable John of St. Samson. This can be seen not only by comparing their writings, but from their exchange of letters. On one occasion, writing to Brother John, Dominic says:

Because I need your prayers and I owe so much to your kindness I am writing this letter to thank you for giving me so much help in educating me in the way of the Lord. Because of you I have been born in Jesus Christ. Would that, with the grace of God, I shall faithfully respond to the holy teaching with which you have imbued me. Do not doubt, brother, that anything is more dear or pleasing to me than the interior life in which you have directed me.[45]

---

[44] *BC*, I, col. 404. Donatian of St. Nicholas, "Vita Ven. Dominici a S. Alberto:" *AOC*, 11 (1940-1942), 19. This life is edited by Father Brenninger with copious notes.

[45] Letter of Nov. 3, 1624. Consult the correspondence of Dominic of St. Albert edited by S. M. Bouchereaux in *AOC*, 15 (1950), 99.

After the death of Dominic, Brother John did not hesitate to write that Dominic of St. Albert had reached in his life a degree of sanctity that hardly had been seen in the Church.[46]

A study of Dominic's writings shows that, like his spiritual director, Brother John, he was an experienced mystic. His most important work has never been published, but manuscripts of it have been preserved. One of these bears the title: *Exercise mystique qui conduist jusques au plus haud degré de la vie spirituelle par le dict St. P. Dominique*.[47] This work comprehends a study of all degrees of mental prayer up to the highest union with God. Besides this, there is another small treatise entirely on mystical theology and in manuscript form entitled: *Théologie mystique du R.P. Dominicque de S. Albert, Carme de d'Observance de Rennes*.[48]

Another work of Dominic, and one which we shall use in this study, is the *Exercitatio spiritualis fratrum tam novitiorum quam professorum in nostro Carmelo Rhedonensis novitiatu degentium*. This little book together with three other small treatises was published in Paris in 1650 and again in 1665. It was translated into German by Father Charles of St. Athanasius, a German Carmelite.[49] A copy of the German translation has not been found. The original Latin text was found a few years ago and published again by Father John Brenninger, O. Carm.[50]

Basing our study on the *Exercitatio spiritualis* of Father Dominic in the new edition of Father Brenninger we shall try briefly to outline his teaching on the ways of ordinary prayer, and compare them with the ways of prayer in the *Méthode*. First of all, let us remember that both Dominic and Bernard of St. Magdalen were disciples of John of St. Samson. Moreover, Bernard surely had in his hands his manuscript of the *Exercitatio spiritualis* (which was also given to the novices) when in 1634 he began to prepare the *Directoires des novices*.

---

[46] *Ibid.*, 126.

[47] John Brenninger, O. Carm., "Dominicus a Sancto Alberto, Carmelita Provinciae Turonensis," *AOC*, 8 (1932-1936), 294. A manuscript copy is preserved in the Archive of the Postulator General of the Carmelite Order, Rome, Codex T, ff. 278r-315v. The original in the Public Library of Tours has been destroyed.

[48] This was published by Fr. Brenninger in *Études carmélitaines*, 22 (1937), 258-269.

[49] *BC*, I, col. 310.

[50] "Opuscula pro novitiis et professis studentibus," in *AOC*, 11 (1940-1942), 15-92. A complete bibliography of Dominic of St. Albert's works can be found in the dissertation of Eugene Tonna, O. Carm., *De doctrina spirituali Ven. Dominici a S. Alberto, Ord. Carm.* unpublished dissertation for the degree of Doctor of Sacred Theology in the Gregorian University, 1951.

Furthermore, according to the *Bibliotheca carmelitana*, both Dominic and Bernard had collaborated in preparing directories.[51] Finally, the *Méthode* cites the writings of Dominic on various occasions. It recalls how Dominic teaches in his exercises that love can be a continual source of knowledge and good thoughts. In other words, not only does the intellect inflame the will, but the will inflamed with love suggests wonderful and sublime thoughts.[52] The *Méthode* also recommends Dominic's writings for their aspirations that will aid the novices to live in the presence of God.[53] Let us examine more closely this influence of Dominic on the *Méthode*.

The *Exercitatio spiritualis* is composed of a prologue and seven chapters. In the first chapter the novices and young professed are informed that their principal exercise is the study of prayer, which consists in a loving conversation with God. The means to acquire this end are outlined in the second chapter. The third chapter presents a method of meditation. The fourth chapter explains the fruits of ordinary mental prayer, that is, the prayer of union which is a pure gift of God. Chapter five is a meditation on the passion of Christ. It is not for beginners but for the advanced who enjoy affective prayer. Chapter six is an exercise on the presence of God, and is also meant for those experienced in mental prayer. The last chapter is dedicated to the end toward which these different grades of prayer should dispose us, that is, simple and unique conversation with God. This is mystical prayer.

Let us examine the first few chapters more minutely. Speaking of prayer Dominic says that it is a union of the whole soul in God with Whom we speak in a loving manner. He describes prayer in its perfect state. That is, he gives the goal toward which the novices must tend. This goal is a total, actual attention to God – a loving extension of the soul in God.[54]

We should choose certain subjects such as death, judgment, the life and passion of Christ, gifts of God, etc., and meditate and reflect upon them in the manner of a most tender colloquy, an internal conversation with God.

All their [novices and young professed clerics] internal exercises are reduced to internal conversations with God, so that they may learn to live interiorly and to speak with Him frequently on different subjects of medita-

---

[51] *BC*, I, col. 406.
[52] *Méthode*, chap. xxiv, p. 372.
[53] *Ibid.*, chap. xxvi, p. 597.
[54] *AOC*, 11, 24.

tion, e. g., death, final judgment, eternal glory, the passion of Our Lord, particular and general benefices, and especially on their conversion to religious life. They should often ask themselves what God demands of them, why they have come to religious life, and think often of the goodness of God in leading them to a life of penitence.[55]

In what does this internal conversation with God consist?

This internal conversation, by which they shall strive to live with God, does not consist in an imaginary, sensible or violent application of the senses or of the expansion of the head, but in a rational, voluntary, affectionate, ardent, desirous, longing adhesion of the spirit which by loving colloquies, inflamed aspirations and ejaculations unites them to God, their supreme good.[56]

This high state of intimate conversation with God can hardly be expected of novices. But this is the goal which they will surely attain, if they are faithful to the practise of prayer and the means to it. What are the means? Dominic demands firm perseverance in our religious vocation, contrition for sins, unfailing confidence in the mercy and goodness of God, humble resignation to the mortifications of religious life, a general confession, if necessary.[57]

In chapter three Dominic presents a method of meditation. A book of meditations should be used by the novices and beginners, such as that of Louis de la Puente or Louis de Granada. They should follow these three steps in meditation: 1) Let them offer to God as a bouquet the material they are about to meditate upon. Let them ask Him to help them obtain the desired fruit (*preparation*). 2) Let them consider the points of the meditation in an orderly manner (*meditation*). 3) Affections and resolutions should come after each point, and not be delayed until the end of the whole prayer (*affections*). Ardent inflammation of the will is the end of prayer and not mere acts of the intellect. At the conclusion of the meditation they can produce more frequent affections, for good prayer should finish with affections. However, novices in the beginning will find it difficult to carry out the *discursus* and colloquies, and therefore it will be wise for them to help their memory and intellect by adding the following parts which are affections, namely, oblation, petition and thanksgiving. For those advanced in prayer these parts are not necessary, and they really have only two parts to their prayer, that is, meditation and affections.

---

[55] *Ibid.*
[56] *Ibid.*, 25.
[57] *Ibid.*, 25-26.

Beginners will find it necessary perhaps to make up conversations (colloquies) with God, since they will have few affections. Thus, rather than waste time with trying to produce sensible affections, let them speculate on the subject of their meditation and elicit affections in the form of a conversation, asking God questions, objecting, answering and consenting. In this way they will mix the *discursus* with the affections, so that they cannot be distinguished one from the other. Sensible affections are to be discouraged. The novice master will avoid this fault by giving his students abstract subjects of meditation, such as the divine perfections, creation, the redemption, etc.

If prayer is dry and sterile and full of distractions, the novice should be resigned, and by short prayers make known to God his miserable state, begging for help. "Help me, O Lord God, if you desire me to progress."[58] Above all they should avoid violence to their sensible faculties. Reading may be joined to prayer, and mixed prayer and oral prayer may be tried. Or let them pray and produce their internal acts vocally, or recite a psalm or the rosary.[59] However, those advanced in prayer finding themselves in this arid state should retain the presence of God, acting as sheep before the shearer. For them perseverance must prevail, and they should follow the advice of a spiritual director.[60]

If we compare Dominic's method of meditation with that of the *Méthode*, we find they both present the same goal to the novices and use the same expression: *continual and loving interior conversation with God.*

The *Méthode's* second definition of prayer, "every elevation of the heart to God," is clearly following the mind of Dominic.[61] Moreover, both consider prayer as the "life of the soul," and believe that our whole life on earth is given to us by God in order to be continually occupied with God. We were created to live a life of prayer, to use our minds to think of God and about God, and our will to love God and to be always occupied with Him. In a word, to live means "vacare Deo." We see this similarity of thought, if we compare the following passages:

This study of prayer is nothing else than a true, total, actual attention to God, and a loving extension in God of all the faculties of the soul, which

---

[58] *AOC,* 11, 31.

[59] *Ibid.*

[60] Father Brenninger says Dominic admits different grades of mental prayer: 1) artificial meditation (discursive prayer), 2) prayer of pure colloquies, i.e., affective prayer, 3) prayer of simple intuition of faith, 4) prayer through the essential conversion of the whole soul which seems to be the beginning of the mystical life. *AOC,* 8, 299 ff. and 11, 52, note 41.

[61] Tonna, *De doctrina spirituali Ven. Dominici,* 123.

so joins and unites them all to God, that nearly always, in every hour and place, the soul speaks with Him.[62]

The *Méthode* repeats this thought, but does not cite Dominic.

Prayer is truly the life of the soul and the food of the spirit. For this reason we boldly dare to say that if God has created us with a rational soul, He did so in order that we may use it with all its powers and faculties to know and to love Him continually and without cease.[63]

The development of the parts of meditation in the *Exercitatio spiritualis* is not as lengthy, complete and orderly as the method of meditation in the *Méthode* but the methods are identical. Both Dominic and the *Méthode* divide meditation into three parts: preparation, meditation and affections. Both speak of meditation as an exercise of the three faculties of the soul, memory, intellect and will. In both we find the three ages of the spiritual life, beginners, advanced and the perfect. What is still more important, we find both subordinating the intellect (*discursus*) to the will (*affections*) and orienting the prayer toward affective prayer. Both advise the *discursus* in the form of a colloquy, the art of prolonging the colloquial *discursus* when affections are less frequent, the affective colloquy, the production of affections after each consideration, or the intermingling of the *discursus* with affections (affective prayer), the general affections of petition, thanksgiving and oblation (Dominic shows here the influence of Granada), the advice to those suffering distractions and aridity, and the recommendation of mixed prayer for those who find a method of meditation too rigid.

Among these different points we call attention to the manner of making the *discursus* in the form of a conversation. We have seen that Alvarez de Paz has recommended such a practise, but it seems that the *Méthode* would depend more directly upon Dominic because of his singular importance in helping to form the spirit of Touraine. Dominic, as we have seen above, says all the interior exercises of the young religious should be made in the form of conversation, and that they should meditate on death, judgment, etc. Then he adds:

On these and similar subjects each one shall dwell in the presence of God, and try to reduce what they reflect or meditate upon to the form of a colloquy. Thus joined to God by internal colloquy they may perform acts of virtues, such as humility, patience, obedience, resignation for the purpose that they may be pleasing to God with Whom they converse in spirit.[64]

---

[62] *AOC*, 11, 24.
[63] Chap. 11, pp. 24-25.
[64] *AOC*, 11, 24.

The *Méthode* says:

> To help them continue their reflection, they may speak to themselves or to some other being—to God or to one of the Three Persons of the Trinity, or to our Saviour, Jesus Christ, to the Blessed Virgin Mary, to the angels and especially to their guardian angel. They can do this by proposing questions, or by asking and answering questions, following the examples of conversation that we have given [in the first volume of the *Directoires*] on the vocation of novices and the misery of the world, or the examples we shall give in the next volume where we shall propose some exercises of compunction.[65]

There are some differences, of course, between the two methods. The *Méthode* is more orderly and complete. It gives better detailed instruction. It insists more on the place of the Holy Spirit in prayer. It gives many practical formulas of meditation, and tells the novice not to use other books in the beginning. Dominic, on the other hand, recommends the ready-made meditations of Puente and Granada. Both, however, recognize Granada as an authority on meditation. The *Méthode* considers resolutions as an essential part of every meditation. Dominic does not make such a demand, although he expects novices to make resolutions at the end of prayer.

How do we explain the similarity between the two methods? There is certainly a dependence of the *Méthode* on the writings of Dominic. We have shown that the *Méthode* cites explicitly the writings of Dominic. Secondly, we believe that the comparison of passages in their works, which we have just given, shows more emphatically this influence. Nor should we be surprised. Dominic had been a novice master and naturally would have taught a method of meditation to the novices. His method should have been the same as that in the *Méthode*, because the preface of the *Méthode* informs us that it contains the same methods of prayer that were taught in the reform from its beginning. However, there are some differences to be noted between the meditation in the *Méthode* and Dominic's.

The teaching of the *Méthode* has enlarged the teaching of the *Exercitatio spiritualis* on methodical prayer and has made it more understandable and adaptable to the novices. Dominic seems always to be in haste to write about the higher degrees of prayer. Like many spiritual masters, his words on methodical prayer are brief. The *Méthode* lacks the personal touch and warmth that is found in the writings of Dominic, but it is written in a more simple and polished style.

---

[65] Chap. vi, pp. 87-88. The two tracts referred to here are: 1) *Directoires des novices*, vol. I, and 2) *Traité de la componction*, ed. by Michael Joseph of St. Mark (Tours, 1696).

It would be wrong to say that the method in the *Méthode* is compiled from the writings of Dominic. As we have already seen, other spiritual writers within the Order and outside the Order have left their influence on the method of meditation in the *Méthode*. This method, therefore, does not represent the teachings of one man, but the teaching of many, studied and organized into one system with the sole purpose of leading souls to continual, loving conversation with God.

The Exercise of the Presence of God

Dominic of St. Albert recommends meditation (discursive and affective) and mixed prayer for the novices. Has he also (in harmony with John of St. Samson and the *Méthode*) recommended and explained aspirative prayer for them? A simple reading of the *Exercitatio spiritualis* is sufficient to convince anyone that aspirative prayer played an important part in the spiritual life of Dominic, and that he recommended it most highly to the novices and young professed of the reform. This is seen especially in chapter six of the *Exercitatio spiritualis* which is entitled: "*Alia conversatio interna*."[66] It is an exercise of the presence of God to which is joined aspirative prayer and loving colloquies. Dominic does not give a complete analysis of this exercise, and beginners will find him difficult to follow. He is solely occupied with a very advanced kind of presence of God, that is, affective presence of God, that leads directly to mystical prayer. This chapter, he says, is written for those in the illuminative way.[67]

Despite the personal touch that is obvious in this chapter, and which reveals the high state of intimacy that Dominic attained in his own conversations with God, he nevertheless directed it to the novices and young professed, stating in the first place what they should do in order to arrive at the state of affective presence of God.

The novices must first practise mental prayer, giving much time to the consideration of divine truths. After profound consideration they should arrive at resolutions, and then converse with God about these good desires.

Subjects of meditation should be: the infinite goodness of God which we have offended, consideration of the days spent in youth far from God, God's mercy toward us, our vocation, our probable state of

---

[66] *AOC*, 11, 43-57.
[67] *Ibid.*, 53. One must remember that Dominic had not only novices but professed clerics in mind.

sinfulness had God not called us to religious life, and God's goodness in leading us to penance. Finally, creation, redemption, conservation, justification and divine judgment.[68]

Good and firm resolutions should follow these considerations.[69] After meditation the novice should try to practise the presence of God. Let him think of God as present everywhere, especially in the depths of the soul.

After this he shall try to walk recollected in God, often invoking God in all his actions. He shall seek His pardon, for having loved Him so little. He shall try to conserve the presence of God by considering God's presence in every place, in every creature, especially in his own soul, where God is present not just as in other creatures, but as in the representative image of Himself. Let him understand that if his heart is prepared, and his passions are subject to reason, that God dwells in him as in a throne, or (if the soul is immaculate) that God dwells within him as a spouse in the marriage chamber. With these devout thoughts he shall try to prepare his heart for God.[70]

The three faculties of the soul should be used in this exercise: the memory, to recall God and all His graces; the intellect to know God, the highest good; the will to embrace, love and enjoy God's goodness. All means that lead to this presence should be used, especially fervent prayer and mortification.[71]

Whoever possesses a strong and burning desire to cling to God above all things will find material to speak with Him from the things which he hears, does, speaks or omits. The depth of love will prompt the soul concerning the nature of the aspirations. It is useless to go outside of oneself looking for material from which the soul aspires to God. Let the soul speak from the love that burns within it.

If one hears something pious, holy and stimulating read or mentioned, one can use this as a means to elevate oneself to God through the following or a similar act: "O Lord God, when shall I do this? When shall I embrace it? Give me the grace, O Lord, to practise what you are now teaching me to do."

On the contrary, if one hears an insult, or something vain and foolish, and it moves him, he can turn to God and say: "O Lord, take me from this

---

[68] *AOC*, 11, 43-44.

[69] *Ibid.*, 44.

[70] *Ibid.*

[71] *Ibid.* L. Blosius, speaking of aspirations, has this same idea. (*Institutio spiritualis* (London, 1925), chap. v, p. 52). Dominic of St. Albert recommended the works of Blosius because they contain many colloquies with God which are an aid to internal conversation with God. Cf. *Regulae exteriores, AOC.* 11, 69.

place! In you alone do I find delight; speak to me, O Lord, because Your servant listens."

From these two examples it is clear that if anyone has a great and vehement desire to cling to God alone, he can find the opportunity to do so in everything that he hears, does, speaks or omits...

But one should never look for external things to express his love, for example, to look for something beautiful, and then say: "O Lord, how beautiful You are? How infinitely more beautiful!"

To act in this way is not bad in itself, but for those who wish to acquire true and internal purity it is a great defect, because a true lover ought not to seek for love except in the depths of his heart, reducing by an internal desire all things to love.[72]

The exercise of the presence of God taught by Dominic lacks the pedagogical value of the same exercise in the *Méthode*. Dominic is concerned only with the affective presence of God (which is usually beyond the ability of novices), whereas the *Méthode* considers the imaginative, intellectual and the affective presence of God, and gives precise rules to be followed for the use of each way. The *Méthode* explains the exact relation of the exercise of the presence of God with aspirative prayer. Dominic seems to presuppose this knowledge. The *Méthode* not only gives well-planned exercises of aspirations, but explains in detail four different ways of living in God's presence. Such detailed teaching, which is excellent for beginners, is lacking theoughout the *Exercitatio spiritualis* of Father Dominic. He does recommend the elevation of the mind to God through creatures, although it is not the simple elementary practise found in the *Méthode*.[73] Likewise, he presents the novices with many examples of aspirations and colloquies which explain in a very concrete manner the kind of aspirations he believes should emanate from their souls. It seems that it is to these exercises that the *Méthode* refers when it advises those who are unable to draw aspirations from their own hearts to have recourse to the writings of the two distinguished contemplatives of the reform. "Let them have recourse to the writings of our excellent contemplatives Venerable Father Dominic and Brother John of St. Samson, who have written many exercises on this subject."[74]

The exercise of the presence of God which includes aspirative prayer as found in the *Méthode* seems far more suited to the ability of novices than the writings of Dominic. But again we must remember

---

[72] *AOC*, 11, 47-48.
[73] *Ibid.*
[74] Chap. xxxvi, p. 597.

that Dominic wrote also for professed clerics. Yet, whatever their differences and comparative value, the same spirit dominates both works, namely, to teach the young reformed members of Touraine how to live continually in the presence of God, talking with Him in a loving affective conversation.

Dominic received his spiritual formation from Brother John of St. Samson. Both the writings of John and Dominic have influenced the doctrine of the *Méthode*. The influence of Dominic is plainly seen in the third part of the *Méthode* on aspirative prayer, just as in the first part on meditation. The exercise of the presence of God in the *Exercitatio spiritualis* and the same exercise in the *Méthode* have an identical purpose, and the *Méthode* not only cites Dominic as an authority on aspirations but borrows the thought and the language of this venerable father. It recommends to the novices the exercises of aspirations written by Dominic. Both the *Exercitatio* and the *Méthode* find aspirative prayer to be an advanced form of prayer that presupposess that the novice has already practised meditation. The *Méthode*, however, adapts the practise to beginners in so far as this is possible. Both agree that aspirative prayer is best suited to one who is versed in affective meditation. Furthermore, they use almost the same language to explain the state of the soul that has progressed in prayer. The *Exercitatio* says:

> It is clear that to attain the perfection of true prayer and internal conversation, the soul divested of terrestrial desires, should exercise itself in the loving, actual and continual presence of God, fulfilling faithfully both externally and internally the divine will. For otherwise neither the reading of many books, nor the violent application of the senses nor deep reflection is able to be of help...
>
> Wherefore, since it is true that God is good and to be desired above all things, as faith teaches us, and each one has experienced, nothing else remains for them than to desire Him above all things, following Him, thirsting for Him and embracing Him with all the faculties of the soul, placing Him in their hearts as a thing of infinite value, as their unique and supreme treasure, being attentive always to Him not as an astrologer contemplates the stars or as a philosopher reflects upon the things of nature, but as an avaricious man is intent upon his treasures.
>
> All his care, solicitude and affection consists in a desire for his treasure: ... wherever he is, whether he drinks or sleeps or does anything else he always has his eyes fixed on his treasure.[75]

---

[75] *AOC*, 11, 34-35.

In like manner the *Méthode* says:

To those who have made some advance in prayer and the love of God this exercise becomes almost second nature. Almost without realizing it their heart, like a burning furnace, continually sends forth to God most fervent aspirations like so many sparks. Hence, whatever they do, or wherever they are, either inside or outside the monastery, day or night, alone or in company, while working or resting, they are always in continual thought and love of God. They speak to Him and address many ardent desires to Him. They are like an avaricious man whose thought is continually on his treasures, and whose heart is always fixed on them.[76]

The *Méthode* develops three ways of prayer: methodical meditation, mixed prayer and aspirative prayer (the exercise of the presence of God). Mark of the Nativity, who edited the *Méthode,* tells us that it should not be considered the work of any one man, since it incorporates the spirit of the members of the reform. Indeed, we have traced the influence of Brother John of St. Samson and of Father Dominic of St. Albert through every part of these three ways of prayer. The *Méthode* itself cites these two Carmelites as authorities on more than one occasion and calls them the renowned contemplatives of the reform. Yet, we have shown that Dominic admits his dependence upon Brother John for his spiritual doctrine. Thus, we may say that the blind mystic of Rennes, John of St. Samson, was not only the guiding spirit of the reform, but that his spirit lived after him, and is reflected in every page of the *Méthode*. L. van den Bossche spoke the truth when he wrote:

When John of St. Samson died at Rennes in 1636, his thought survived him, because a whole group of religious who venerated him as the most beloved of their masters spread his doctrine, taught it to the novices whom they educated, and proposed it in their writings as the doctrine itself of their Observance.[77]

---

[76] *Méthode*, chap: xxviii, pp. 433-434.

[77] *Actes de la vie chrétienne – Jean de Saint Samson* (Les Éditions du Cerf, Paris [1938], 152.

CONCLUSIONS

The reform of Touraine was an attempt to restore the primitive spirit of Carmel, that is, to make life an interior and continual occupation with God. For this purpose the *Directoires des novices* in four volumes was prepared by Father Bernard of St. Magdalen during his forty years as master of novices, but it was completed and edited by Father Mark of the Nativity of the Blessed Virgin. The fourth volume, the *Méthode,* is entirely dedicated to mental prayer in which we find the spirit of the Order and of prayer expressed in terms of "introversion" and "continual, loving conversation with God." It is a clear orderly manual of prayer.

Three ways of mental prayer are developed in the *Méthode,* namely, methodical meditation, mixed prayer and aspirative prayer (the exercise of the presence of God). They are not proposed as three different degrees of prayer, but as three ways of ordinary prayer that lead to "loving conversation" with God.

These ways of prayer are predominantly affective. That is, the affections are given the greatest part in prayer, although the intellect must supply the considerations which move the will. The will is the queen of the faculties. Love is an inexhaustible source of holy thoughts. Affective union is the end to be obtained.

This affective tendency is the result of the reform's personal interpretation of chapter seven of the Carmelite Rule "to meditate day and night on the law of God." In the *Méthode* (and this is the mind of the reform) the word "meditate" does not refer to the act of the intellect but to the act of the will. The act of the intellect is necessary, but it is only a means to help the Carmelite keep his heart, that is, the will, elevated continually to God. If the instructions of the *Méthode* are carefully heeded and diligently practised, they will lead the novice to affective prayer. Affective prayer will gradually dispose him to more simplified prayer that will lead to the threshold of the contemplative or mystical state.

The method of meditation is methodical. It is composed of three parts: *preparation, meditation* and *affections,* which correspond with the three faculties of the soul, the memory, intellect and will. These parts are again subdivided. The meditation or body of the prayer differs according to the subject matter. And the subject, according as it is sensible (the birth of Christ) or spiritual (the goodness of God), will determine the relative role played by the three faculties.

This method is structurally complete, and gives the impression of being formal, rigid and artificial. But such is not the case. The novice is reminded time and again that the Holy Spirit is his principal director, and that great freedom is given in prayer, However, he is asked to follow the method at least for the first three months in order to learn it. He is advised that methods are only a means to an end, and many parts of the structure of meditation can and should be omitted provided that the purpose of meditation, which is progress toward loving conversation with God, is obtained. For this purpose resolutions in meditation are necessary.

Mixed prayer, the second way of prayer, is only one of the more simplified forms of meditation for beginners and others who find the methodical meditation unsuitable to their nature. It is presented as an affective prayer that leads to more intimate conversation with Gad.

The methodical meditation of Touraine is not original. All the parts have been taken from other methods. The influence of the *Spiritual Exercises* of St. Ignatius is recognized, if not directly, then at least through his disciples. The fundamentals of the meditation, that is, the exercise of the three faculties (perhaps even the remote, proximate and immediate preparation), the body of the meditation (contemplation of the mysteries of Christ, the colloquies throughout the meditation, though not at the end of meditation), and the examen after meditation are all taken from the Ignatian School.

The influence of Louis of Granada is also recognized, especially in regard to the affective character given to meditation and to the parts of the general affections with the exception of the resolutions.

St. Teresa has also influenced the *Méthode* especially in regard to the nature of prayer, its necessity, excellence and its difficulties. Both the method of the *Méthode* and that of the Discalced Carmelite, John of Jesus and Mary, although differing somewhat in plan, have the same fundamental *affective* orientation, and show the influence of St. Teresa and of Louis of Granada.

St. Francis of Sales, who owes much to St. Ignatius and Louis of Granada, has a method very similar to that of the *Méthode*. The differences are accidental, and do not seem to be of practical importance. It cannot be said that the *Méthode* depends upon St. Francis, although both emphasize the importance of resolutions more than the previously cited authors.

The two outstanding mystics of Touraine, Brother John of St. Samson and Father Dominic of St. Albert, have left their influence on the method of meditation. Their influence is not shown so much in the structure or form of the meditation as in the affective nature and purpose of the meditation. They both recommend highly Louis of Granada and writers of the Ignatian School (Louis de la Puente and Francis Arias) in their writings.

The third part of the *Méthode* contains the practise of the presence of God and aspirative prayer as parts of one way of prayer called the exercise of the presence of God. This exercise is for all grades of the spiritual life. The more frequently one thinks of God, the more will his soul be given to elicit loving aspirations. Aspirations, in their full sense, are burning desires, transports of love that flow from actual charity, that is, from a soul that is a burning furnace of charity. In this sense aspirations are not for beginners, but presuppose the habit of meditation. The Carmelite should aspire to this high form of aspirative prayer, because it will help him to fulfill the precept of the Rule which commands him "to meditate day and night on the Law of God," that is, to elevate his heart to God continually. This loving elevation of the heart to God leads to the threshold of the mystical life, to the simple and loving intuition of God.

The exercise of the presence of God is found in many spiritual writers at the beginning of the seventeenth century, such as: Louis of Blois, St. Francis de Sales, the Venerable John of Jesus and Mary, Rodriquez, Francis Arias, etc. Prior to these Henry van Herp, who depends on Hugh of Balma, had great influence in the seventeenth century and his aspirative prayer was greatly favored in the reform of Touraine. It is difficult to say which of these writers on aspirative prayer and the presence of God have influenced the *Méthode* and to what extent. But we do know for certain that aspirative prayer as developed in the *Méthode* was under the direct influence of John of St. Samson and to a lesser degree his disciple, Dominic of St. Albert. John of St. Samson not only inspired the authors of the *Méthode,* who were also his spiritual children, with a knowledge of this type of prayer, but he taught them to use it, and they in turn incorporated it into the *Méthode* as representing the true spirit of the Carmelite Order. John of St. Samson had developed the prayer of aspirations in his own writings and in his own spiritual life. It embodies the spirit of the interior life which he tried to impart to the reform of Touraine.

The blind mystic of Rennes is not original in his exposition of aspirative prayer. He borrows especially from Henry van Herp, whose work he warmly recommends. Yet, aspirative prayer became such a part of his own life, such a living experience, that he explains it in a masterly and personal way.

In conclusion, we may say that the reform of Touraine did not present ways of mental prayer to its novices that were taken verbatim from other books and incorporated wholly and entirely into the *Méthode*. Therefore, it is not a compilation of the methods of others. Rather, its methods of prayer represent the essential elements of mental prayer taken from the great spiritual writers of the sixteenth and seventeenth centuries, including the great writers within the Order. These elements were studied, weighed, judged and examined by the authors of the *Méthode*, and after mature consideration organized into a plan of prayer that was considered suitable to obtain the contemplative purpose of the Order—continual and intimate occupation and conversation with God.

BIBLIOGRAPHY

For editions, translations, compendia and adaptations of the *Directoires des novices* see pp. 34-38.

Acta Capitulorum Generalium Ordinis Fratrum B. V. Mariae de Monte Carmelo, Edited by Gabriel Wessels, O. Carm. 2 Vols. Rome, 1912-1934.

ALVAREZ DE PAZ, J., S. J. *Opera Jacobi Alvarez de Paz.* 6 Vols. Paris, 1875-1876.

ANTOINE MARIE DE LA PRÉSENTATION, O.C.D. "La Réforme de Touraine", *Études carmélitaines.* Vol. XVII, 1932.

———. *Le Carmel en France; Étude historique.* 7 Vols. Toulouse, 1936-1939.

ARIAS, F., S. J. *Aprovechamiento espiritual. . . compuesto por el P. Francisco. Arias de la Compañia de Jesús.* Madrid, 1603.

———. *Traité de l'oraison mentale.* Translated by Francis Solier, S. J. Rouen, 1614.

BELLINTANI DE SALO, MATHIAS, O.F.M. CAP. *Practica orationis mentalis seu contemplativae.* A translation into Latin from Italian by Anthony Volmarum, O. Carth. Cologne, 1609.

BLOIS, L. (BLOSIUS), O.S.B. *Ludovici Blosii opera omnia.* Edited by Anthony de Winghe, O.S.B. Antwerp, 1632.

BOSSCHE, L. VAN DEN. *Actes de la vie chrétienne - Jean de Saint-Şamson.* Paris, 1938.

BOUCHEREAUX, S.M. *Directions pour la vie intérieure par Jean de Saint Samson.* Paris, 1948.

———. "Dominique de Saint Albert: sa vie et sa correspondence avec Jean de Saint Samson," *Analecta Ordinis Carmelitarum.* Vol. XV, 1950.

———. *La Réforme des Carmes en France et Jean de Saint-Samson.* Paris 1950.

BRANDSMA, T., O. CARM. *Carmelite Mysticism; Historical Sketches.* Chicago, 1936.

———. "Carmes (Spiritualité de l'Ordre des)," *Dictionnaire de spiritualité.* Vol. II, Fasc. VII. 1937.

BREMOND, H. *Histoire littéraire du sentiment religieux en France.* Vol. II, *L'Invasion mystique.* Paris, 1916.

BRENNINGER, J., O. CARM. "De Ven. Joanne a S. Samsone, insigni mystico Ordinis Carmelitarum," *Analecta Ordinis Carmelitarum.* Vol. VII, 1930-1931.
———. *Directorium carmelitanum vitae spiritualis.* Vatican City, 1940.

———. "Dominicus a Sancto Alberto Carmelita Provinciae Turonensis," *Analecta Ordinis Carmelitarum.* Vol. VIII, 1937.

———. "Joannes a S. Samsone de animo et ingenio Ordinis Carmelitarum, *Analecta Ordinis Carmelitarum.* Vol. VIII, 1937.

CATENA, C., O. CARM. "La meditazione in comune nell'Ordine carmelitano: origine e sviluppo," *Carmelus,* Vol. II, Rome, 1955.

CIOLI, T., O. CARM. *Fondamenti di spiritualità carmelitana.* Rome, 1951.

COGNET, L. "Les origines de la spiritualité française au XVIIe siècle," *Culture catholique,* No. 4, Paris, 1949.

CONSTANTINE OF BARBANSON, O.F.M. CAP. *Secrets sentiers et de l'amour divin esquels est cachée la vraye sapience céleste et la royaume de Dieu en nos âmes.* Rome, 1932.

DAGENS, J. *Bérulle et les origines de la restauration catholique* (1575-1611). Paris, 1952.

DANIEL OF THE VIRGIN MARY, O. CARM. *Vinea Carmeli.* Antwerp, 1662.

———. *Speculum carmelitanum.* 4 Vols. Antwerp, 1680.

DOMINIC OF ST. ALBERT, O. CARM. *Exercitatio spiritualis fratrum tam novitiorum in nostro Carmeli Rhedonensis novitiatu degentium.* Paris, 1650, 2nd ed. 1665; 3d edition by J. Brenninger, *Analecta Ordinis Carmelitarum.* Vol. XI, 1940. This is the general title of four tracts edited together, although the above title belongs only to the first. The other three bear the following titles: *Regulae exteriores seu Praxis externa praecipuarum virtutum. Regulae generales magistri novitiorum de directione fratrum, Directio spiritualis pro studentibus.*

———. *Théologie mystique du R. P. Dominique de Saint Albert religieux Carme de l'observance de Rennes.* Edited by J. Brenninger, *Études carmélitaines.* Vol. XXII, 1937.

———. *Letters of Dominic.* Edited by S. M. Bouchereaux. "Dominique de Saint-Albert, sa vie et sa correspondence avec Jean de Saint-Samson," *Analecta Ordinis Carmelitarum.* Vol. XV, 1950.

DONATIAN OF ST. NICHOLAS. *Vie du Père Dominique de Saint Albert.* Edited by S. M. Bouchereaux. *Analecta Ordinis Carmelitarum.* Vol. XV, 1950.

———. *Vita Doninici a S. Alberto.* Edited by J. Brenninger. *Analecta Ordinis Carmelitarum.* Vol. XI, 1940-1942.

DUDON, P. "Dans son *Traité de l'oraison, S.* Pierre d'Alcantara a-t-il demarqué Louis de Grenade?" *Revue d'ascétique et de mystique.* Vol. II, 1921.

ÉTIENNE DE S. MARIE, O.C.D. "La pratique de la presence de Dieu," *Spiritualité carmélitaine.* Vol. III [Brussels, 1938].

FLORENCIO DEL NIÑO JESÚS, O.C.D. *El V. P. Fr. Juan de Jesús María prepósito general de los Carmelitas Descalzos,* 1564-1615; *su vida, sus escritos y sus virtudes.* Burgos, 1919.

FONCK, A. "Puente (Luis de la)," *Dictionnaire de théologie catholique.* Vol. XIII, 1936.

FRANCIS DE SALES. *Oeuvres de Saint François de Sales.* Vol. III, *Introduction à la vie dévote.* Annecy, 1893. Vols. IV and V. *Traité de l'amour da Dieu.* Annecy, 1894.

FRANÇOIS DE STE: MARIE, O.C.D. *Le plus vieux textes du Carmel. Traduits et commentés.* Paris, 1944.

GABRIEL OF SAINT MARY MAGDALEN, O.C.D. *La mistica teresiana.* Fiesole, 1935.

———. "L'École d'oraison carmélitaine," , *Études carmélitaines.* Vol., XVII, 1932.

GAVA, G. COAN, A. *Carmelo.* Rome, 1950.

GRANADA, LOUIS OF, O. P. *Obras de Fray Luis de Granada.* Critical edition by Justo Cuervo, O. P. 14 Vols. Madrid, 1906-1927.

———. *Summa of the Christian Life.* 2 Vols. Trans. and adapted by Jordan Aumann, O.P. St. Louis, 1954-1955.

GRATIAN, J., O. CARM. *Della disciplina regolare opera.* Venice, 1600. Translated into Italian from Spanish by George Bovio, O. Carm.

GRAUSEM, J. P: "Rodriguez (Alphonsus)," *Dictionnaire de théologie catholique.* Vol. XIII, 1937.

GREGORY OF ST. MARTIN, O. CARM. *Apologie pour l'antiquité des religieux Carmes, tenans légitimement leur origine et succession héréditaire des Saints prophêtes Élie et Elizée.* Douay, 1685.

GUIBERT, J. de, S. J. *Theologia spiritualis ascetica et mystica.* 4th ed., Rome, 1952.

———. *Documenta ecclesiastica christianae perfectionis.* Rome, 1931.

———. *"Arias (François)," Dictionnaire de spiritualité.* Vol. I, 1937.

HARPHIUS, H. (Van Herp), O.F.M. *Spieghel der Volcomenheit.* Edited by L. Verschueren, O.F.M. Antwerp, 1931.

HUGH OF BALMA. *Mystica theologia.* Falsely attributed to Saint Bonaventure and published under the title—*Seraphici Doctoris Bonaventurae opusculorum theologicorum tomus secundus.* Venice, 1634.

HUGH OF ST. FRANCIS, O. CARM. *La véritable idée d'un supérieur religieux, formée sur la vie et les conduites du vénérable père Philippe Thibault avec les maximes et instructions spirituelles pour acquérir la perfection chrétienne et religieux.* 2 Vols. Angers, 1663-1665.

HUIJBEN, J., O.B.S. "Aux sources de spiritualité française du XVIIe siècle," *Vie spirituelle supplement.* Vols. XXV-XXVII, 1930-1931.

HYACINTH OF THE MOTHER OF GOD, O. CARM. *Nova schola virtutum exhibens regulas, praxim, et usum vacandi Deo per meditationes, considerationes, actus virtutum, victoriam passionum, nec non praesentiae divinae et alia consueta religionis, praesertim novitiatus exercitia.* 2nd ed. Bamberg, 1764.

IGNATIUS OF LOYOLA. *The Spiritual Exercises of St. Ignatius.* Translated by Louis Puhl, S.J. Westminster, Md., 1951.

IPARRAGUIRRE, I., S. J. *Introduzione allo studio degli Esercizi.* Translated by Mario Lonero, S. J. Rome, 1951.

JOHN OF JESUS AND MARY (ARAVALLES), O.C.D. *Tratado de oración:* (1587). Edited by Evarist of the Virgin of Carmel. Toledo, 1925; 2nd ed. Madrid, 1952.

JOHN OF JESUS AND MARY (OF CALAHORRA), O.C.D. *Opera omnia.* 3 Vols. Florence, 1771-1774.

JOHN OF ST. SAMSON. *Oeuvres spirituelles et mystiques du divin contemplatif F. Jean de S. Samson, religieux Carme de la réforme et observance de Rennes en la Province de Touraine.* Edited by Donatian of St. Nicholas, O. Carm. 2 Vols. Rennes, 1658-1659.

JOHN 44, PATRIARCH OF JERUSALEM. *De institutione primorum monachorum in lege veteri exortorum et in nova perseverantium ad Caprasium monachum.* Pars ascetica. Edited by G. Wessels. *Analecta Ordinis Carmelitarum.* Vol. III, 1916.

LANSPERGIUS, J., O. CARTH. *Opera omnia.* 5 Vols. Cologne, 1630.

LAVOGAT, M. H. "Louis de Grenade," *Dictionnaire de théologie catholique.* Vol. IX, 1926.

LEO OF ST. JOHN, O. CARM. *Delineatio observantiae Carmelitarum Rhedonensis in Provincia Turonensi.* Paris, 1645.

———. *Studium sapientiae universalis.* Lyon, 1664.

LÉZIN DE SAINTE SCHOLASTIQUE, O. CARM. *La vie du V. P. Philippe Thibault, pére et principal auteur de la réforme des Carmes de l'observance de Rennes en la Province de Touraine.* Paris, 1673.

MARK OF THE NATIVITY OF THE VIRGIN, O. CARM. *La directoire des petits offices.* 4 Vols. Angers, 1677-1679.

———. *Traité de la camponction.* Tours, 1696. Edited by Michael Joseph of St. Mark, O. Carm. The preface is a biography of Father Mark by the editor.

MATTHIAS OF ST. JOHN, O. CARM. *Genius carmelitanae reformationis in antiquo Ordinis coetu institutae.* Bordeaux, 1666.

MICHAEL OF ST. AUGUSTINE, O. CARM. *Introductio ad vitam internam et fruitiva praxis vitae mysticae.* Edited by G. Wessels, O. Carm. Rome, 1925.

MOLINA, A. DE, O. CARTH. *Exercisios espirituales de la excelencias provecho y necessitad de la oración mental reducido a doctrina y meditaciones, sacado de los santos padres y doctores de la Iglesia.* Burgos, 1613.

PEERS, E. A. *Studies of the Spanish Mystics.* 2 Vols. London, 1927-1930.

PETER OF THE RESURRECTION, O. CARM. *Le manuel des religieux profez.* Vol. IV, Nantes, 1666.

PHILIPPE P., O. P. "Mental Prayer in the Catholic Tradition," *Mental Prayer and Modern Life, a Symposium.* Translated by Francis C. Lehner, O. P. New York, 1950. This book is a partial translation of *L'Oraison. Paris,* 1947.

PIER GIORGIO DEL S. CUORE, O.C.D. *La contemplazione secondo il Ven. P. Giovanni di Gesù Maria, O.C.D.* Cremona, 1950.

POULAIN, A., S. J. *The Graces of Interior Prayer.* Translated by Leonora Smith. 6th ed. London, 1928.

———. "Alvarez de Paz," *Dictionnaire de théologie catholique.* Vol. I, 1909:

POURRAT, P. "Affective (Spiritualité)," *Dictionnaire de spiritualité.* Vol. I, 1937.

———. *La spiritualité chrétienne.* Vols. II, IV, Paris, 1927-1930.

———. "Thérèse de Jésus (Sainte)," *Dictionnaire de théologie catholique.* Vol. XV, 1946.

PUENTE, LUIS DE LA, S. J. *Méditatións sur les mystères de notre sainte foi avec la pratique de l'oraison mentale.* Translated by P. Jenesseaux, S. J. Edited by R. P. Uguarte, S. J. 6 Vols. Paris, 1932-1933.

PUNIET, P. DE. "Blois (Louis de)," *Dictionnaire de spiritualité,* Vol. I, 1937.

Regula et Constitutiones Fratrum beatae Dei Genetricis et Virginis Mariac de Monte Carmelo. Pro conventibus reformationis Gallicae in Provincia Turonensi. Paris, 1636.

RODRIQUEZ, A., S. J. *The Practice of Christian and Religious Perfection.* 3 Vols. [n. d.].

SARACENI, P. T., O. CARM. *Dell'oratione mentale.* Bologna, 1636.

SERNIN-MARIE DE SAINT ANDRÉ, O.C.D. *Vie du V. frère Jean de S. Samson religieux Carme de la réforme de Touraine.* Paris, 1881.

SERVIÈRE, J. DE LA. "Clement VIII," *Dictionnaire de théologie catholique.* Vol. III, 1911.

SILVERIO DE SANTA TERESA, O.C.D. *Historia del Carmen Descalzo.* Vol. VIII, Burgos, 1937.

SORETH, J. O. CARM. *Expositio paranaetica in regulam Carmelitarum.* Paris, 1625.

TERESA OF AVILA. *The Complete Works of Saint Teresa of Jesus.* 3 Vols. New York, 1946. A translation by E. A. Peers of the critical edition of *Obras de Sta. Teresa de Jesús.* Edited by Silverio de Santa Teresa. 9 Vols., Burgos, 1915-1924.

THEODORE OF ST. JOSEPH, O.C.D. *L'Oraison d'aprés l'école carmélitaine.* 2nd ed. Bruges, 1929.

TIMOTHY OF THE PRESENTATION, O. CARM. "Vita Ven. P. Philippi Theobaldi," *Analecta Ordinis Carmelitarum. Vol.* VII, 1930-1931.

TRUHLAR, C., S. J. *De experientia mystica.* Rome, 1951.

VANSTEENBERGHE, E. "Aspiration," *Dictionnaire de spiritualité.* Vol. I, 1937.

VENTIMIGLIA, M., O. CARM. *Historia chronologica priorum generalium Ordinis B. M. Virginis de Monte Carmelo.* Edited by G. Wessels, O. Carm. Rome, 1929.

VILLIERS, C. DE, O. CARM. *Bibliotheca carmelitana notis criticis et dissertationibus illustrata.* Orléans, 1752. New edition G. Wessels, O. Carm. Rome, 1927.

Vita carmelitana. Edited by J. Brenninger, O. Carm. Rome, 1933. Translated into English by Leo J. Walter, O. Carm., under the title: *Life in Carmel.* Chicago, 1934.

ZIMMERMAN, B., O.C.D. "Les réformes, dans l'Ordre de Notre Dame du Mont Carmel," *Études càrmélitaines.* Vol. XIX, 1934.

UNPUBLISHED MATERIALS

MARK OF THE NATIVITY OF THE VIRGIN, O. CARM. Ten Letters to Father General and to Father Louis Perez at Rome. Written from La Flèche and Poitiers between 1674-1686. Archives of the Carmelite Order, Rome. II AO37.

———. Six letters to Father General and Louis Perez at Rome. Written between 1674-1686. Some refer to the origin of the *Directoires des novices.* Archives of the Carmelite Order, Rome. II AO42; Nos. 56, 67, 69, 70.

———. Nine letters written to Father General and to Louis Perez at Rome. Written between 1671-1684. Archives of the Carmelite Order, Rome, II AO94.

———. One letter on the American Missions. No date, etc. Archives of the Carmelite Order, Rome. II AO221.

———. Seventeen letters written to Father General, to Louis Perez and Seraphin of Jesus and Mary. Written from La Flèche, Orléans, Poitiers, Rennes, Tours between 1670-1688. Many refer to his writings and to news in the province. Archives of the Carmelite Order, Rome, II AO222.

POTENZA, S. O. CARM. *Introduttione nella mistica terra del Carmelo o' sia il novitio carmelitano istruito nella perfettione della sua regola.* Archives of the Carmelite Order, Rome, Ms. S. 275A.

TONNA, E., O. CARM. *De doctrina spirituali Ven. Dominici a S. Alberto, Ord. Carm.* Unpublished dissertation presented for the doctorate in theology in the Gregorian University, Rome, 1951.

INDEX

Abram, Nicolas, historian, 3
Acarie, Barbe Madame, influenced by Blosius, 17
Affections: in mental ptayer, 46-48; importance, 90; according to Louis of Granada, 114
Affective prayer. *See* Prayer
Aimo, Jerome of St. Clement, translator of *Directoires*, 36, 38
Alvarez de Paz, James: writings on prayer, 105-106
Angelus of St. Paul, pioneer of reform, 6
Angers, monastery of, 2, 4, 5
Anthony de Molina, Carthusian, method of meditation, 92
Antoine-Marie de la Présentation, explanation of Touraine reform, 15
Aquitaine, province of, 1, 11
Aravalles, John of Jesus and Mary, method of prayer of, 132
Ari, Jerome, translator of *Directoires*, 29-32
Arias, Francis: life and writings, 91-92; influence on *Méthode*, 93-97
Arnauld, Anthony, dispute with Mark of the Nativity, 31-32
Aspirative prayer. *See* Prayer
Aubron, Mathurin, pioneer of reform. 5
Augustine, St., quoted in *Méthode*, 78-79
Aulnay, monastery of, 2
Auray, monastery of, 2

Basses-Loges, monastery of, 2
Beaucousin, Richard: influence on French spirtuality, 3; on Thibault, 3-4
Behourt, Peter: organizer of reform, 2; provincial, 5
Bellintani, Matthias de Salo, method of prayer, 92
Bernard of St. Magdalen: life, 24-27; writer of reform, 21; instructed to complete *Directoires*, 23
Berthelot, Robert, Carmelite bishop, 9
Bertot, Abbé, influenced by Maurus of the Child Jesus, 13
Bérulle, Pierre de, cardinal, origin of Oratory, 31
Bethléem, Carmelite convent of, 2
Blessed Sacrament in Paris, monastery of, 2, 25

Blois, Louis de (Blosius): influence in France, 121; on French Carmelites, 121; teaching on prayer, 121-123; influence on *Méthode*, 124
Boniface of St. Euphrasia, member of reform, 149
Bossuet, Jacques Bénigne, bishop, method of prayer, 13
Bouchereaux, S. M., history of reform, 17
Brazil, province of, 30, 32
Brenninger, John, author of *Directorium Carmelitanum*, 38

Carmelite Rule of St. Albert of Jerusalem, 8, 79
Carmelites of the Ancient Observance: provinces in 17th century, 1; members in 18th century, 13
Carthusians, relation of Thibault with, 3
Cassian, John, quoted in *Méthode*, 78
Ceva, Theobald of the Annunciation, translator of *Lo spirito di azioni religiose*, 36
Chalain, monastery of, 2
Chalumeau, Peter, provincial, 7
Charles of St. Agatha, pioneer of reform, 5
Charles of St. Athanasius, writer of German province, 160
Charpentier, Louis, organizer of reform, 2, 5
Cisneros, García de, influence on Louis of Granada, 109
Clement VIII, pope: absolution of Henry IV of France, 1; grants audience to Thibault, 4
Climacus, John, quoted in *Méthode*, 78
Colloquies in prayer, 86, 89
Constantine of Barbanson, influence on reform, 151
Constitutions, Carmelite, 8, 12, 44
Conversation with God, loving, 161
Cospéan, Philip, bishop of Nantes, 10, 31

Daniel of the Blessed Virgin Mary, historian of reform, 12, 19
Directoires des novices: on nature of reform, 18; origin of reform, 25; edited, 29; editions, translations, adaptations, 34-38
Les Directoires des petits offices de la religion, 26, 30
Direttorio spirituali de' Carmelitani. *See Directoires des novices*

Discalced Carmelite friars: arrival in France 1; influence on Thibault, 3, 9, 11, 83; dependence on Louis of Granada in method of prayer, 111; early methods of meditation, 131-132
Discalced Carmelite nuns, arrival in France, 1
Dol, monastery of, 2
Dominic of St. Albert: life, works and doctrine, 159-170; spirit of reform according to, 19; exercises on aspirations, 71; affective meditation, 90
Donation of St. Nicholas, secretary of John of St. Samson, 148
Dupuy, Anthony, pioneer of reform, 5
Duval, André, adviser of Thibault, 3
Duvergier de Hauranne (Abbé Saint Cyran), teaching, 31-32

Ejaculations. *See* Prayer
Elias, prophet, father of Carmel, 18
England, Carmelite missionaries in, 32

Fantoni, Sebastian, prior general of the Order, 8, 11
Flanders, province of, 11
Fontainebleau, monastery of, 2, 32
Fouquet, Christopher, benefactor of reform, 7
France, province of, 1, 11
Francis de Sales, St.: influenced by Beaucousin, 3; by Louis of Granada, 109, writings, 141; influence on Carmelites, 142; doctrine on prayer, 142-144; influence on *Méthode,* 143-146
French Revolution, effect on Carmelites, 13

Gabriel of Mary Magdalen, Carmelite method of prayer, 132
Gabriel of the Annunciation, pioneer of reform, 6
Garrigou-Lagrange, R., on methods of prayer, 53
Gascony, province of, 1, 11, 30
George of the Queen of Angels (George Gaillard), translator of *Méthode,* 36, 38
Germany, Carmelite provinces of, 12
Giuliani, Tarcisio, translator of *Directorium Carmelitanum,* 38
Gratian, Jerome: commentator on Rule, 82; method of meditation, 132
Gregory of St. Martin, writer of reform, 8
Gregory Nazianzenus, quoted *in Méthode,* 78
Guerchois, William, pioneer of reform, 5
Guibert, J. de: Christian perfection, 39; resolutions in meditation, 56
Guyon, Madame, Quietist, 13

Harphius, Henry, influence on John of St. Samson, 158, 173

Hennebont, monastery of, 2, 7
Henry IV, king of France: absolution of, 1; relation with Carmelites, 4
Herp, Henry van. *See* Harphius
Holy Sepulchre, Carmelite convent of, 2
Hugh of Balma, influence on *Méthode,* 157
Hugh of St. Francis, historian of reform, 18, 29
Humanity of Christ, its place in prayer, 69
Hyacinth of the Mother of God, author of compendium of the *Directoires,* 37

Ignatius, St. *See Spiritual Exercises*
Imaginaton, importance in prayer, 89, 113
Institutio primorum monachorum: influence on *Méthode,* 80; spirit of Order, 81
Intellect, use of in prayer, 90
Introversion, way of prayer, 122, 151
Italy, Carmelite provinces of, 30

Jansenism, conflict of Mark of the Nativity with, 31
Jesuits: influence on Thibault, 3; on Carmelite Constitutions, 8; teachers of Carmelites, 10, 159; attacked by Jansenius, 32
Joannes XLIV. *See Institutio primorum monachorum*
John of Jesus and Mary Aravalles. *See* Aravalles
John of Jesus and Mary of Calahorra: life, 132-133; writings, 133-134; on meditation, 134-138; similarity of teaching with *Méthode,* 138-140; on presence of God, 139; on aspiration, 139
John of St. Samson: life, 147-148; spirit of reform, 18, 22; soul of reform, 147; writings, 148; doctrine on meditation, 149-152; influence on *Méthode,* 150, 156-158; aspirative prayer, 153-158
John of the Cross: quoted in *Directoires,* 125; method of meditation, 132
Joseph of Jesus, collector of manuscripts of John of St. Samson, 149
Josselin, monastery of, 2
Joyeuse, Cardinal de, relation with Carmelites of reform, 4

La Flèche: monastery of, 2, 25; Jesuit college at, 10, 27
La Flocelière, monastery of, 2
La Rochelle, monastery of, 2
Le Boudon, monastery of, 2
Le Guildo, monastery of, 2
Leo of St. John: writer and preacher in reform, 13; testimony on spirit of reform, 19; provincial, 25, 81; panegyric of St. Francis de Sales, 142
Lercaro, Giacomo, cardinal, writer on methods of prayer, 54

INDEX

Le Roy, Christopher, provincial, 6
Levesque, M., writer on Bossuet, 13
Liturgy, Carmelite in Touraine, 9
Loudun, monastery of, 2, 7
Louis XIII, king of France, relation with Carmelites, 4, 13
Louis XIV, king of France, relation with Carmelites, 13, 32
Louis of Granada: life, 108; writings and general influence, 108-110; influence on meditation in *Méthode*, 112-118, 172; on exercise of presence of God in *Méthode*, 119; influence on St. Teresa, 127; on John of St. Samson, 151; on Dominic of St. Albert, 162

Maillard, Peter, provincial, 10
Mantua, Carmelite reform of, 1
Marie de Medicis, queen mother of France, relation with Carmelites, 11
Mark of the Nativity of the Blessed Virgin: life, 27; formation of his spiritual life, 28; studies, 28; general visitator, 30; novice master, 30; relation with Arnauld, 31; writings, 30-31; provincial, 32
Mary of St. Teresa (Petyt), Marian mystic, 21
Mathurin of St. Anne; translator of writings of John of St. Samson, 148
Maurus of the Child Jesus: writer in reform, 12, 21; connection with *Directoires*, 23, 28
Meditation. *See* Prayer
Mental prayer. *See* Prayer
Méthode: affective prayer, 50-51; aspirative prayer, 60-64; difficulties in prayer, 52; division of, 38; editions, translations, adaptations, 34-38; influence of Arias, 93-97, of Carmelite Rule, 80, of Constitutions, 82-83, of Dominic of St. Albert, 159-170, of Fathers, 78-79, of Francis de Sales, 142-146, of *De Institutione primorum monachorum*, 80-81, of John of Jesus and Mary of Calahorra, 132-140, of John of St. Samson, 147-158, 170, of Louis de Blois, 124, of Louis of Granada, 111-120, of de la Puente, 102-105, of Rodriguez, 99, of Soreth, 81-82, of *Spiritual Exercises*, 84-91, of Sacred Scripture, 77-78, of St. Teresa, 127-131; meditation and parts in, 41-50; meditative reading, 50; mixed prayer, 57; outline of meditation, 43; prayer of recollection, 51; prayer of simple regard, 51; presence of God, 64-70; purpose of, 39-40, 74; style of, 38
Merkelbeek, monastery of, 35
Michael Joseph of St. Mark, biographer of Mark of the Nativity, 23, 28, 33
Michael of Ave Maria, pioneer of reform, 5
Michael of St. Augustine, writer in reform, 12, 21

Mixed prayer. *See* Prayer
Molina, Anthony de, method of meditation, 92
Molinos, Michael de, false teaching, 69
Mortification, 74-75, 122

Nantes, monastery of, 2, 4, 159
Narbonne, province of, 1, 11, 30
Nazareth, Carmelite convent of, 2
Notre Dame des Couëts, Carmelite convent of, 2

Odiau, Francis: pioneer of reform, 5; prior, 7
Orléans, monastery of, 2

Paris: university of, 5, *See* Blessed Sacrament
Paz, Alvarez de, James. *See* Alvarez, de Paz, James
Perez, Louis, regent of Carmelite studies, Rome, 30
Perfection, Christian, 39
Peter of Alcantara, St.: dependance on Louis of Granada, 109; method of prayer praised by St. Teresa, 127
Peter of the Resurrection, writer in reform, 21
Philippinus, John, prior general of Order, 34
Pinault, Matthew: pioneer of reform, 5; novice master, 10, 159; adviser of John of St. Samson, 148
Place Maubert: general house of studies, 10; resists reform, 11, 28
Ploërmel, monastery of, 2, 10
Poitiers, monastery of, 2, 28
Poland, Carmelite province of, 12, 30
Pont-à-Mousson, university of, frequented by Thibault, 2
Pont-L'Abbé, monastery of, 2
Porras, Anthony, influence on Louis of Granada, 109
Prayer: affective, 50-51; aspirative, 60-64, 119, 153-158; contemplative, 132, 134; difficulties in, 52; divisions of, 40-41; ejaculations, 67-68; meditation and its parts, 42-50, 130; meditative reading, 50; mixed, 57-59, 130-131; necessity of, 55-56; parts of, 40; of recollection, 51; resolutions in, 56, 143; of simple regard, 51; of simplicity, 13
Preparation in meditation, 93
Presence of God: definition, 60, 64, 161; imaginary, 65; intellectual, 66; affective, 66, 154, 166; way to exercise the, 67-70
Provence, province of, 1, 11
Pseudo-Dionysius, quoted in the *Méthode*, 78
Puente, de la, Luis: writings and influence, 99-100; influence on *Méthode*, 100-105

Quietists, esteem for writings of Maurus of the Child Jesus, 13

Quintin, monastery of, 2

Reading in meditation, 113
Recollection, prayer of. *See* Prayer
René of St. Albert, Carmelite confessor of Bossuet, 13
Rennes, monastery of, 2, 5, 16
Richelieu, Armand de, cardinal: relation with Leo of St. John, 13; interest in reform, 28
Rodriguez, Alphonsus: influence in 17th century, 97; teaching on exercise of presence of God, 98-99
Rule of St. Albert of Jerusalem. *See* Carmelite Rule
Ruysbroeck, John, influence in France, 92

Sacred Scripture, uses in *Méthode*. See *Méthode*
St. Malo, monastery of, 2
St. Pol-de-Leon, monastery of, 2
Sancta Maria in Traspontina, monastery of, 30
Self-denial. *See* mortification
Seraphino de Fermo, influence on Louis of Granada, 109
Silverio de Santa Teresa, historian of Discalced Carmelites, 1
Simple regard. *See* Prayer
Simplicianus of St. Francis, translator of writings of Dominic of St. Albert, 141
Simplicity, prayer of. *See* Prayer
Soreth, John, Blessed: inspired Thibault, 9; on meditation, 67; commentary on Rule, 81; influence of commentary, 81
Spirito delle azioni religiose, 36
Spiritual Exercises: influence on Thibault, 3, 84; mixed prayer in, 58; influence on methods of prayer, 84; influence on *Méthode*, 87-91, 106-107; methods of prayer in, 85-86; in writings of Arias, 92, 96; in Rodriguez, 98; in de la Puente, 100-101, 103; in Alvarez de Paz, 105
Statutes, of reform, 7
Strictior Observantia, relation to reform of Touraine, 14
Sylvius, Henry, prior general, interest in reform, 4, 82

Tauler, John, influence on Blosius, 121
Teresa of Avila, St.: quoted by *Méthode*, 42-47; prayer of active recollection, 51; mixed prayer, 58; spirit of, 80; influence on Thibault, 83; influence on *Méthode*, 125-126, 130-131, 172; concept of prayer, 127-131
Thibault, Philip: life, 2-11; preparation of reform, 3-5; first steps of reform, 6; prior of Rennes, 7; preparation of the Constitutions, 8-9; provincial, 10; in Flanders, 11; last days, 11; influenced by St. Teresa, 83
Toulouse, province of, 1, 11
Touraine: province of, 1; reform of, 1-14; spiritual life of, 15-21; contemplative ideal of, 21
Tours, monastery of, 2
Traité de la componction, style of, 33
Trent, council of, 3
Truhlar, Charles, on humanity of Christ in prayer, 69

Urban of the Ascension, provincial, 12

Valenciennes, monastery of, 11
Vitae Patrum, quoted by the *Méthode*, 78
Vivonne, monastery of, 2

Walter, Leo J., translator of *Directorium Carmelitanum*, 38
Wessels, Gabriel, source of the *Directoires*, 81
Will, in prayer, 90, 113

BIOGRAPHY OF
KILIAN HEALY (1912-2003)
FORMER PRIOR GENERAL

On May 18, 2003, Father Kilian John Healy, a member of the American Province of the Most Pure Heart of Mary, returned to the house of the Father. He had held the helm of the Order for twelve years; we remember him with appreciation, with affection and with gratitude.

Kilian was born in Worcester, Massachusetts, on November 15, 1912; he died shortly before he was to have completed his ninetieth year. He entered the novitiate of the Province of the Most Pure Heart of Mary in Niagara Falls, Ontario, on August 15, 1930, and made his first profession on August 15 of the following year. His Solemn Profession took place on August 15, 1934. Shortly thereafter he was sent to Rome to take his theological studies in the *Studium Generale*; at the end of his program - four years, at that time - he earned a Lectorate in Theology. In the meantime, following the reception of tonsure, minor orders, subdiaconate and diaconate, he was ordained to the priesthood on July 11, 1937.

He was forced to interrupt his studies for a doctorate in Theology due to the war; and returned to his province on June 1, 1940. There he began to teach Theology, first at Mount Carmel College in Niagara Falls, then at Whitefriars Hall in Washington, D.C., where he was named prior in 1945. During this period he was a member of the Catholic Theological Society of America and of the Mariological Society of America.

He returned to Rome, to *Sant'Alberto*, on October 15, 1951; he received the Doctorate in Theology at the Pontifical Gregorian University on February 9, 1952. His dissertation was *The Methods of Prayer and Their Sources in the Directory of Novices in the Carmelite Reform of Touraine*; this work was published in 1956, the first volume of the Spiritual Theology Series of the Institutum Carmelitanum of Rome.

Fr. Kilian taught dogmatic theology at the *Studium Generale* of the Order - the *Collegio Internazionale di Sant'Alberto* - from 1953 to 1959, and spiritual theology at the Pontifical Institute *Regina Mundi* in Rome from 1954 to 1959. He was appreciated for his clarity of presentation and especially for his characteristic application of the matter under consideration to practical daily living. It was also during this period that he wrote the majority of his published academic articles, in particular those on such Marian themes as the Assumption and the Immaculate Conception.

He was a renowned preacher and also an examiner of the Roman clergy. On March 2, 1954, he was named a Fellow of the *Institutum Carmelitanum*, in the area of Spiritual Theology.

During the 1953 General Chapter of the Order he was elected Assistant General for the English-speaking provinces; in the following Chapter of 1959 he was elected Prior General of the Order, a position he held until 1971.

On several occasions in the history of the Order, Priors General have been elected less due to their administrative or political abilities than to their recognition as distinguished scholars and eminent theologians. Kilian was one of these. As noted above, before his election as Prior General, he had passed the greater part of his life in the halls of academe. His great interest, without question, was Theology, Spiritual Theology in particular. He taught it not as something abstract but as material that served as the very lifeblood of the Church.

Fr. Kilian was, moreover, one of the few Priors General in the history of the Order who was privileged to participate in an Ecumenical Council of the Church, Vatican Council II. He was assisted by Fr. Bartholomew Xiberta, a theologian who was a *peritus* of the Council, and he was supported by several Carmelite Bishops, such has the Most Reverend Donal Lamont.

For Kilian participation in the Council was a deeply intellectual and spiritual experience. Reviewing the official Acts of the Council, one learns that even in its preparatory phase he had presented a series of reflections and proposals. Among his more relevant suggestions in the area of doctrine was his intervention on Christian unity, and his proposal favoring the universal mediation of Mary. Alongside his observations about certain dogmas of faith, he insisted on the need for a revision of the criteria for the relations between Church and State. In the area of morality, he underlined the need for major improvements in certain aspects of priestly life; he suggested not only more clear criteria for preaching during the sacred liturgy. He also put forth a proposal demonstrating his love for the Blessed Virgin: to add the invocation "Blessed be the Immaculate Heart of Mary" to the prayers after Mass and Benediction of the Blessed Sacrament.

During the course of the Council he was especially active when dealing with the *Schema* on *De Ecclesia*. He wrote out a series of observations on Chapter 2 - on the hierarchical constitution of the Church - and, along with 126 other Fathers of the Council, he signed the intervention of John Hervás y Benet in the 133rd General Congregation on *De Ecclesia in mundo huius temporis*. He also approval and signed other interventions of various Fathers on several points of this same *Schema*, including one written by the Bishops of England and Scotland on the role of the Blessed Virgin Mary within the Church. Finally, along with other Superiors General, he put forward a series of considerations for updating the Consecrated Life.

This was a period of disturbing changes within the Church. Kilian, conservative by temperament and by education, was neither rigid nor intransigent; he understood how to be open to new ways. His loyalty to the Church, his Mother, give him the courage to embrace and to faithfully carry out all the decisions of the Council. This posture was also evident in meetings of the General Council of the Order: he had his own clear, precise ideas, but he also had the wisdom to recognize others' valid points of view. It is generally acknowledged that Kilian suffered a great deal because of the number of people who left the Order. He maintained contact with many up until his death.

Already by the end of 1964, for the sake of renewal and updating, he had recognized the need to revise the Constitutions of the Order. This proposal was set in motion during the General Chapter of 1965, continued in the extraordinary Chapter of 1968, and brought to a conclusion in the General Chapter of 1971. At that time - following a long and tortuous itinerary marked with a deep-seated identity crisis as to the very nature of being Carmelite' - Kilian had the satisfaction of witnessing the approval of the Constitutions renewed according to the spirit of Vatican II.

It is within this context that his circular letters to the entire Order are to be read: they are vibrant, even passionate appeals for fidelity within Carmel, with particular emphasis on the spiritual life, on the biblical figures of Elijah the Prophet and of Mary the Virgin Mother, on poverty, and on the Rule of Carmel.

In 1967 Kilian joyfully received the results of a Congress of experts on the *Ratio Ordinis* that he had enthusiastically supported. It was the fruit of this Congress, the document *Delineatio vitae carmelitanae*, that provided the solid foundation for subsequent renewal.

Still within the context of the renewal sought by Vatican II, he had a special concern for the Liturgy. He provided guidelines and regulations in support of the coral recitation of the Liturgy of the Hours and of vibrant Eucharistic celebrations. From the very beginning of his generalate Fr. Kilian had expressed special concern for the Sacred Liturgy. As early as 1960 he had ordered the publication of the

Antiphonale for Mass according to the Carmelite Rite; he thus continued the work of his predecessor, the Most Reverend Kilian Lynch, who had inaugurated the renewal of the Order's liturgical texts with the publication of its own *Rituale*. In 1961 Fr. Healy published the renewed *Ordo Hebdomadae Sanctae*. Finally, in 1965, he requested and received from the Pontifical Council for the Implementation of the Constitution on the Sacred Liturgy a dispensation from the celebration of the Canonical Hour of Prime, whether in choir or in private, for the entire Order.

Among other developments during the generalate of Fr. Kilian Healy, the following are noteworthy: the affiliation of the *Studium Generale di Sant'Alberto* to the Pontifical Lateran University, beginning with the 1960-1961 academic year (a relationship that lasted until the *Studium generale* ceased to function in 1968); the transfer in 1966 of the General Curia to its new seat in the *Collegio Pio XI*; in this same year the creation of *CITOC*, an agency for disseminating the news within the Order; the erection of the General Commissariat of Indonesia in 1960 and seven years later its elevation to the status of a Province; similarly the erection of the Provinces of Lower Germany and England (now Great Britain) in 1969; the aggregation to the Order of the Secular Institute *The Leaven* in 1965; his support for the activities of the *Institutum Carmelitanum* and the Lay Carmelites.

Moreover, in 1962 the Prelature *Nullius* of Chuquibamba, Peru, was entrusted to the Province of Malta; its first Prelate was the Most Rev. Redemptus Gauchi, O.Carm. In the same year the Prelature *Nullius* of Paracatù, Brazil, became a Diocese, whose first Ordinary was the Most Rev. Raymond Lui, O.Carm.

His terms as Prior General completed, Fr. Kilian retired to the Priory in Washington where he could take advantage of its library. He wrote several articles on spirituality and republished *Walking with God,* a short book on the Presence of God first published in 1948 which had proved very popular and had been translated into Spanish. Fr. Kilian's interest in the topic stemmed from his earlier study on the Carmelite Reform of Touraine.

According to the Constitutions of the Order then in force, as a former Prior General he had the right to choose the friary where he wished to live; however his Provincial made known his need for another priest in the friary of Peabody, Massachusetts, a community served a chapel located in a shopping center where people could pause during their shopping to assist at Mass, especially on Saturdays, go to confession, or seek advice with regard to their spiritual problems.

Kilian, humble as always, readily accepted the Provincial's suggestion. Thus he spent the final years of his life in prayer and in the service of the faithful. An optimist by nature, he was always in good spirits and well-loved by all. He was a man of great spirituality who, as a true Carmelite, lived continually in the presence of God.

The Mass of Christian Burial for him was held in the chapel of the Carmelite monastery in Danvers, Massachusetts. The current Prior general of the Order, Fr. Joseph Chalmers, was the main celebrant. Fr. John Malley, a former Prior general, preached. Many Carmelites from aorund the country concelebrated. Bishop Francis X. Irvin, Auxiliary Bishop of the Archdiocese of Boston, was also present. many family and friends as well as formers Carmelites were also present.

Fr. Kilian was buried in the Carmelite plot at st. Mary's cemetery in Salem, Massuchusetts.

Joachim Smet, O.Carm. - Emanuele Boaga, O.Carm.
Centro Internazionale di Sant'Alberto

www.carmelites.info

Finito di stampare nel mese di novembre 2005
dalla Tipografia Città Nuova della P.A.M.O.M.
via San Romano in Garfagnana, 23 - 00148 Roma
Telefono & fax 06.65.30.467